ALAN GAULD

Mediumship and Survival

A Century of Investigations

Series Editor: Brian Inglis

Published on behalf of the Society for Psychical Research

PALADIN
Granada Publishing

Paladin Books
Granada Publishing Ltd
8 Grafton Street, London W1X 3LA

Published by Paladin Books 1983

First published in Great Britain by
William Heinemann Ltd 1982

Copyright © Alan Gauld 1982

ISBN 0-586-08429-0

Reproduced, printed and bound in Great Britain by
Hazell Watson & Viney Limited,
Member of the BPCC Group,
Aylesbury, Bucks

To Sheila

Who uncomplainingly put up with a
difficult summer

THE SOCIETY FOR PSYCHICAL RESEARCH

The Society for Psychical Research is the oldest learned society in this field. Its aim is to investigate apparently inexplicable phenomena scientifically. It organizes monthly lectures in London and other activities; it publishes a *Journal*, *Proceedings*, and *Newsletter*. An extensive library and archives are held at the Society's London headquarters where all enquiries, including membership, should be directed to:

The Society for Psychical Research
1 Adam & Eve Mews
Kensington
LONDON W8 6UG

Contents

List of Illustrations

Acknowledgements

For their kindness in reading a draft of this work, and for many helpful comments and suggestions, I am much indebted to Ian Stevenson, Brian Inglis, John St John, Louise Bloomfield and John Beloff. For valuable help in various related matters I have to thank Bernard Carr, Tony Cornell, Sam Grainger, Eleanor O'Keeffe, D. N. Clarke-Lowes, Emily Williams Cook, and Bert Haylett.

A number in parentheses in the text refers to the source listed opposite that number in the Bibliography (pp. 268–282).

Foreword

Around the year 1873, Frederic Myers was to recall in his *Human Personality*, a small group of Cambridge friends came to the conclusion that neither religion nor materialism had provided satisfactory answers to questions that were puzzling them:

> Our attitudes of mind were in some ways different; but to myself, at least, it seemed that no adequate attempt had yet been made even to determine whether anything could be learnt as to the unseen world or no; for that if anything were knowable about such a world in such fashion that Science could adopt and maintain that knowledge, it must be discovered by no analysis of tradition, and by no manipulation of metaphysics, but simply by experiment and observation – simply by the application to phenomena within us and around us of precisely the same methods of deliberate, dispassionate exact inquiry which have built up our actual knowledge of the world which we can touch and see.

Along with his friends – chief among them Henry Sidgwick and Edmund Gurney – Myers became one of the founder members of the Society for Psychical Research, when it was formed in 1882 to put these ideas into practice, and this series is being published to mark the Society's centenary.

The phenomena of the 'unseen world' to which Myers referred were originally for convenience put into five categories, each of which a committee was set up to investigate: telepathy, hypnotism, 'sensitives', apparitions and 'the various physical phenomena commonly called Spiritualistic'. Over the years the emphasis has to some extent shifted – in particular hypnotism, which at that time was dismissed as an occult delusion, was just about to be accepted as a reality, so it ceased to be on the psychic side of the fence. But broadly speaking, the phenomena under investigation are the same, and the ways in which they have been investigated have remained as Myers planned.

The terminology, however, was changed – and changed rather often, which made for some confusion. Myers himself introduced 'telepathy', as 'thought reading' was ambiguous; it could refer to the way in which Sherlock Holmes picked up what was in Watson's mind by watching his expression. 'Supernormal', however, which Myers thought preferable to supernatural to describe the class of phenomena with which the Society would be dealing, has since itself been replaced by 'paranormal'; and 'parapsychology' has been easing out 'psychical research' – though some researchers prefer to restrict its use to laboratory-type work, leaving 'psychical' for research into spontaneous phenomena. 'Psi' has also come in as an all-purpose term to describe the forces involved, or to identify them – for example, in distinguishing a normal from a paranormal event.

If evidence were lacking for 'parascience' – as it might now more embracingly be described, because the emphasis of research has been shifting recently away from psychology to physics – it could be found in the composition of the Society, from its earliest beginnings. There can be few organizations which have attracted so distinguished a membership. Among physicists have been Sir William Crookes, Sir John Joseph Thomson, Sir Oliver Lodge, Sir William Barrett and two Lord Rayleighs – the third and fourth barons. Among the philosophers: Sidgwick himself, Henri Bergson, Ferdinand Schiller, L. P. Jacks, Hans Driesch, and C. D. Broad; among the psychologists: William James, William McDougall, Sigmund Freud, Walter Franklin Prince, Carl Jung and Gardner Murphy. And along with these have been many eminent figures in various fields: Charles Richet, a Nobel prizewinner in physiology; the Earl of Balfour, Prime Minister from 1902–6, and his brother Gerald, Chief Secretary for Ireland in 1895–6; Andrew Lang, polymath; Gilbert Murray, Regius Professor of Greek at Oxford and drafter of the first Covenant of the League of Nations; his successor at Oxford, E. R. Dodds; Mrs Henry Sidgwick, Principal of Newnham College, Cambridge; Marie Curie; the Hon Mrs Alfred Lyttleton, Delegate to the League of Nations Assembly; Camille Flammarion, the astronomer, and F. J. M. Stratton, President of the Royal Astronomical Society; and Sir Alister Hardy, Professor of Zoology at Oxford.

Such a list, as Arthur Koestler pointed out in *The Roots of Coincidence*, ought to be sufficient to demonstrate that ESP research 'is not a playground for superstitious cranks'. On the contrary, the standards of research have in general been rigorous – far more rigorous, as psychologists have on occasion had to admit, than those of psychology. The reason that the results have not been accepted is basically that they have not been acceptable: extra-sensory perception and psychokinesis have remained outside science's domain, in spite of the evidence. And although the prejudice against parapsychology has been breaking down, so that it is being admitted as an academic discipline in universities, it is still very far from securing a firm base in the academic world.

Sceptics have sedulously propagated the notion that psychical researchers believe in ESP, PK, apparitions, and so on because they long to believe, or need to believe. Anybody who has studied the Society's *Journals* and *Proceedings*, or attended its meetings, will testify that this is a ludicrous misconception. Many of the most assiduous and skilled researchers have originally been prompted by *dis*belief – by a desire, say to expose a medium as a fraud. It has to be remembered, too, that many, probably the great majority, of the members have been and still are desirous of showing that paranormal manifestations are *natural*, and can be explained scientifically – though admittedly not in the narrow terms of materialist science, which in any case the nuclear physicists have shown to be fallacious.

No: insofar as a Society containing such a diverse collection of individuals can be said to have a corporate identity, it could almost be described as sceptical; certainly as rational, as this series will show. Not, though, rational*ist*. Unluckily rationalists, in their determination to purge society of its religious and occultist accretions, often failed to draw a distinction between superstitions and the observed phenomena which gave rise to them – which led them into such traps as refusing to accept the existence of meteorites, because of the association with Jove's thunderbolts; and to this day, they are prone to lapse into support for dogmas as rigid, and as ill-founded, as any of those of the Churches. If the series does nothing else, it will show how rationally – using that term in its proper sense – the writers have examined and presented the evidence.

Of all the issues which have been of concern to psychical researchers, Survival – commonly spelt with a capital S to indicate that it means the survival of the soul or spirit after death – has been the hardest to come to terms with. From the start, the SPR has included some members who are Christians, some who are members of other religions, some who believe in reincarnation, and some who flatly reject the existence, or even the possiblity of the existence, of a discarnate spirit life. As the holders of these different views are apt to hold them to be of transcendental importance – none more so than those who regard themselves as rationalists – it has always been difficult to survey the evidence for (and against) Survival as agnostics would like to see it; with the same detachment as, say, the evidence for (and against) telepathy. Many members of the Society, in fact, have felt inhibited about considering it at all.

Yet for obvious reasons Survival cannot be pushed to one side. If psychical research has any light to shed on it, then that light ought to be shed, because whether or not there is spirit life independent of the body is indeed of transcendent importance, to all of us. 'The question for man most momentous of all', as Myers put it, was 'whether or not his personality involved any element which can survive bodily death'; and he went on to state his belief that the answer should be sought through the method of science, a method 'never yet applied to the all-important problem of the existence, the powers, the destiny of the human soul'. Nobody is better qualified than Alan Gauld to take a dispassionate look at the evidence from the metapsychical – the term coined by Charles Richet to describe the new science, as he believed it to be – rather than from the metaphysical or religious point of view. Dr Gauld has for many years been a member of the Council of the Society, his account of its early years established him as a historian in his own right. *The Founders of Psychical Research* was a well-documented and objective but very readable account of the Society's early years, and the problems its members faced. In *Mediumship and Survival*, he has set himself the same high standards.

Brian Inglis

1 Introduction

People have believed or disbelieved in human survival of bodily death for various reasons, philosophical, theological, religious, emotional, moral, intuitive or factual. This book deals with the factual reasons with the empirical evidence (or some of it) on which belief in survival, and also disbelief in the very possibility of survival, has been grounded. Philosophical issues will be (briefly) raised only when they bear upon the interpretation of the evidence.

The gathering of evidence, or supposed evidence, for survival is no new endeavour. Many anecdotes that might be thought to bear upon the question are strung together in lives of the early saints, in the *Dialogues* of Pope Gregory the Great, in various late mediaeval collections of ghost stories, in post-Reformation books of remarkable 'providences' illustrative of God's mercies, in the works of early nineteenth century German mesmerists influenced by Schelling and a romantic philosophy of nature. These materials were, however, only rarely subjected to critical scrutiny, and were generally presented not as curious natural phenomena in need of an explanation, but as support for religious beliefs antecedently favoured by the writers.

It was not until the last quarter of the nineteenth century that a large-scale attempt was set afoot to collect and critically assess ostensible evidence for survival, and to interpret that evidence in a scientific spirit and without any prior commitment to religious or survivalistic hypotheses. This attempt began with the foundation of the British Society for Psychical Research (the 'SPR') in 1882 and of its American counterpart (the 'ASPR') in 1884 (refounded 1907). Both are still active, and I have drawn heavily upon their publications in the preparation of this volume. These societies, it should be noted, do not hold corporate opinions, and the views advanced by members (including myself) are entirely their own.

The SPR was not founded to pursue the problem of survival as such. The aim expressed by its founders was 'to investigate that large group of debatable phenomena designated by such terms as mesmeric, psychical, and Spiritualistic', and to do so 'without prejudice or prepossession of any kind, and in the same spirit of exact and unimpassioned inquiry which has enabled science to solve so many problems, once not less obscure nor less hotly debated' (148, pp. 3 and 4). These objectives sound – indeed are – a little vague, but in the context of 1882 it was reasonably clear what were the phenomena intended. First of all there were certain alleged findings that had increasingly caught public attention in the wake of the mesmeric movement of the late eighteenth and early nineteenth centuries (see 32; 122c; 122d). The facts (or supposed facts) of mesmerism (or 'animal magnetism') were at first sight themselves sufficiently surprising – striking cures of cases given over by orthodox medicine, the 'rapport' between mesmeric operator and his subjects, the induction in good subjects of a trance state in which subjects might 'perceive' the nature of their own ailments, predict their course and give prescriptions for them. Out of happenings of the last kind, further peculiar phenomena developed. Certain subjects began to manifest the ability to 'see' not just diseased and malfunctioning aspects of their own internal workings, but those of other people, sometimes even of distant people. A class of professional and semi-professional sensitives grew up, whose members, usually female and usually under the influence of one particular mesmeric operator, would diagnose, predict and prescribe for all comers. Now if the 'clairvoyant' vision of these ladies could reach inside people, or reach distant people, or predict the course of diseases, why should it not reach inside other kinds of closed containers, e.g. sealed boxes, or reach distant or even future scenes and events? Before long, entranced clairvoyantes were purportedly giving demonstrations of just these abilities. Some, indeed, believed that their vision extended beyond this world altogether, and regaled admiring wonder-seekers with visions of heaven, angels, other planets, guardian spirits, and the souls of deceased human beings.

Out of the 'rapport' between mesmeric operator and mesmeric subject (supposedly due to the transmission of the quasi-electrical 'magnetic fluid' from the former to the latter) arose other alleged 'paranormal' phenomena. Subjects could, it was believed, read the thoughts of the operator, feel pinpricks inflicted upon him, taste substances placed in his mouth. An operator might be able to entrance or influence the subject by the sheer exercise of his will – it was supposed that he exercised this control by directing the magnetic fluid into appropriate parts of his subject's nervous system. Indeed, towards the middle years of the nineteenth century, some mesmeric subjects purportedly fell under the 'control' of departed spirits and other exalted beings, and thus became 'mediums' for communication between this world and the next.

The second category of phenomena falling within the SPR's field followed immediately from the first and was closely related to it. What may be called the spiritualistic wing of the mesmeric movement, the wing that took seriously the tales of contact with angels and departed spirits (there was, incidentally, a materialist, even atheist, wing, which allied itself with phrenology), had by the late 1840s become moderately well known, and had, especially in America, achieved some degree of harmony with the Swedenborgians, who were likewise well known, and in some quarters influential. Thus it came about that when what looked at first like an unremarkable poltergeist case, of a kind common enough down the centuries, and usually attributed to diabolic influence, took a peculiar (but not unprecedented) turn, a new religious movement was born. During the early months of 1848, the small wooden cottage of Mr J. D. Fox, a blacksmith of Hydesville, New York State, was disturbed by a variety of odd events. The most notable were sustained and imperious rapping sounds of unknown origin, which resounded night after night, fraying the family's nerves and spoiling its sleep. Eventually, in despair, Mrs Fox and her daughters began to address questions and commands to the invisible agent, and to their shock and astonishment received intelligent replies, rapped out by means of a simple code. Neighbours were summoned. The rappings assumed the form of communications from deceased persons, and showed a surprising knowledge of local affairs. An enterprising local publisher, Mr E. E. Lewis, brought out a pamphlet containing the signed statements of twenty-two witnesses (90). Sight-seers began to come from miles around to witness the wonders.

Eventually it became apparent that the phenomena centred not upon the house, but around the two youngest Fox children, Margaretta (aged fifteen) and Kate (aged eleven), described by Slater Brown (19, p. 99) as 'simple, corn-fed country girls'. Others discovered that they had similar gifts. The phenomena spread by a kind of infection. Persons who visited Hydesville found on their return home that the spirits would also rap for them. The Fox sisters went on the road, exhibiting their 'mediumship' in New York and other large cities, and by the early 1850s 'Spiritualism' had begun to spread quite

widely through the Eastern United States. Spiritualist associations and
Spiritualist newspapers sprang up, and soon the phenomena were
exported (with somewhat limited success) to Britain and the Continent
of Europe. (On the early history of Spiritualism, see 19 and 122c.)

The relationship between mesmerism and Spiritualism was twofold.
The mesmeric movement had accustomed the public to the supposed
phenomena of clairvoyance, and to the idea that certain gifted
sensitives might perceive, or be influenced by, the inhabitants of the
next world. Thus it had prepared the ground for the acceptance of
Spiritualism. But the mesmeric movement also had its own press and
its own supporters, its own operators and its own clairvoyantes. These
were very readily transferred to or absorbed by the growing Spiritualist
movement. Mesmeric clairvoyantes, or the type of person who would
previously have become such, now emerged as the first 'mental
mediums' – mediums whose contact with the spirits was through
'interior' vision or hearing, or through the spirits 'taking over' and
controlling their bodies or parts thereof, especially, of course, the parts
required for speech and writing.

'Physical mediumship' – the sort in which communication with the
departed proceeds through paranormal physical events in the
medium's vicinity – diversified during the remainder of the nineteenth
century a great deal more than did mental mediumship. From simple
raps, the spirits, or the mediums, or both, graduated to 'table-tipping'
with, and sometimes without, contact of hands with table (an
upturned top-hat made an acceptable substitute for a small table); to
movement of other household objects, including musical instruments;
to actual playing on those musical instruments; to the visible
'materialization' of hands with which to move objects and play
instruments (these materializations were held to be made of a fluidic
substance, later known as 'ectoplasm', descended from the old
magnetic fluid of the mesmerists, and generated by the peculiarly
constituted organism of the medium); to the materialization of vocal
apparatus through which the spirits could speak directly (the 'direct
voice'), often with the aid of a speaking trumpet; and at last to the
materialization of complete ectoplasmic replicas of the bodies which
deceased persons had formerly inhabited. Of course many of these
phenomena required darkness or near-darkness for their production
(delicate ectoplasmic structures were, it was claimed, liable to be
damaged by light, especially short-wavelength blue light), a fact which
led cynics to suggest that darkness was merely a cover for fraud. This

suggestion received support, especially in and after the 1870s, from a series of unsavoury 'exposures'.

Other phenomena of physical mediumship included: levitation of the medium, elongation of the medium's body, the production of 'spirit lights', 'apports' (small objects brought into the seance room by the spirits), the precipitation of paintings onto blank cards or canvases, and 'psychic photography' (the appearance of 'extras', often veiled in clouds of 'ectoplasm', on studio photographs of paying sitters). Exposures of psychic photographers were numerous and devastating.

The third category of phenomena falling within the provenance of psychical research was less directly linked with the other two, though still having some connections with them. It was that of traditional ghost stories – apparitions, hauntings, and linked perhaps thereto, assorted cases of visions, crystal visions, and so forth.

It was thus, I think, in the historical setting of 1882, fairly clear what phenomena could be designated as the subject matter of 'psychical research'. They included the phenomena of mesmerism and hypnotism; of paranormal healing; of clairvoyance, thought-transference and precognition; of mental and physical mediumship; and of apparitions and hauntings. There is no doubt, of course, that many of the founders of the SPR hoped for a positive outcome to their inquiries; hoped, that is, that impartial investigation would prove that some at least of the phenomena under scrutiny were genuine. The 1870s had been a decade in which 'scientific' materialism of a rather crude kind had made unparalleled advances at the expense of all varieties of religious belief. Huxley, Tyndall, Clifford, Bastian, drew upon the Continental materialism of Büchner and Haeckel, and upon Darwinian evolutionary theory, to produce a 'materialist synthesis' which shook the faith of the older generation and drove many of the younger into agnosticism. Under these circumstances the work of the SPR assumed in the eyes of some a peculiar urgency and importance (see 44b). Perhaps it would be possible to answer materialism with science and to show that not all the findings of science tended to the support of materialism. However one must not let the hopes of certain early psychical researchers obscure the fact that they were committed to investigating the phenomena 'without prejudice or prepossession, and in a scientific spirit.' Others who joined the enterprise were dedicated to demolishing the evidence for survival and for the miraculous in general. What we have to consider here is the validity of data and of arguments, not the religious and philosophical views of those who proferred them.

Without doubt the SPR answered a contemporary need. Some of the ablest people of the period devoted a great deal of time, energy and money to running it, and to carrying out the very extensive investigations reported in its early publications. They included Henry Sidgwick (1838–1900), professor of moral philosophy at Cambridge, and first president of the SPR; his wife Eleanor (1845–1936), second principal of Newnham College, Cambridge; F. W. H. Myers (1843–1901), a poet and classical scholar, author of *Human Personality and its Survival of Bodily Death* (1903), a two-volume survey of the first twenty years of the Society's work; Edmund Gurney (1847–1888), who wrote *Phantasms of the Living* (two volumes, 1886), a work on apparitions that is still frequently referred to; Sir Oliver Lodge (1851–1940), a physicist and pioneer of wireless telegraphy; and Frank Podmore (1856–1910), the historian of Spiritualism, who consistently played the role of *advocatus diaboli*, examining and rejecting all evidence which others had presented as tending to prove human survival of bodily death. Mrs Sidgwick was the niece of a Prime Minister, the sister of a Prime Minister, and the sister-in-law of the wife of the Archbishop of Canterbury. I mention this not because I think that sharing the genes of prime ministers is a guarantee of intelligence (Mrs Sidgwick's intelligence was in any case manifest), but to bring out the point that psychical research was thought important by members of the intellectual, literary and even political 'establishments'. Among the early members and honorary members of the SPR were Tennyson, Ruskin, Gladstone, 'Lewis Carroll', A. J. Balfour, Lord Rayleigh, Couch Adams, William James, J. J. Thomson, Sir William Crookes, G. F. Watts and Alfred Russel Wallace. Tennyson expressed what may have been his thoughts about the enterprise in lines first published in 1889:

> The Ghost in Man, the Ghost that once was Man,
> But cannot wholly free itself from Man,
> Are calling to each other thro' a dawn
> Stranger than earth has ever seen; the veil
> Is rending, and the Voices of the day
> Are heard across the Voices of the dark.

It is probable that several of the early leaders of the SPR – and most especially F. W. H. Myers – took a similarly exalted view of the achievements and potentialities of psychical research. I wonder what they would make of the present state of the art. Investigations of mediumship, apparitions, and other survival-related phenomena have been to a considerable extent displaced by laboratory experiments on telepathy, clairvoyance and precognition. Problems of statistics and experimental design loom large in the literature. Computers and other electronic gadgets are widely used in both the running of experiments and the assessment of the results.

There have been innovations in terminology. The Continental and American term 'parapsychology' is beginning to replace 'psychical research', to which it is largely equivalent. From America has come the term 'extrasensory perception' (ESP) to cover any instance of the apparent acquisition of non-inferential knowledge of matters of fact without the use of the known sense organs. ESP is usually said to have three varieties: 'telepathy', in which the knowledge is of events in another person's mind, 'clairvoyance', in which the knowledge is of physical objects or states of affairs; and 'precognition' (telepathic or clairvoyant), where the knowledge relates to happenings still in the future. The word 'knowledge' is, however, not entirely appropriate, for there may be telepathic or clairvoyant 'interaction', in which a person's mental state or actions may be influenced by an external state of affairs, though he does not 'know' or 'cognize' it.

Another American term is 'psychokinesis' (PK), the direct influence of mental events on physical events external to the agent's body. The term 'psi' (Greek letter Ψ) is sometimes used to cover both ESP and PK.

I cannot, in the space available to me, undertake a general review and assessment of the evidence for psi-phenomena. That a fairly good case can be made out for ESP will be taken for granted in much of the rest of this book. (For a survey of ESP research I recommend Palmer, 118a.) Lest this be thought a sign of such credulity as to undermine the remainder of my argument, I should perhaps point out, what will I trust became clear later on, that if there were *no evidence at all* for ESP, the 'case for survival' could well be *much stronger than it is*.

Despite changes of emphasis the parapsychological enterprise today is recognizably continuous with the undertaking set afoot by those distinguished and earnest Victorians one hundred years ago. There has in fact been in the last decade or so something of a revival of interest among parapsychologists in the problem of survival. It is my task in

this book to review some of the factual evidence, old and new, which
has been thought to bear one way or another upon this problem. I
emphasize the 'some', for it is both impossible and undesirable to
attempt to be comprehensive. The quantity of potentially relevant
material is enormous (a select bibliography will be found in 44e), and
those who have not taken a serious look at complete sets of the
Proceedings and *Journal* of the SPR and the ASPR have perhaps little
idea of its extent. Some of this material I can cut out at once, because it
consists mainly of evidence for fraud and self-deception. I omit it with
regret, for much entertainment is to be derived from studying the
methods of psychic photographers and fraudulent physical mediums.
Another class of material which I shall omit is much harder to define
satisfactorily. It consists of evidence, maybe sound, maybe not, for
phenomena which, if genuine, could with some degree of plausibility
be interpreted in terms of the survival hypothesis if that were
antecedently established, but which do not by themselves even begin
to constitute evidence for that hypothesis. Phenomena such as the
production of 'spirit lights' at a seance, or the elongation of the
medium's body, or the levitation of the medium into the air, will
perhaps serve as examples. Such phenomena have often been
attributed to the activities of 'the spirits', and they may well be very
difficult to explain; but there is nothing about them, taken just in
themselves, to suggest to us that they are manifestations of a
personality, still less of the personality of a deceased human being.

Let us go one stage further. Suppose that at a seance or in a haunted
house there appears and is photographed a perfect simulacrum of a
certain deceased person, and that there is no sign of trickery; or let us
suppose that the recognizable voice of a certain deceased person is
tape-recorded, and that the 'voice-print' matches up with that of his
voice when alive. Would these astonishing phenomena *by themselves*
constitute evidence that the person himself has survived the dissolution
of his body? They would not. A simulacrum or shell, or a hollow voice
mouthing empty words, need have 'behind' them no personality, no
surviving sentient mind. Further evidence would be required before
we could begin to take the survivalist explanation seriously. And it is
easy, up to a point, to see what such evidence would have to consist in.
We would need evidence of intelligence, of personality characteristics,
of goals, purposes and affections, and of a stream of memory, that are
largely or recognizably continuous with those once possessed by a
certain formerly incarnate human being. That is the sort of evidence

we are concerned with, and a materialization, 'direct voice', or tape-recorded spirit voice, would have to provide it *in addition to* mere physical similarity before we could begin to take it seriously as evidence for survival. For that reason phenomena of these classes will not often be mentioned in this book.

I shall instead, and by the same token, concentrate upon classes of phenomena – certain sorts of apparitions, and some cases of mental mediumship and of ostensible reincarnation – which do sometimes appear to provide evidence for the survival of a personality. Of course the notion of personal identity is a complex and elusive one, and some people would say that personal identity is logically as well as factually linked to bodily continuity, so that it makes no sense to talk of a person surviving the dissolution of his body. I shall touch briefly on this issue later on. Another possibility to be borne in mind – one with which not a little of the evidence could be squared – is that there is survival, but survival only of a diminished and truncated something, capable of manifesting as a quasi-person in certain circumstances, but not ordinarily to be thought of as a person at all. The late professor C. D. Broad discussed this idea under the name of the 'psychic factor' or 'psi-component' hypothesis (18a, pp. 536-551; 18c, pp. 419-430). I do not, however, want to spend too much time discussing such issues in the abstract before I have given some concrete examples of the evidence, or supposed evidence, with which we have to deal.

Most of the material which I shall cite will, as I have said, come from the publications of the SPR and the ASPR. Occasionally I shall draw upon evidence of comparable quality from other sources; and where I cite cases of more dubious authenticity, it will be mainly to illustrate possibilities. Of course the question immediately arises of what, in this context, would constitute evidence of appropriate quality. Some writers of sceptical tendency are apt to deny not just that we have, but that we ever could have, evidence strong enough to establish the genuineness of such paranormal phenomena as telepathy or precognition, let alone to establish human survival of bodily death. The position of these extreme disbelievers was discussed by Edmund Gurney in an illuminating essay first published in 1887 (54). Many of them have implicitly based themselves on principles derived from a celebrated essay on miracles by the eighteenth century Scottish philosopher, David Hume. Hume's argument (suitably emended) is, in essence, this. The cumulative evidence in favour of certain basic 'laws of nature' is immensely strong, so strong, in fact, that no evidence in favour of an event contravening one of them, in favour, that is, of a paranormal phenomenon, could ever outweigh it. Hence whenever we encounter supposed evidence for a paranormal event, we are always justified in dismissing that evidence. The 'laws of nature' taken by upholders of this doctrine as 'basic' are commonly ones which they think fundamental to a rather crudely materialistic view of the universe.

If practising scientists as a body had ever come to take this argument seriously we would, I suppose, still believe ourselves to inhabit a universe whose leading features would be conceived precisely as they were conceived at the moment of mass conversion to Hume's doctrines. Of course scientists do not take it seriously, and we no longer believe that the earth is flat. The argument errs in the first place by equating 'paranormal' events with events which violate currently accepted laws of nature. If, at a seance, an object (or a person!) suddenly floats up into the air, this does not necessarily constitute a violation of the law of gravity. The first reaction of an observing scientist (or say his second reaction, because his first reaction would certainly be astonishment) would be to look for the unknown force or the unknown structure (a force or a structure perhaps in no conflict with the accepted principles of mechanics or physics) which had raised it up. But in any case there can be no law of nature that is so solidly established as to be immune from revision. Consider the following possibility. A law of nature changes overnight. Following Hume's argument we refuse to accept any evidence whatever that it has changed. We say 'that can't be right!', 'that can't be right!', and so on. Consequently all our predictions and calculations continue to be hopelessly wrong. Where did we err? The answer is obvious. First of all we assumed that the evidence in favour of the old law grew stronger by a constant amount with each successive verification; hence we could hardly expect it to be overthrown in any period of time shorter than that already taken to build up this massive accumulation of evidence. It is, however, clear that what, as a matter of psychological fact, each one of us acts upon is not some conspectus of the accumulated wisdom of the ages, but a kind of running average of the more recent observations. Nor (though I cannot go into this further) is it irrational to act upon such a basis. Secondly, we did not allow this evidence in favour of the new law to accumulate. We dismissed each piece of evidence separately on the grounds that since it conflicted with an established law it *cannot really have been sound evidence.* And this is wholly irrational. Evidence is good if it fulfils certain criteria appropriate to evidence (e.g. the witness or experimenter is of good repute, he made recordings with instruments generally agreed to be reliable, and so on). It does not become bad evidence just because the phenomenon it is evidence for is regarded as antecedently improbable.

It has, in fact, been peculiarly characteristic of those hostile to the claims of parapsychology to adopt the second of the above-mentioned stratagems. They say in effect (I am quoting Gurney here), 'The fact is so improbable that extremely good evidence is needed to make us believe it; and *this* evidence is not good, for how can you trust people who believe such absurdities?' (54, p. 264). Comment would be superfluous. It is not superfluous, however, to point out that though extreme sceptics have pushed their arguments to the verge of paranoia, it is none the less vital when examining the alleged evidence for novel and debatable phenomena to maintain a strict watch for certain recurrent sources of error. These sources of error can arise in all the areas which I propose to discuss, so it will be as well to say something now about each of them in turn. If they can be eliminated from the evidence under review, we shall be able to present that evidence, at least provisionally, as being of a quality which merits serious attention. They may be taken under two headings: hoaxing and fraud; and mistaken testimony.

1. Hoaxing and Fraud
Hoaxing and fraud could vitiate the evidence we have to deal with in one of two ways:

(a)   the supposed witnesses of apparitions, and other experients in cases of 'spontaneous' ESP or PK, might have concocted their stories for amusement, notoriety, or even for what they conceive to be the good of humanity;

(b)   mediums who stand to profit financially from successful sittings might take steps to deceive their clients.

The first of these possibilities does not strike me as a very serious one, at least so far as the cases investigated by the SPR are concerned. It is true that several hoaxes have come to light after the publication of the case reports. But in the great majority of cases the witnesses have been persons of unblemished reputation, with no apparent motive for deceit. They have as a matter of routine given signed statements to the Society's representatives, they have submitted to questioning, their friends have given corroborative testimony, all relevant supporting documents, e.g. death certificates, have been obtained and put on file; and so forth. I do not think that under these circumstances it is reasonable to postulate wholesale hoaxing as a general explanation of the inflow of case reports.

The matter stands somewhat differently with regard to possible fraud by mediums. Many physical mediums, and some mental mediums, have been caught in the most egregious trickery. Still, I shall not in this book be dealing with physical mediumship to any extent, and the mental mediums whom I shall principally discuss – most notably Mrs Piper and Mrs Leonard – were never caught in fraud despite some rigorous precautions. In the case of Mrs Piper these precautions included opening her mail and having her shadowed by detectives to ascertain whether or not she employed agents. Mrs Leonard was also at one time shadowed by detectives. I do not think that the fraud hypothesis will help us here.

2.   Mistaken Testimony

That eyewitness testimony, especially as to unusual or bizarre happenings, cannot be relied upon, is a commonplace of sceptical assaults upon the credibility of evidence for the sorts of phenomena we are considering; and it is a commonplace which can be substantiated by an appeal to a large body of psychological findings. These findings, however, bear somewhat unequally upon different parts of our subject-matter. Testimony concerning the phenomena of physical mediumship, which are commonly exhibited under conditions of near darkness and of emotional stress, is notoriously unreliable. However I shall present very little of such testimony. When it comes to mental mediumship the case is different. We usually have complete contemporary records of what such mediums say or write, so that the question of mistaken testimony rarely arises. It is over stories of apparitions and related phenomena that the problem impinges most directly upon the subject-matter of this book.

Some writers (see, e.g., 169a) appear to want to dismiss almost all testimony concerning apparitions on the following grounds:
(a)   In only a few cases did the percipients immediately write down a full account of their experience. Stories told months or even years after the event are likely to be seriously in error, for memory is notoriously fallible, and tall stories tend to grow with retelling. In one celebrated case, the principal witness, Sir Edmund Hornby, claimed that he saw

an apparition whilst he was in bed with his wife, who also confirmed the story. However it was later established that at the date of the supposed apparition Sir Edmund was not yet married.

(b)   Numerous experimental investigations have cast doubt on the reliability of eyewitness testimony even when that testimony has been given immediately after the event.

I do not think that these objectives are very powerful. With regard to (a) we do have the witnesses' contemporary statements in a modest number of cases. Furthermore there is no reason to believe that percipients of apparitions have a general tendency towards retrospective exaggeration. Stevenson (153b) gives a number of instances in which witnesses have written a second account many years after the first without introducing substantial changes or exaggerations. This finding receives support from experimental studies. Recent fresh evidence concerning the Hornby case rather suggests that Sir Edmund Hornby and his wife had simply forgotten that they were not yet married at the time when the apparition was seen (44a). (b) These investigations show that eyewitnesses are liable to be mistaken over details important for forensic purposes, e.g. who fired first, or what colour jacket the accused was wearing. They do not show that witnesses are likely to be mistaken upon points crucial to the assessment of apparition stories, e.g. whether the figure which stood before one was that of one's maternal grandfather.

Suppose, then, that we accept, provisionally and for the purposes of argument, that we do possess some quantities of evidence, not so inferior in quality as to be instantly dismissible, which seems *prima facie* to suggest that certain formerly incarnate human beings have survived the dissolution of their carnal bodies, and continue to exhibit some at least of the memories and personal characteristics which they possessed in life. How are we to interpret this evidence? Discussions of the pros and cons of the 'survival' hypothesis will occupy much of the rest of the book. There are, however, two recurrent counter-hypotheses which merit a mention at this point.

Chance Coincidence

The first, and less important, is what may be called the chance coincidence hypothesis. It is seen at its simplest in connection with allegedly precognitive dreams. There are in print quite a number of cases in which a dreamer has apparently dreamed, with considerable correspondence of detail, of an event which, at the time of the dream, had not yet happened. Is this proof of precognition? The following counter-explanation might be offered. There are in the world, or even in that limited part of the world where the publications of the SPR and the ASPR circulate, many millions of persons, each of whom probably dreams several dreams a night. A year's total of dreams will add up to thousands of millions. Given so many dreams, surely we would expect that now and again, and *simply by chance*, one or two of them will correspond, to a marked extent, with some immediately subsequent event? These dreams will be remembered and talked about, while the others – which we may call the 'forgotten also rans' – will simply pass into oblivion. Thus it comes about that the publications of certain learned societies are swelled with a growing number of accounts of dreams falsely thought to have been precognitive.

A very similar argument can be applied to certain stories of apparitions. Two sorts of apparition case that figure prominently in the literature are cases of apparitions coinciding with the death of the person seen, and cases of apparitions simultaneously seen by more than one person. Now suppose we make the assumption that some people have hallucinations of a certain type (i.e. see apparitions) more frequently than they let on. They keep quiet about it for fear of being thought unbalanced. Then we might expect that now and again one of these hallucinations would, just by chance, coincide with a death, or coincide spatially and temporally with someone else's hallucination. The percipients will be prepared to talk about *these* hallucinations, because they will not think such talk will endanger their reputations for sanity. Hence stories of 'crisis' apparitions and of collectively perceived apparitions will get into circulation. The 'forgotten also rans' will not be heard of again.

This issue will recur later. Here I shall simply remark that a number of surveys, old and new, suggest quite strongly that what may be called the 'spontaneous hallucination rate' in the population at large is not nearly high enough to support the argument (see 57; 58; 83; 118b; 146; 169b).

A variant of the chance coincidence hypothesis is often applied to explain away the 'hits' so often scored by mental mediums. Many mediums, it is held, deal to a considerable extent in banalities. They deliver 'messages' from the beyond which would probably be appropriate for a high percentage of likely sitters, especially sitters of the sex, age and class group of the current client. Naturally the messages appear 'evidential' to the sitter; but they are not. The medium has succeeded by a mixture of chance and skill.

The problem touched on here can be a very real one, and attempts have been made to devise statistical methods of assessment to circumvent it. I do not, however, think that the problem is an important one for our immediate purposes, for I do not believe that in the majority of examples of apparently successful mental mediumship which I shall actually cite anyone would seriously raise the chance coincidence hypothesis.

'Super-ESP'

The second commonly proferred counter-hypothesis to the survivalistic one is what Hart (60b) has called the 'super-ESP' hypothesis. It is that all the phenomena which we are tempted to take as indicating the survival of the memories and personalities of certain deceased persons can be more simply and satisfactorily explained in terms of ESP by living persons – by the mediums who deliver the messages, the percipients who see the apparitions, and so on. This hypothesis, pushed to its limits, lands us in the following dilemma. If a piece of putative evidence for survival is to be of use, it must be verifiable – we must be able to check by consulting records or surviving friends that the information given by the ostensible communicator was correct. But if the sources for checking it are extant, they might in theory be telepathically or clairvoyantly accessible to the medium or percipient. Since we do not know the limits of ESP we can never say for certain that ESP of the extraordinary extent that would often be necessary – 'super-ESP' – is actually impossible. This is the central dilemma in the interpretation of ostensible evidence for survival, and it will crop up again and again throughout the rest of this book. I have no convenient sword with which to cut this Gordian knot. But as a guiding principle in approaching it I propose the following. One should, whenever possible, avoid maintaining any hypothesis by engaging in speculations which do not, so far as we can at the moment see, commit one to propositions which can be tested against the facts. It is, for example, quite unprofitable, because barren of further consequences, to maintain the super-ESP hypothesis by postulating telepathy between the unconscious mind of the medium and the unconscious mind of some distant person, for this is a process unobservable in principle, and nothing further can be done to check up on it; and it is equally barren to explain away mistakes and inconsistencies by a purported mediumistic communicator by suggesting that the error came not from the supposed communicator but from lying and malicious impersonating spirits.

Finally, I must emphasize that this book is only a brief introduction to some exceedingly difficult and complex problems. Large volumes could be – indeed have been – written upon topics or cases to which I have been able to devote only a chapter, or a paragraph, or a sentence. Though I try to develop certain lines of argument, and to reach certain conclusions – the book would be very flat if I did not – I am more concerned to present the data and the issues than to promote a particular set of views. The conclusions that I in fact offer are fairly modest. I profess no overwhelming certainty as to the true explanations of the phenomena under review. I am, however, certain of two things. The first is that we are here confronted with a great range of unsolved problems and unexplained phenomena, all of which are potentially of great psychological and philosophical interest. The second is that these issues are not of merely academic concern. They are important to anyone who thinks and feels about the human situation. I have heard many people of a bluff and fiddlesticks turn of mind talk somewhat as follows. 'Of course we all perish utterly at our deaths. But one life, lived to the full, should be enough for anyone.' Such people have, I think, commonly had comfortable and prosperous lives. Those – the majority – who have been less fortunate, often through no fault of their own, might express other feelings.

2 Mediumship: General

With the phenomena of mediumship, which will occupy the next seven chapters, we at once reach the very heart of the debate concerning the alleged evidence for survival. I gave in the first chapter a brief account of modern Spiritualist mediumship and its origins within the animal magnetic movement of the early nineteenth century. But these forms of mediumship – known at least by hearsay to most members of contemporary Western society – are only local and culturally shaped versions of phenomena which have, and have had, their equivalents in many societies, past and present. This point will be forcefully brought home to anyone who glances at some of the quite numerous field studies of possession and kindred phenomena published by social anthropologists (e.g. 7; 25; 38; 65; 124; 168). I am talking here about 'possession' in a strong sense – the ostensible controlling of someone's speech and behaviour by a discarnate entity capable of intelligent communication. In some societies all kinds of diseases and ailments are attributed to possession by malevolent spirits; but with 'possession' in this sense we are not concerned.

Possessed persons may be divided into two broad categories: those who are the victims of possession, who are involuntarily taken over and manipulated by discarnate entities (usually hostile); and those who invite and indeed cultivate possession by better-disposed beings through whose agency good works of one kind or another may be performed. Among the latter class of persons are the shamans, witchdoctors, cunning men, seers and spirit mediums who fulfil similar roles in so many widely different and widely separated societies. The discarnate entities which possess persons of these two categories include in many cultures not just deceased human beings (as in Western Spiritualism), but all sorts of gods, godlings, demons, devils, and animal spirits. These last, I think, are usually not the spirits of individual deceased animals, but are either the spirits of tiger-in-general, crocodile-in-general, and so forth, or superhuman entities which assume the form of animals, as in the numerous oriental tales of fox spirits, monkey spirits, etc.

Anthropologists of an earlier generation were prone to write off shamans and witchdoctors as impostors or hysterics or some amalgam of the two. Sir James Frazer, for example, wrote in 1913 (42, p. 15):

> ... these persons more or less crazed in their wits, and particularly hysterical or epileptic patients, are for that very reason thought to be peculiarly favoured by the spirits, and are therefore consulted as oracles, their wild and whirling words passing for the revelations of a higher power, whether a god or a ghost, who considerately screens his too dazzling light under a thick veil of dark sayings and mysterious ejaculations. I need hardly point out the very serious dangers which menace any society where such theories are commonly held and acted upon.

Despite Frazer's prognostications of doom, many societies in which shamans and witchdoctors play a leading role have survived very well, and look like continuing to do so. This suggests that, whatever appearances there may be to the contrary, such persons possess a far greater degree of worldly efficiency than Victorian anthropologists allowed. Modern anthropologists recognize this, and tend to regard shamanism not as a form of mental alienation, dangerous to the sufferer and to his society, but as a phenomenon with many facets, requiring, perhaps, explanation on a number of different levels. One level of explanation may, indeed, in some cases be the psychopathological. The 'classical' Eskimo or Siberian shaman often undergoes during his training or initiation a period of emotional instability and mental disturbance; but from this he may emerge a stronger and more integrated person than he was before (37, pp. 23–32). He has been cured through suffering, or rather has cured himself through suffering. For novice shamans in other parts of the world even this period of suffering and disturbance may not be necessary. After conducting in-depth interviews with ten Shona *ngangas*, Michael Gelfand concluded that all were 'physically and mentally normal' (47, p. 133), whilst the editors of a standard anthropological work on spirit mediumship in Africa, state (7, p. xxiv) that in Africa mediums are by no means crazed in their wits. 'On the contrary they are usually shrewd, intelligent, and accepted members of their communities.'

Although being 'possessed' by discarnate entities, and the converse phenomenon, namely quitting the physical body to visit the spirit world and talk and negotiate with its inhabitants, are the most spectacular of the shaman's skills, they form only a part of his repertoire. The shaman (I am using the word now in an extended sense to include not just Eskimo and Siberian shamans but all kinds of witchdoctors, mediums, and so forth) is in many societies first and foremost a repository of cosmological and theological doctrines. He knows his tribe's corner of the universe, the unseen powers which occupy and rule it, and the proper means for approaching and propitiating them. This knowledge may be thought vital to the management of weather, crops, and game. The shaman can communicate with and obtain information from the ancestral spirits of his tribe. He plays a leading part in all sorts of religious ceremonies and *rites de passage*, which may have in turn not just inner symbolic meanings, but recreational aspects, so that his dramatic and artistic skills may be of great importance to the community. Above all the shaman is a healer. He diagnoses, perhaps clairvoyantly, the nature and causes of afflictions, drives out the evil spirit responsible, prescribes herbs to cure the residual physical damage. He may be especially successful with what we should regard as mental illnesses, and if these take the form of ostensible possession, we may have the curious spectacle of a possessed shaman treating a possessed patient. His clairvoyant capacities and his ability to dream dreams may be in demand for locating lost property and detecting thieves. He may thus come to be involved in the maintenance of social order. A good shaman obviously requires many gifts other than just that of entering trance and uttering wild and whirling words while 'possessed'. He requires knowledge, intelligence, dramatic flair, tact, social skills, and a thorough understanding of the individuals with whom he has to deal.

The successful exercise of these gifts may bring a shaman commensurate rewards in the shape of wealth and social status. This fact has led some writers (see especially 92) to lay emphasis upon the possibilities for advancement which a career as a shaman may open up to persons from normally underprivileged sections of a society – for instance women, homosexuals, the very poor, and members of minority groups. No doubt there is an element of truth in this view, as in many other views of this complex phenomenon. One must, however, beware of supposing that shamans from underprivileged backgrounds have in all, or even most, cases adopted this course of life from conscious policy. Behaviour like that of an entranced or possessed shaman, which from a certain point of view may appear irrational and arbitrary, may conceal a deeper rationality and a strategy which is not fully comprehended even by the agent himself.

A question of particular interest to parapsychologists is of course that of whether shamans (using the word still in an extended sense) may sometimes include among their other gifts the 'paranormal' ones of ESP and PK. This is a difficult issue. It is only quite recently that a few anthropologists have given serious consideration to the possibility that there may be elements of the paranormal in the performances of shamans, but adequate investigations remain largely to be carried out (see, for instance, 4 and 94; and for older material 87a and 113). Meanwhile we have a fair number of travellers' tales of varying credibility, and a much smaller number of footnotes and incidental observations by anthropologists. I wish that I had the space to review this highly entertaining literature. My personal impression of it is that there is some evidence that certain shamans occasionally exhibit ESP and perhaps also PK; and that there is rather more evidence that certain shamans (sometimes the same ones) may work wonders by adroit conjuring – not necessarily, it should be added, with any criminal intent, but simply as part of a dramatic performance designed, for instance, to manipulate a patient's mind in directions favourable to a cure.

There are very few studies from an anthropological perspective of spirit mediumship in Western society. This might seem surprising, since the phenomenon is relatively common. Most accounts of mediumship come either from dedicated believers, or else from parapsychologists chiefly interested in assessing the ostensible evidence for ESP. It may be that anthropologists are afraid of being tarred with these brushes. I think, however, that most people who have any substantial acquaintance with Western Spiritualism will recognize that many of the above observations about shamans and shamanism apply equally to Spiritualist mediums in our own society. It is true, of course, that the discarnate entities which are alleged to 'possess' or otherwise communicate through Spiritualist mediums usually (though not always) claim to be just the spirits of deceased humans rather than of the gods, demons, animal spirits and other beings which additionally manifest through shamans. But the outward forms of the phenomena present many analogies which it would be superfluous to pursue in detail. In fact there are few mediumistic phenomena for which the literature of shamanism cannot provide parallels, and few shamanistic performances to which Spiritualism provides no counterpart. I have not heard of any shaman who has allegedly produced full-form materializations clad in flowing white ectoplasmic drapery; nor, to my regret, do I know a contemporary Spiritualist church in which the officiating medium dances wildly when under spirit control. But these, and a few others, are the exceptions which prove the rule.

Just as Victorian anthropologists were apt to think shamans merely crazy, so some psychiatrists and clergymen have dramatically or unreflectingly asserted that many mediums are mentally disturbed and probably certifiable. Such assertions are as mistaken in the latter case as in the former. Most mediums exhibit in their ordinary lives no symptoms of hysteria, epilepsy or mental disturbance. There are, of course, exceptions, but I should hesitate to say that these are more numerous than in the ordinary run of the population. In fact several mediums are among the most practical people I know. None the less some mediums claim to have gone through a period of suffering and emotional disturbance due to early psychic experiences which they did not understand and which led them to fear they were going mad. As with shamans, these initial problems disappeared after contact with and training by other and more developed mediums.

Again it is quite clear that although communication with the dead is the principal function which a medium performs, he or she (usually the latter) may fulfil many other functions too. Like shamans, mediums are repositories of, or vehicles for, assorted theological and cosmological teachings, though the importance of this role is somewhat diluted in our society by the existence of a large body of readily accessible Spiritualist literature. Mediums who are the ministers of Spiritualist churches may, like shamans, officiate at such *rites de passage* as weddings and funerals (arguably the most significant *rite de passage* of all!). Healing and mediumship go hand in hand almost as much as do shamanism and the treatment of disease. Physical diseases are treated in healing sessions by dedicated spiritual healers, many of whom believe that spirits channel healing forces through their hands. Most mediums are apt to suggest homely (often herbal) remedies for minor ailments. Many in effect function as psychotherapists and general counsellors, and it would not surprise me to learn that with a clientele possessing appropriate background beliefs they achieve a success rate quite as high as that of qualified professionals. A reputable medium, like a reputable shaman, is apt to be shrewd, balanced and well-meaning, to have perhaps a touch of vanity and a liking for the dramatic, but to do overall much more good than harm.

It has, as I pointed out, not infrequently been suggested that shamanism offers a road to status for talented persons who might otherwise find themselves condemned to remain in underprivileged or even despised obscurity. Similar arguments might be put forward in connection with Spiritualist mediumship. Female mediums greatly outnumber male (which is not the case with shamans, but shamanism *is* a career – almost the only career – open to women). In fact it must be easier for a woman to become a minister or church leader within the Spiritualist movement than within almost any other religious organization. Furthermore these ladies often come from relatively poor and uneducated backgrounds. Not a few male mediums are (like certain shamans) reputedly homosexual, which might be construed as further evidence for the thesis under discussion. It is not a thesis which I personally would attempt to push very far, but whatever can be said in its favour so far as shamanism is concerned, can probably also be said in connection with Spiritualist mediumship.

I expressed above a fairly qualified belief that some shamans may in the exercise of their craft at times exhibit ESP or PK. My belief that certain mediums sometimes exhibit paranormal abilities is much less qualified – I was almost rash enough to write that it is unqualified – but since most of the next five chapters will be devoted to the sort of evidence on which my belief is based, I shall not further discuss the matter at this point.

I have tried, in this brief and inadequate account of the relevant anthropological material to show that Spiritualist mediumship, as we know it in Europe and America, has such clear affinities with what I have somewhat loosely chosen to call shamanism that it can only be regarded as a culturally conditioned variety of the latter. It is, if you like, the local variant of a general human potential. This conclusion can now be shelved and temporarily forgotten. It will be brought out again when I come to attempt a general assessment of the nature of mediumship. To a more detailed account of mediumistic phenomena we must now turn.

As I pointed out in the first chapter, Spiritualists themselves commonly distinguish two categories of mediumship, physical mediumship and mental mediumship. In physical mediumship, the spirits of deceased persons communicate through ostensibly paranormal physical happenings in the medium's neighbourhood. The 'power' for these happenings (raps, object movements, materializations, etc.) is supposedly obtained from the medium's own, peculiarly endowed, organism. In mental mediumship, the spirits either impress pictures and sound-images upon the medium's psychic perceptivity ('clairvoyant' mediumship), or else use her hand or vocal apparatus to communicate by speech or writing.

Both kinds of mediumship have many varieties, and are carried on in many different settings. Some mediums function as ministers of Spiritualist churches, and regularly enliven church services with a demonstration of clairvoyant mediumship; others see individual clients by appointment; others lead small groups of enquirers in so-called 'home circles'; some do all of these things. The initial aim is always the same. Sitters are to be convinced by the force of evidence that the communicating personalities are indeed the surviving spirits of particular formerly incarnate human beings. Thereafter the pronouncements of these spirits concerning the status and prospects of the post-mortem individual, and upon religious matters in general, will be accorded the weight due to genuine inside information. It is this emphasis upon evidence and proof that underlies Spiritualism's frequent claim to be a 'scientific' religion.

Physical Mediumship

By far the greater part of the ostensible evidence for survival comes from the phenomena of mental mediumship. This is, as I pointed out in the first chapter, because it is the *content* of what is communicated, rather than the *means* by which it is communicated, that yields (if anything does yield) evidence for the survival of personality. If paranormal raps resound in the vicinity of a medium, and hammer out intelligent sentences by means of a simple code (a phenomenon, incidentally, which I have several times witnessed myself in good light), this is no doubt very curious and interesting, but it does not *per se* constitute evidence for human survival of bodily death. However the raps *might* convey an 'evidential' message. In fact we have firsthand accounts of a number of cases in which they have apparently done so. Several of these concern D. D. Home (1833–1886), perhaps the most remarkable of all physical mediums. Thus, in a seance held at Edinburgh in 1870, and recorded by Mr P. P. Alexander (1, pp. 35–6), raps spelled out the name 'Pophy Sophy'. It transpired that this was the pet name of a child whose mother and aunt were present. The aunt burst into tears. The raps then spelled out, 'You were not to blame, and I am happy.' The aunt had blamed herself for supposed carelessness in allowing the child to catch scarlet fever.

The only form of physical mediumship of which I shall subsequently cite examples is the so-called 'direct voice'. The Spiritualist theory of the direct voice is that spirits construct for themselves vocal organs out of 'ectoplasm' supplied by the medium. With these vocal organs they are able to speak to the sitters, often directing their remarks into a speaking trumpet provided for the purpose. If the sitting is held in the dark, the trumpet, usually marked with luminous paint, may move around the circle, so that the voices speak from different positions. The possibilities for fraud here are limitless – one medium known to me used to conceal the reaching rods with which he manipulated his trumpets in the hollow legs of a small bamboo table – but some curious observations have none the less been made. For instance in the early part of this century an American direct voice medium, Mrs Etta Wriedt (1859–1942), of Detroit, greatly intrigued several leading members of the SPR. Sir William Barrett (1845–1925), one of the founders of that Society gives (103, pp. 83–84) the following account of a sitting with Mrs Wriedt:

> When after my examination of the room Mrs Wriedt and Miss Ramsden entered, the door was locked, and one of the electric lights over our head was left on to illuminate the room. We sat on chairs adjoining each other; I sat next to Mrs Wriedt and held her hand. Miss Ramsden sat on my left. We asked Mrs Wriedt to let us try in the light first, and at her suggestion Miss R. held the small end of a large aluminium trumpet to her ear; the larger end I supported with my left hand. My body therefore came between the trumpet and the medium. I had previously looked into the trumpet, which was perfectly bare and smooth. Presently Miss Ramsden said she heard a voice speaking to her, and entered into conversation with the voice. I only heard a faint whispering sound, but no articulate words. To avoid the possibility of Mrs Wriedt being the source of the whispering, I engaged her in talk, and while she was speaking Miss Ramsden still heard the faint voice in the trumpet, but begged us to stop speaking, as it prevented her hearing distinctly what the voice said. Miss Ramsden assured me afterwards that there could be no doubt whatever that the voice in the trumpet was independent of Mrs Wriedt, and I can testify that I watched the medium and saw nothing suspicious in the movement of her lips. She did not move from her place, and no accomplice or concealed arrangement could possibly have produced the voice.

Miss Ramdsen adds a note concerning the (evidential) message which she received. She says further, 'While holding the trumpet I could feel the vibration of the little voice inside.'

Mental Mediumship

Of mental mediumship there are numerous kinds, and I can mention only the more important. The most frequently seen, both in private consultations, and on the public platform, is that of 'clairvoyant' mediumship, which I mentioned above. The medium or sensitive may be in a slightly dissociated state, but is usually not entranced. She claims to 'see' or 'hear' deceased friends and relatives of persons present, and to transmit messages from them. Occasionally the 'seeing' and 'hearing' seem to reach an hallucinatory vividness, and the experience resembles that of seeing an apparition (see Chapter Fourteen). Sometimes the medium's guides (spirits who are alleged to direct her activities from the 'other side') may present the information in the form of symbolic visions which she must learn to interpret. Something of the flavour of such demonstrations may be gleaned from the following verbatim transcript (64a, pp. 163–164):

> *Medium* . . . See, a boy comes in your surroundings. He looks to me to be about 17 or 18, and I think there will have been a good deal of sorrow over the passing away of this boy. A lady brings this boy, and she wants the parents to know about him. Whether he passed away in weakness or not, I don't know. He is a very beautiful boy; she is telling me that it is Herbert Ernest. There is somebody belonging to him called Seth. I cannot get along with it. Do you know anybody called Seth and Mary that had a boy called Herbert Ernest Hobson?
>
> *Answer.* You are right, friend.
>
> *Medium.* They want you to know.
>
> Right in the corner there [pointing]. I don't know what to make of this at all. It is a youth. I should take him to be about 18. There is a gentleman with this youth; and I have a very curious feeling. I rather think this youth will have been killed from shock. Now he comes and shows me. He is without jacket, and his clothes are covered with colour. He is holding out his hands and there is a reddish dye on them. He may have worked in a dye works. I feel I would fall over. He may have met with his death in a dye works. It is Mrs Miller's boy, William Henry Miller; lived in Valley Place, and I think he would be killed in a dye works. Not more than four or five years ago, as far as I can see in the surroundings. This gentleman comes with him. He is Henry Mitchell, and he used to belong to Yeadon. He is helping the boy forward.
>
> (*All correct, except that Henry Mitchell is unrecognized. Mr Holden, my informant, knew William Henry Miller. Leg hurt at dye works, blood poisoning, died about 1911. Valley Dye Works.*)
>
> *Answer.* I know this man.

Clairvoyant mediumship has been less extensively studied by psychical researchers than it perhaps deserves. I shall give what are in effect some examples of it in Chapter Eleven. More attention has been focused on the kinds of mental mediumship that manifest through what F. W. H. Myers christened 'motor automatisms'. Motor automatisms are actions of an intelligent, purposive and even symbolic kind which go on outside the automatist's conscious control. They may include speech and writing, and then communication can sometimes be established with a quasi-personality ostensibly different from that of the automatist. In our society such quasi-personalties very readily take on the guise of deceased persons, and then, of course, automatism passes into ostensible mental mediumship.

A simple and well-known form of such mediumship is that of writing with an ouija or planchette board. Several persons sit round a table with the fingers lightly resting on an upturned glass or other pointer, or on a small, heart-shaped piece of wood, into the apex of which a downward-pointing pencil is inserted. The glass may then move so as to spell out words on letters of the alphabet encircling it ('ouija'), or the board writes with its pencil on an underlying piece of paper ('planchette'). In neither case need the outcome be deliberately brought about by one of the operators. It is as though each sitter, knowing that others are also involved, no longer feels tempted to analyse the situation and ask, 'Am *I* doing this?' Under these conditions one's hand may 'run by itself', under the control of systems outside the main stream of consciousness. Sometimes the sitters simply rest their hands on top of a small table, which then 'tips' to spell out words and sentences by means of a simple code. In Victorian times upturned top-hats often served instead of tables – yet another use for this versatile but now, alas, outmoded form of headgear.

To the participants in such seances, the mere fact that the devices move often seems surprising, indeed uncanny, and should coherent sentences be written they may be accorded the respect due to the deliverances of an oracle. I have myself come across a number of cases in which an ouija board wrote copiously and fluently and produced material which was quite alien to the conscious minds of the persons operating it. In each case, however, it appeared highly likely that the material was coming from some hidden level of the mind of a particular sitter. Thus I was once a sitter in a circle which received pungent communications from Goering and Goebbels and other deceased Nazi leaders. They favoured us with such interesting pieces of information as that Hitler was alive and well and operating a petrol pump in the town of Clifton, Arkansas, and that Martin Bormann was in Gothenburg disguised as a priest by the name of Father Odo. They favoured us also with various apologias for Nazism. After several sessions it became apparent that this little band of unrepentant sinners only communicated when the finger of one particular person was on the glass. Very reluctantly he admitted that many years before he had gone through a phase of admiration for certain features of Hitler's Germany, and had joined an extreme right-wing political organization. Now he repudiated, indeed abhorred, his former paltering with Nazisim. None the less these views were clearly still alive in him somewhere, and slipped out when his conscious censorship was circumvented by the ouija board. I am absolutely certain that he was not deliberately manipulating the glass – his embarrassment was too great, and he refused to participate further.

I have also come across a number of instances of ouija and planchette writings in which correct information was given which was *prima facie* unknown to any person present. Some examples will be given in a later chapter.

A rarer form of motor automatism is that of automatic writing by a single individual (see 63; 107). Such writing may develop as a symptom of mental disturbance, or it may be encouraged by a psychologist or psychotherapist as a means of reaching memories or emotions which have become dissociated from consciousness. Very often, however, it has been deliberately cultivated by normal persons bent upon 'psychical development'. The state of mind of an automatist during the production of automatic writing may be anything from normal wakefulness, with full knowledge of what is being written, to profound trance, with subsequent loss of memory for the events of the trance.

In most cases automatic writing does not progress beyond the production of crude and repetitive squiggles. Sometimes, however, the automatist may come in time to write more fluently and to exhibit skill or knowledge beyond her ordinary capacities. Automatic writing has been known to report events forgotten or unnoticed by the waking self, and to exhibit what look like flashes of ESP. The writing may profess beliefs and opinions differing from those of the automatist; may display literary fluency greatly exceeding hers; may compose long romances or religio-cosmological treatises (concerning the merits of which opinions differ considerably); and may claim to come not from the automatist but from a deceased person or supernatural being who has gained control over her neuromuscular apparatus. Claims to have a discarnate origin are, of course, in most cases not to be taken seriously;

they simply reflect the dramatizing tendencies, and the responsiveness to suggestion and to cultural influences, characteristic of automatic writing in general.

Some examples of automatic writings which have ostensibly been the vehicles of ESP will be given in later chapters.

Two important ideas crop up again and again in discussions of automatic writing and kindred motor automatisms.

(a)   Automatic writing, or at any rate automatic writing which exhibits literary and artistic abilities, the capacity to converse rationally, etc., is clearly the product of an intelligence. The intelligence, however, is not that of the automatist's waking mind, for the automatist does not consciously control what is written, and she may be as surprised as anyone else when she reads it. We must therefore suppose that whatever psychoneural system underlies, underpins or constitutes this intelligence must be of a nature not fundamentally different from that of the system which underlies the conscious activities of the ordinary waking intelligence. We are driven, in short, to postulate the existence of what may perhaps best be called *dissociated* or *subliminal* streams of consciousness.

(b)   Automatic writing is sometimes the vehicle for ostensible ESP, and it is so to an extent which makes it plausible to allege that ESP is more likely to manifest itself through a motor automatism than through the normal channels of waking activity.

The former of these proposals is hard to reject, though one might perhaps accept it only with some qualifications. The latter is very difficult to assess. F. W. H. Myers supports it simply by advancing numerous apparent examples of ESP manifested in automatic writing (110a, II, pp. 81–188). The problem, however, is that even if his examples are individually acceptable, this does not prove that the mental state (whatever it may be) which accompanies automatic writing is more favourable to the occurrence of ESP than is any other mental state. The necessary controlled experiments to discover whether or not this is so have still not been carried out. However, if we accept that Myers has made a preliminary case, we may proceed to some further considerations.

Parapsychologists who have collected and studied large numbers of cases of spontaneous ESP – cases in which the ESP has manifested itself in dreams, intuitions, hallucinations, visions, etc. – have often been driven to the conclusion that the information concerned is generally received (if that is the right word) and initially analysed, at a level beneath the threshold of ordinary consciousness. Furthermore it has trouble in forcing its way into the main stream of consciousness. It may only be able to do so when the latter is relaxed or idle, or in one of those 'altered states' (such as dreams) which seem to permit a freer passage of hitherto excluded material into consciousness. From this point of view motor automatisms, and especially automatic writing, represent a path by which dissociated or subliminal material, *including information acquired by ESP*, can find direct expression without having to crash whatever barrier it is that hinders its transition into consciousness. Motor automatisms are thus outpourings of the same levels of the personality which produce the dreams, visions, etc., by which spontaneous ESP is commonly manifested. Indeed F. W. H. Myers labelled the dreams, visions, etc., *sensory automatisms*. Just as the bodily movements in motor automatisms are made without the initiation, and generally without the concurrence, of conscious thought and will, so do these dreams, visions, etc., arise without it; and Myers regarded both motor and sensory automatisms as means by which subliminal streams of consciousness, often possessing enhanced dramatic abilities and powers of memory, and in receipt of extrasensory information, can make their deliverances available to the ordinary workaday mind.

It is impossible adequately to assess these complex, plausible, but controversial notions here. I introduce them mainly because they constitute a pervasive background to much parapsychological thinking in this area.

To return now to my exposition of the various kinds of mental mediumship. The most 'advanced' form of mental mediumship is without doubt what is generally termed 'trance' mediumship. Here the normal personality is, as it were, completely dispossessed by the intruding intelligence, which achieves a varying degree of control over the medium's speech, writing, and entire neuromuscular apparatus. The medium herself retains little or no recollection of what has been said or done in her 'absence', though sometimes she may on awakening seem to remember scenes and persons from some other sphere of existence.

This kind of trance mediumship (trance in the sense of unconsciousness of surroundings may accompany other forms of mediumship, including physical mediumship) tends to develop not, as it were, by the piecemeal advance of sensory automatism, so that now one hand is under external control, now both hands, and so on. Usually it evolves out of the 'clairvoyant' mediumship which I touched on earlier. The clairvoyant may feel herself to be overshadowed, influenced, gradually 'taken over' by another personality, while her own awareness of her surroundings progressively diminishes. With repetition, the passage to full trance becomes quicker and easier. Sometimes a sensitive discovers her gift when she is suddenly and completely entranced during a casual visit to a seance.

Usually there will be only a few deceased persons who can ostensibly control the medium's hand or vocal apparatus directly. They are generally referred to as 'controls'. Controls will often relay messages from other deceased persons, spoken of as 'communicators', with whom they purport to be in touch. The term 'communicator' is also used generically, to cover both controls and communicators. Use of these terms must not be held to imply a belief that the 'controls' and 'communicators' are anything other than aspects of the medium's own personality; I shall therefore hold myself excused from too frequent a use of such phrases as 'ostensible communicator', 'alleged control', etc.

Trance mediumship will figure somewhat prominently in the chapters that follow; more prominently than its actual frequency would indicate. This is because the fullest manifestations of the personalities of ostensibly deceased persons have often been obtained through trance mediums, and because psychical researchers have shown a corresponding interest in collecting detailed records of this kind of mediumship. Among prominent trance mediums who have been subjected to extensive and careful study are: Mrs L. E. Piper, Mrs 'Smead' (Mrs W. L. Cleaveland), Mrs 'Chenoweth' (Mrs M. M. Soule), Mrs R. Thompson, Mrs E. J. Garrett and Mrs G. O. Leonard. Several of these ladies will be discussed in more detail later on.

I talked just now of the manifestation through mediums of the personalities of deceased persons; and the question inevitably arises of what these manifestations could possibly consist in. This problem was in effect raised in the first chapter, where I pointed out that some philosophers would say that one's personal identity is logically linked to the continuity of one's physical organism, so that to talk of the manifestation of the personality of a deceased human being is nonsense. This issue will be mentioned again later on. Here I can only point out that if, for instance, one had to identify a person, whose body one could not see, by conversing with him over a somewhat noisy telephone line, one could not identify him unless his conversation exhibited certain distinctive features – unless, for example, he could remember certain things that he ought to be able to remember if he is the person he purports to be (one's individual memories must be far more specific even than one's fingerprints); and unless he exhibited certain motives and purposes, skills and personality characteristics known to be his; and so forth. Rather similarly, evidence of just these kinds is at least evidence *without which* one would have *no grounds at all* for supposing that some human beings may in some sense survive the dissolution of their bodies. Accordingly I shall for the moment defer philosophical worries, and shall in the next few chapters present in turn evidence from communications through mediums for the ostensible survival of memory, of purpose, of intellectual skills and of individual personality characteristics.

3 The Mediumship of Mrs Piper

Mrs Leonora E. Piper (1857–1950) is important in the history of psychical research for at least three reasons. Of the mental mediums subjected to study by members of the SPR and the ASPR she was the first to provide substantial evidence for the possession of some paranormal faculty; the records of her case are still unsurpassed in quantity and detail – if the papers on her published in the *Proceedings* of the British and American SPRs were collected together they would fill a good few volumes; and she is one of the very few mediums whose trance speech and writings have been subjected to a serious and extensive pyschological analysis. The most comprehensive general account of her mediumship is that contained in Holt (67); see also Sage (136) and Piper (121).

Mrs Piper lived in Boston, Massachusetts, where her husband was employed in a large store. Her career as a medium began more or less accidentally. In 1884 she consulted a blind healing medium named J. R. Cocke. At her second visit to him she passed into a trance, and wrote down a message for another of the sitters, Judge Frost, of Cambridge, Massachusetts. The message purported to come from Judge Frost's deceased son, and it impressed him more than any other which he had received during an extensive investigation into Spiritualism.

Mrs Piper then set up a 'home circle'. Her first spirit guide is said to have been a red indian girl named 'Chlorine'. Among other communicators were Bach, Mrs Siddons, Longfellow and Commodore Vanderbilt. These less than convincing *dramatis personae* retired from the scene the following year with the arrival of a new control who rapidly became predominant. This was a soi-disant French doctor who gave the name of 'Dr Phinuit'. In some ways Phinuit was quite as implausible as his predecessors. No trace of him could be found in French medical records, and his knowledge of the French language was scanty indeed. In fact it seemed likely that he was an unconscious plagiarism from Cocke, who possessed an Irish guide named 'Finney'.

But whatever his ultimate status, he was a 'character', and more important he was, as we shall see, a success.

Under Phinuit's regime the general procedure at a sitting would be this. Mrs Piper would pass into a trance. The onset of the trance was in these early days often accompanied by unpleasant spasmodic movements, grinding of the teeth, etc. There was never the least doubt that the trance-state was in some sense, 'genuine' – in it Mrs Piper could be cut, blistered, pricked and even have a bottle of strong ammonia held under her nose without being disturbed. After a few minutes, Mrs Piper would begin to speak with the voice of Phinuit, which was gruff and male and made use of Frenchisms, and also of slang and swearwords, in a manner quite unlike that of the waking Mrs Piper. Phinuit would give sitters accounts of the appearances and activities of deceased (and sometimes also of living) friends and relations, and would transmit messages from them, often with appropriate gestures.

Mrs Piper was 'discovered' for psychical research by William James, of Harvard University, arguably the greatest psychologist of that, perhaps of any, time. James was sufficiently impressed by his sittings to send some twenty-five other persons to her under pseudonyms. In the spring of 1886 he wrote an account of the results in which he stated (111, p. 653), 'I am persuaded of the medium's honesty, and of the genuineness of her trance; and although at first disposed to think that the 'hits' she made were either lucky coincidence, or the result of knowledge on her part of who the sitter was, and of his or her family affairs, I now believe her to be in possession of a power as yet unexplained.'

'Lucky coincidence' was not, I think, an explanation ever seriously considered by anyone who had extensive firsthand acquaintance with Mrs Piper's performances. It was true that on an off-day, Phinuit would ramble and flounder hopelessly, would fish for information, and if given any, would blatantly serve it up again as though it had been his own discovery. But when he was on form he could, with hardly any hesitation or fishing, relay copious communications from the deceased friends and relatives of sitters, communications which would turn out to be very accurate even in tiny details, and far too accurate for the hypothesis of chance or of guesswork from the appearance of the sitters to seem in the remotest degree plausible.

As a result of James's report, a leading member of the British SPR, Richard Hodgson (1855–1905), came out to Boston in 1887 and assumed charge of the investigation (66a). He was looked upon as an expert in the unmasking of fraud. He arranged for the careful recording of all sittings, and took the most extensive precautions against trickery. Sitters were introduced anonymously or pseudony-mously, and were drawn from as wide a range of persons as possible. Especial notice was taken of first sittings. For some weeks Mrs Piper was shadowed by detectives to ascertain whether she made enquiries into the affairs of possible sitters, or employed agents so to do. She was brought to England where she knew no one and could have had no established agents. During her stay there in the winter of 1889–90, all her sittings were arranged and supervised by leading members of the SPR. Sitters were for the most part introduced anonymously, and comprehensive records were kept (111). And still Mrs Piper continued to get results.

Dr Phinuit remained Mrs Piper's chief control until the spring of 1892. Thereafter he was gradually superseded by a control who, whatever his ultimate nature, was at least not fictitious. This was George Pellew ('GP'), a young man of literary and philosophical interests who had been killed in New York a few weeks previously. He was known to Hodgson, and five years previously had had, under a pseudonym, one and only one sitting with Mrs Piper. He first manifested at a sitting to which Hodgson brought a close friend of his (Pellew's). Then and thereafter the GP communicator showed a most detailed acquaintance with the affairs of the living Pellew. Out of 150 sitters who were introduced to him, GP recognized twenty-nine of the thirty who had been known to the living Pellew (the thirtieth, whom he recognized after an initial failure, was a person who had 'grown up' in the interval). He conversed with each of them in an appropriate manner, and showed an intimate knowledge of their concerns, and of his own supposed past relationships with them. Only rarely did GP slip up badly, as he sometimes did when discussing, for instance, the philosophical questions which had so much interested Pellew in life. During the period of GP's ascendency, Hodgson became convinced (he had not previously been so) that Mrs Piper's controls and communicators were, at least in many cases, what they claimed to be, namely the surviving spirits of formerly incarnate human beings (66b).

GP, like Phinuit, would pass on messages from other deceased persons who wished to communicate; but now it apparently became easier for other deceased persons to 'communicate' directly by speaking or writing through Mrs Piper's organism. Writing in trance became much commoner, and ultimately predominant, and sometimes two different spirits would communicate simultaneously, one by the hand and one by the voice.

The later history of Mrs Piper's mediumship requires only a brief account. GP remained the principal communicator until early in 1897 (during this period Hodgson had almost complete charge of her sittings, and very full records were kept). Thereafter for some years her principal controls were a band of spirits of the mighty dead who disguised their illustrious identities under such appropriately solemn sobriquets as 'Imperator', 'Doctor', 'Rector', 'Prudens', etc. Evidence figured somewhat less in the proceedings, and elevated teachings somewhat more, than they had previously done. In 1905 Hodgson died, and, predictably, became himself one of Mrs Piper's controls. The purported communications from him were discussed in an interesting paper by William James (74). Later on Mrs Piper played a part in the famous 'cross-correspondences' (which are discussed later). Her trance mediumship ended in 1911, perhaps in consequence of the harsh treatment which she received at the hands of two American psychologists, Professor G. Stanley Hall, and Dr Amy Tanner (156). However she continued to do automatic writing.

As I implied a moment ago, I am prepared wholly to dismiss chance hitting as an explanation of Mrs Piper's achievements. Although on his off days, Phinuit's ramblings, fishings and platitudes were such as to provide invaluable ammunition for hostile critics, he was capable even at his most banal of springing a surprise. Thus at a sitting on 3 June 1889 (66a, p. 130), Mr J. Rogers Rich gave Phinuit a dog's collar. After a while Phinuit said he saw the dog coming, and then went on: 'Here he comes! Oh, how he jumps! There he is now, jumping upon and around you. So glad to see you! Rover! Rover! No – G-rover, Grover! That's his name!'. The dog was once called Rover, but his name was changed to Grover in 1884, in honour of the election to the American Presidency of Grover Cleveland.

With Phinuit at his best, chance hitting is an impossible explanation. Another general explanation which I am prepared to dismiss is that of fraud. I have already indicated some of the considerations which tell against it. The thought of fraud was never far from Mrs Piper's early investigators. The case against it was powerfully summarized in 1889 by Frank Podmore (122b), a highly sceptical writer. Podmore points out that despite careful overseeing amounting at times to invasion of privacy, Mrs Piper had never once been detected in dishonesty or found to have employed agents. She could not in any case have afforded to employ agents. Furthermore arrangements had commonly been made to preserve the anonymity of sitters; these arrangements were made not just by Hodgson, but at various times by a number of other responsible people. Nor was the information communicated through Mrs Piper generally of the sort which could have been obtained from public records, cemeteries, or talkative servants. Names and dates were very difficult to 'put through'. Despite the fact that she had given sittings to hundreds of people, material relating to different individuals was hardly ever mixed up. In delineation of character Mrs Piper far outreached anything which could have been constructed from an accumulation of such facts as might have been unearthed by snooping or by bribery. Successful communicators would often address sitters in exactly the right tone, and might unmistakably refer to trivialities of a wholly private significance. The charge of credulity, said Podmore, rested with those who, without consideration and without enquiry, could lightly attribute all the results to imposture.

Some of these considerations also tell against another 'naturalistic' explanation that is sometimes propounded. It may be called the 'grapevine' theory and goes like this. Mrs Piper before long became quite well known in Boston, and built up a network of clients each of whom was in turn likely to recommend her to friends. By this means, and without any question of deliberate trickery or the employment of agents, she could have built up a store of information about numerous interlinked Boston families, and could often have made a good guess at the identities even of sitters introduced anonymously. Add to these suppositions the possibility that she possessed a 'flypaper' memory for personal details, and we can begin to see a way of accounting for her remarkable successes.

At least one thing may be said in favour of these ideas. There was not a little evidence to suggest that when in trance Mrs Piper possessed a remarkably good memory for what had been said during previous trances. And this fact could clearly have a bearing upon the interpretation of certain cases. For example in May and June 1905, shortly after Hodgson's death, Mrs Piper's Hodgson-control made some references to correspondence between Hodgson and a certain Miss Densmore ('Huldah') of Chicago, and stated that Hodgson had proposed marriage to her. None even of Hodgson's closest Boston friends had any inkling of this, but it turned out to be true. Unfortunately it also transpired that Hodgson had mentioned the matter to Mrs Piper's controls *ten years previously* when he was hoping that the lady would accept him (74, pp. 20–26). So this apparently striking case must be dismissed as evidence for the paranormal: or almost dismissed, since it must be added that a living person (a New York lady) to whom Hodgson had confided his disappointment – certainly not at a Piper sitting – was located through information given by the Hodgson-control.

In general, however, I think that this theory may be safely rejected. The chief investigators of the Piper case were well aware of the dangers in question, and made every effort to avert them by anonymously bringing to her a substantial sprinkling of sitters from as far afield as possible, and by taking her on several extended trips to England. It was abundantly clear that whatever part the local grapevine may have played in marginally improving Mrs Piper's results, it was not her chief source of inspiration.

On the face of it the 'grapevine plus sticky memory' theory should have been on its strongest ground with the alleged post-mortem communications from Richard Hodgson himself. For not merely had Mrs Piper known Hodgson for eighteen years; she could also have learned a good deal about those friends of his who were most likely to attempt to make contact with him after his death. She would therefore (it might be said) have been able to produce those Hodgson-reminiscences which had a particular appropriateness for each sitter.

In his report on Mrs Piper's Hodgson-control, William James considers and rejects this hypothesis, saying of Hodgson (74, p. 6): 'Gifted with great powers of reserve by nature, he was professionally schooled to secretiveness; and a decidedly incommunicative habit in the way of personal gossip had become a second nature with him, – especially towards Mrs Piper.' In fact one has only to consider a few of the incidents described in James's report to see just how implausible is the grape-vine hypothesis as a general explanation of Mrs Piper's successes. I shall give three examples:

1. *The Pecuniary Messages*
Hodgson's salary as secretary of the American branch of the SPR, though small, was often irregularly paid. The result was that he was

sometimes left in circumstances of great financial embarrassment. On one occasion he was rescued by a wholly unexpected remittance from a friend. To this remittance, says James (74, p. 26),

> ... he replied by a letter which ... cited the story of a starving couple who were overheard by an atheist who was passing the house, to pray aloud to God for food. The atheist climbed the roof and dropped some bread down the chimney, and heard them thank God for the miracle. He then went to the door and revealed himself as its author. The old woman replied to him: 'Well, the Lord sent it, even if the devil brought it.'
>
> At this friend's sitting of 30 January, [Hodgson] suddenly says:
>
> Do you remember a story I told you and how you laughed, about the man and woman praying.
>
> SITTER: Oh, and the devil was in it. Of course I do.
>
> HODGSON: Yes, the devil, they told him it was the Lord who sent it even if the devil brought it ... About the food that was given to them ... I want you to know who is speaking.
>
> The sitter feels quite certain that no one but himself knew of the correspondence ...

Later another friend agreed to make up any deficit in Hodgson's salary, provided this action should remain anonymous, and Hodgson should ask no questions. On the first sitting which this friend had after Hodgson's death, the ' spirit' of Hodgson immediately referred to the matter and thanked the sitter. 'The donor is of opinion,' says James (74, p. 27), 'as I am also, that Hodgson may have suspected the source of the aid while receiving it, and this his "spirit" may therefore naturally have thanked the right person. That Mrs Piper's waking consciousness should have been acquainted with any part of this transaction is incredible.'

2. *The 'Fist-Shaking' Episode*

I quote James's own account of this episode (74, p. 109):

> The following incident belongs to my wife's and Miss Putnam's sitting of 12 June 1906: – Mrs J. said: 'Do you remember what happened in our library one night when you were arguing with Margie [Mrs J.'s sister]? – 'I had hardly said "remember",' she notes, 'in asking this question, when the medium's arm was stretched out and the fist shaken threateningly,' then these words came:
>
> R. H. Yes, I did this in her face. I couldn't help it. She was so impossible to move. It was wrong of me, but I couldn't help it.
>
> [I myself well remember this fist-shaking incident, and how we others laughed over it after Hodgson had taken his leave. What had made him so angry was my sister-in-law's defence of some slate-writing she had seen in California. – W. J.]

3.   *'Buying Billy'*
Again I quote James's own account (74, p. 112):

> On 30 January 1906, Mrs M. had a sitting. Mrs M said:
>   Do you remember our last talk together, at N., and how, in coming home
> we talked about the work?
> (R. H.) Yes, yes.
> Mrs. M. And I said if we had a hundred thousand dollars –
>   Buying Billy!!
> Mrs. M. Yes, Dick, that was it – 'buying Billy'.
>   Buying only Billy?
> Mrs. M. Oh no – I wanted Schiller too. How well you remember!
> Mrs. M., before R. H.'s death, had had dreams of extending the American
> Branch's operations by getting an endowment, and possibly inducing Prof.
> [W. R.] Newbold (Billy) and Dr [F. C. S.] Schiller to co-operate in work.
> She naturally regards this veridical recall, by the control, of a private
> conversation she had had with Hodgson as very evidential of his survival.

If one regards the various 'naturalistic' explanations of Mrs Piper's performances as by and large inadequate (and personally I do so regard them), and is further prepared instead to consider the possibility that she may have possessed abilities of kinds not yet generally recognized by science, then the most obvious hypothesis to present itself is undoubtedly that of telepathy between the medium and persons present at the sitting. Clairvoyance will hardly serve, for most of the evidence (not all) transmitted was confirmed by the recollections of living persons rather than by documents, photographs, etc., which might, by a great stretch of imagination, be supposed decipherable by clairvoyance. All the cases so far quoted in this chapter could in principle be explained by telepathy between medium and sitters; and some incidents from the Piper records strongly suggest it. For instance, Hodgson had one day been reading with great interest Lockhart's *Life of Scott*. Next day a ludicrous Sir Walter Scott turned up at a Piper sitting, and gave a guided tour of the solar system, stating that there are monkeys in the sun (145b, pp. 437–448). Mr J. T. Clarke was told by Phinuit that he was in financial trouble, which was correct. Phinuit further asserted that things would improve within four and a half months, and that 'There are parties that haven't dealt honourably with you.' He warned Clarke particularly against a man named H. None of Phinuit's further assertions was justified; but they accurately reflected Clarke's own beliefs at the time (111, pp. 568–571).

Not just isolated incidents, but the overall pattern of whole series of sittings seemed sometimes to favour the hypothesis of telepathy between medium and sitters. For instance, Sir Oliver Lodge gave Dr Phinuit a chain, entrusted to him by a gentleman abroad, which had belonged to that gentleman's father. Phinuit produced a large number of facts and purported facts concerning the father, which Lodge transmitted to the son. The son's reply, according to Lodge (111, p. 461), was

> ... Important and distinct. It recognizes the correctness of those things which I knew, and it asserts the total incorrectness of those things of which I was ignorant. So far as this series of facts goes, therefore, the hypothesis of a direct thought-transferential means of obtaining information is immensely strengthened. I can indeed hardly resist the conclusion that the series of facts purporting to be related by the elder Mr Wilson have no more substantiality than a dream of my own; that I was, so to speak, dreaming by proxy, and imposing upon myself through the mouth of the medium, a number of statements such as it is not difficult to imagine reported to one in a dream.

The theory of telepathy between medium and sitters has thus in certain cases a good deal of plausibility, which is more than can be said for the other theories we have so far considered. But just how far can we push this theory? I shall give now an extract from the first of two sittings with Mrs Piper had by the Rev and Mrs S. W. Sutton, of Athol Center, Massachusetts (66b, pp. 485–486). The sitting was held on 8 December 1893. It was booked by Hodgson, and the sitters were introduced under the pseudonym of 'Smith'. A practised note-taker acted as recorder. It must be understood that throughout Phinuit speaks (and sometimes gesticulates) *on behalf of* the child communicator; she does not 'control' herself. The annotations in square brackets are by Mrs Sutton.

> Phinuit said ... A little child is coming to you ... He reaches out his hands as to a child, and says coaxingly: Come here, dear. Don't be afraid. Come, darling, here is your mother. He describes the child and her 'lovely curls'. Where is Papa? Want Papa. [He (i.e. Phinuit) takes from the table a silver medal.] I want this – want to bite it. [She used to bite it.] [Reaches for a string of buttons.] Quick! I want to put them in my mouth. [The buttons also. To bite the buttons was forbidden. He exactly imitated her arch manner.] ... Who is Dodo? [Her name for her brother, George.] ... I want you to call Dodo. Tell Dodo I am happy. Cry for me no more. [Puts hands to throat.] No sore throat any more. [She had pain and distress of the throat and tongue.] Papa, speak to me. Can you not see me? I am not dead, I am living. I am happy with Grandma. [My mother had been dead many years.] Phinuit says: Here are two more. One, two, three here, – one older and one younger than Kakie. [Correct.] ...

Was this little one's tongue very dry? She keeps showing me her tongue. [Her tongue was paralysed, and she suffered much with it to the end.] Her name is Katherine. [Correct.] She calls herself Kakie. She passed out last. [Correct.] Where is horsey? [I gave him a little horse.] Big horsey, not this little one. [Probably refers to a toy cart-horse she used to like.] Papa, want to go wide [ride] horsey. [She plead this all through her illness.] . . .

[I asked if she remembered anything after she was brought downstairs.] I was so hot, my head was so hot. [Correct] . . . Do not cry for me – that makes me sad. Eleanor. I want Eleanor. [Her little sister. She called her much during her last illness.] I want my buttons. Row, row, – my song, – sing it now. I sing with you. [We sing, and a soft child voice sings with us.]

> Lightly row, lightly row,
> O'er the merry waves we go,
> Smoothly glide, smoothly glide,
> With the ebbing tide.

[Phinuit hushes us, and Kakie finishes alone.]

> Let the wind and waters be
> Mingled with our melody,
> Sing and float, sing and float,
> In our little boat.

. . . Kakie sings: Bye, bye, ba bye, bye, bye, O baby bye. Sing that with me, Papa. [Papa and Kakie sing. These two were the songs she used to sing.] Where is Dinah? I want Dinah. [Dinah was an old black rag-doll, not with us.] I want Bagie [Her name for her sister Margaret.] I want Bagie to bring me my Dinah . . . Tell Dodo when you see him that I love him. Dear Dodo. He used to march with me, he put me way up. [Correct.]

Remarkable though this excerpt is (not more remarkable, however, than the full transcripts of the two sittings, which are, incidentally, documents of social as well as psychical interest), no information was communicated which lay outside the knowledge of the sitters. Does this mean, then, that we can comfortably attribute all Mrs Piper's 'hits' here to telepathy with the sitters? Such a conclusion would be too hasty. I know of no instance of undeniable telepathy between living persons, or for that matter of any other variety of ESP, in which the flow of paranormally acquired information has been so quick, so copious, and so free from error. (I may say that these features are understated by the brief extract which is all I have been able to quote.) Then again there is the question of the point of view from which the information is presented. It appears that Mrs Piper must have obtained parents'-eye information about Kakie from the sitters, and then with a fair degree of dramatic skill have constructed on the basis of this information a Kakie's-eye view of the same facts. Furthermore (and this is exceedingly odd), incidents at both sittings apparently showed associations that seemed to be in the mind of the child, and which did not awaken the corresponding associations in the minds of the sitters. For instance when Kakie asked for 'horsey', and was given a little toy horse, she said 'big, horsey, not this little one.' Mrs Sutton surmised that she referred to another toy horse that she used to like. At the second sitting Kakie requested the horse again, but when given the little horse, said (66b, p. 387) 'No, that is not the one. The big horse – so big. [Phinuit shows how large.] Eleanor's horse. Eleanor used to put it in Kakie's lap. She loved that horsey.' These additional particulars made it clear to Mrs Sutton what horse was meant – one which was packed away and forgotten in another city. In a later passage, not given above, from the first sitting Kakie asked for 'the little book'. Her mother supposed that she meant a linen picture book. At the second sitting it became clear that what was intended was a little prayer book which had been read to Kakie just before her death, and then put in her hands. If we are to say that Mrs Piper could select from the sitters' minds associations conflicting with the ones consciously present and utilize them in order to create the impression that the communicator's thoughts moved along lines distinctively different from the sitter's, we are beginning to attribute to her not just super-ESP but super-artistry as well.

The theory of telepathy from the sitters is, of course, manifestly ruled out when correct information is given which is not at the time known to any sitter. Incidents of this kind are sprinkled throughout the Piper records (and throughout the records of various other mediums too – see 44e, p. 587). I shall end this chapter with summary accounts of two such cases (the original records are too long to be quoted in full).

1. *Sir Oliver Lodge's Uncle Jerry*

This case took place during Mrs Piper's visit to England in the winter of 1889–90. Sir Oliver Lodge's summary of it (111, pp. 458–459) is as follows:

> It happens that an uncle of mine in London [Uncle Robert], now quite an old man, had a twin brother who died some twenty or more years ago. I interested him generally in the subject, and wrote to ask if he would lend me some relic of his brother. By morning post on a certain day I received a

curious old gold watch, which his brother had worn . . . I handed it to Mrs Piper when in a state of trance.

I was told almost immediately that it had belonged to one of my uncles . . . After some difficulty . . . Dr Phinuit caught the name Jerry . . . and said . . . 'This is my watch, and Robert is my brother, and I am here. Uncle Jerry, my watch.' . . . I pointed out to him that to make Uncle Robert aware of his presence it would be well to recall trivial details of their boyhood . . .

'Uncle Jerry' recalled episodes such as swimming the creek when they were boys together, and running some risk of getting drowned; killing a cat in Smith's field; the possession of a small rifle, and of a long peculiar skin, like a snake-skin, which he thought was now in the possession of Uncle Robert.

All these facts have been more or less completely verified. But the interesting thing is that his twin brother, from whom I got the watch, and with whom I was thus in a sort of communication, could not remember them all.

He recollected something about swimming the creek, though he himself had merely looked on. He had a distinct recollection of having had the snake-skin, and of the box in which it was kept, though he does not know where it is now. But he altogether denied killing the cat, and could not recall Smith's field.

His memory, however, is decidedly failing him, and he was good enough to write to another brother, Frank, living in Cornwall, an old sea captain, and ask if he had any better remembrance of certain facts – of course not giving any inexplicable reason for asking. The result of this enquiry was triumphantly to vindicate the existence of Smith's field . . . , and the killing of a cat by another brother was also recollected; while of the swimming of the creek, near a mill-race, full details were given, Frank and Jerry being the heroes of that foolhardy episode.

It should be noted that Uncle Frank could not remember the snake-skin; so that if Mrs Piper got all this information by telepathy, she must have ransacked the memory stores of two separate individuals and collated the results.

2. *The Dog 'Rounder'*

The following is a summary (164a, p. 354) by Miss Helen Verrall (Mrs W. H. Salter) of a case from a long paper in which she describes and analyses some remarkable communications from a recently deceased young man, Bennie Junot, to surviving members of his family:

On 11 February 1902, Mr Junot [senior] sent a message through his son Bennie to a former coachman of his, Hugh Irving, who had been dead some months, asking where 'the dog Rounder' was. Hugh Irving had left Mr Junot's service about two months before his death and taken the dog with him. In the waking stage [i.e., when Mrs Piper was beginning to 'come to'] on 2 April 1902, it is stated that 'John Welsh has Rounder'. Mr Junot succeeded after some difficulty in tracing 'John Welsh', but unfortunately it proved impossible to discover whether he had ever had the dog in his possession. It is certain, however, that he was closely associated with the coachman, who took the dog away, and it was through his attempts to find John Welsh that Mr Junot recovered the dog. Moreover, there seems good reason for thinking that John Welsh, even if he never had the dog himself, knew something of his whereabouts, and could have helped Mr Junot to recover him. Neither Mr Junot nor any of his family had ever to their knowledge heard of John Welsh (at any rate under that name), still less of his connection with Hugh Irving and possible connection with the dog. Doubtless people could have been found to whom all these facts were known, but they were not people with whom Mrs Piper had ever been brought into contact. Until we know to what limitations, if any, telepathy between living minds is subject, we cannot determine whether it is a sufficient explanation of such phenomena as this.

We are, alas, today no nearer knowing the limitations, if any, of telepathy than we were in 1910, when Miss Verrall wrote the above passage. What bearing cases such as these, which go so far beyond telepathy from the sitters, may have upon the survival hypothesis is a question which must be taken up after we have considered some further kinds of case. Miss Verrall goes on to remark:

> . . . if we suppose, as the controls themselves declare, that the source of the information is the minds of the dead, such incidents present no difficulty, and therefore, though they cannot be said to prove their hypothesis, they would, if frequently repeated, render it more probable.

This is, I fear, an oversimplification, but it is an oversimplification of a standpoint that may perhaps be defensible.

To Mrs Piper I shall return again in various places. For the moment I should like to emphasize that the Piper cases which I have presented in this chapter constitute only a tiny proportion of the mass of 'evidential' materials supplied by the records of her mediumship.

At the end of the last chapter I briefly described and discussed several examples of mediumistic communications in which the correct information given was ostensibly not known by normal means to any person present at the sitting. Such cases, in sufficient number, and with sufficient assurances that no sitter had a buried memory of the relevant details, would seriously undermine the theory that mediums' 'hits', when not fortunate flukes, are due to telepathy with the sitters. In this chapter I shall talk about a remarkable medium who made, one might almost say, a speciality of producing evidence of this kind. I refer to the British medium, Mrs Gladys Osborne Leonard (1882–1968).

As a child Mrs Leonard, like so many other mediums, used to have beautiful visions, of which her conventional parents disapproved (89). Much later, when she was already married, she discovered her mediumistic gifts as a result of experimenting in table-tipping with some friends. She passed into a trance, and was afterwards told that her mother, and a young girl named Feda, had spoken through her. Feda became her chief control. She purported to be the spirit of an Indian girl whom an ancestor of Mrs Leonard had married in the early nineteenth century. These statements were naturally unverifiable, though there was a family tradition of such a girl (she had died in childbirth at an early age). Feda spoke in a high-pitched voice, with occasional grammatical errors and misunderstandings of word-meanings, and had sometimes a touch of the archness and childish ways which, in a more extreme form, have endeared numerous child-communicators to middle-aged lady sitters. ('I believe we are going to have a Topsy', such a sitter once exclaimed at a home circle which I used to attend, clasping her hands together in anticipation.) Feda regarded Mrs Leonard with something between tolerance and amused contempt, and would sometimes cause her embarrassment, for example by soliciting small presents, which she thereafter fiercely insisted were her own and not Mrs Leonard's.

As the First World War approached, Feda began to speak of a coming catastrophe, and urged upon Mrs Leonard that it would be her duty to help as many people as possible by her mediumship. Mrs Leonard shortly thereafter became a professional medium, and devoted herself to helping the bereaved. At the same time she was quite prepared to submit herself to critical investigation by members of the SPR, some of whom (as with Mrs Piper) had her shadowed by detectives to ensure that she did not make enquiries about sitters or employ agents so to do. The first parapsychologist to study her in detail was Sir Oliver Lodge, whose book *Raymond* (1916), describing communications from a son killed in the war, made her famous. She continued to be regularly studied by SPR investigators from then until the early years after the Second World War. Throughout that time Feda remained as her principal guide. Most communications were given by speech, with Feda acting as intermediary; sometimes other deceased persons would control the vocal apparatus; and very occasionally communications were made by writing.

A most odd feature of Mrs Leonard's mediumship in later years was this. At times, when Feda was in control, and was transmitting messages from another communicator purportedly in touch with her on the 'other side', she would be interrupted by a whisper coming apparently from the empty air a foot or two in front of the medium. This 'direct voice' (ostensibly that of the communicator whose remarks Feda was relaying) would correct and clarify the statements which Feda was making through Mrs Leonard. Tests made with the acoustic instruments then available did not suffice to determine whether or not this voice was truly independent of Mrs Leonard's vocal apparatus (11). In brief recordings to which I have listened it never overlaps with the voice of Feda.

In many ways the mediumship of Mrs Leonard resembled that of Mrs Piper, and I do not want to go over similar ground twice. I shall therefore concentrate upon those singular aspects of it which, as I mentioned a moment ago, seem irreconcilable with the hypothesis of telepathy from the sitters. Indeed they are not easy to reconcile with anything much less than a form of the super-ESP hypothesis which allows the medium potential extrasensory access to any identifying detail whatsoever relating to any living or recently dead person in the whole of the Western world. The aspects of Mrs Leonard's mediumship concerned are, first, her remarkable successes (or Feda's remarkable successes) with 'book tests', and, second, her quite numerous apparently successful 'proxy sittings'.

The origin of the Leonard book tests is a little obscure, and it seems quite likely that they were first proposed by Feda. If so, they share with the 'cross-correspondences' (to be discussed later) the remarkable feature of being 'tests of survival' ostensibly suggested by deceased persons. There are, however, analogies for them from earlier literature. The principle of book tests is well summarized by Sir Oliver Lodge (50, p. xvi). A communicator, usually passing the message through Feda, has to specify

> the number of a page in a book, itself indicated only by its numbered place on a given shelf in a book-case whose position is described, in a house to which the medium need have no access, though a house presumably, or usually, well-known to the ostensible communicator. The idea is that a sentence shall subsequently be found on that page, by any one who follows the instructions and identifies the book, which sentence shall sufficiently convey an intended message, or shall show a similarity in thought to what has otherwise been said, or shall be appropriate to the actual circumstances or past connection of communicator and intended recipient.

Since the book chosen need not be one known to the sitter, or indeed known in the requisite detail to anyone living, it is plain, as Lodge says, that 'no simple kind of mind-reading can be appealed to or regarded as a rational explanation.' I will take as an example a short but somewhat remarkable case in which the communicator is Edward Wyndham Tennant ('Bim'), a young officer killed on the Somme in 1916. The sitting (50, p. 60) was held on 17 December 1917.

> *Feda.* 'Bim now wants to send a message to his Father. *This book is particularly for his Father*; underline that, he says. It is the ninth book on the third shelf counting from left to right in the bookcase on the right of the door in the drawing-room as you enter; take the title, and look at page 37.'
> We found the ninth book in the shelf indicated was: *Trees* [by J. Harvey Kelman].
> And on page 36, quite at the bottom and leading on to page 37, we read: *Sometimes you will see curious marks in the wood; these are caused by a tunnelling beetle, very injurious to the trees . . .*'
> (Signatures of two testificators to the finding and verifying of this Book-Message).
>
> GLENCONNER
DAVID TENNANT

Bim's father was intensely interested in Forestry; and his obsession with 'the beetle' was a family joke. Thus the message was particularly appropriate, and the bookshelf from which it had been culled was one known to the alleged communicator.

During the period immediately before and after the end of the First World War many successful book tests were carried out (145c, 157a). In a lengthy paper published in 1921 (145c), Mrs E. M. Sidgwick analysed the results of 532 such tests. She classified 92 (17%) as successful, 100 (19%) as approximately successful, 96 as dubious, 40 as nearly complete failures and 204 as complete failures. In a control experiment (138a; cf. 10) 1800 'sham' book tests were subjected to a similar analysis. There were 34 successes (under 2%) and 51 partial successes (under 3%).

Some of the individual successes in these tests were very remarkable. In one case (145c, pp. 253–260) an anonymous sitter (Mrs Talbot) received through Feda a message from her late husband advising her to look for a relevant message on page twelve or thirteen of a book on her bookcase at home. Feda said the book was not printed, but had writing in it; was dark in colour; and contained a table of Indo-European, Aryan, Semitic and Arabian languages, whose relationships were shown by a diagram of radiating lines. Mrs Talbot knew of no such book, and ridiculed the message. However when she eventually looked, she found at the back of a top shelf a shabby black leather notebook of her husband's. Pasted into this book was a folded table of all the languages mentioned; whilst on page 13 was an extract from a book entitled *Post Mortem*. In this case the message related to a book unknown to medium and sitter (indeed, so far as could be told, to any living person), but undoubtedly known to the communicator.

The two book tests which I have just described might be thought to constitute rather striking evidence for survival. Mind-reading does not seem a likely explanation, for it was highly unlikely that the requisite information was possessed in sufficient detail by any living person. On the other hand the existence of the books, and of the relevant passages, could have been, and in the second case certainly was, known to the alleged communicator. Unfortunately the results of many other book tests serve only to confuse the issue; not because they were unsuccessful, but because they were too successful. For the communicators proved equally able to transmit information relating to the contents of books deliberately placed on shelves in houses unknown to them, books, furthermore, having for them no special significance. On the face of it this would imply that the communicators got their knowledge of the contents of these books by clairvoyance (the books, of course, being all closed). Feda certainly talks as though the communicators were independent entities who homed in on the test bookshelves, scanned the books for appropriate passages, and then returned to relay the results through her. But if these communicators can exercise clairvoyance of such remarkable degree, why should not Feda? Why should not Mrs Leonard herself? The information given is no longer such as the alleged communicators are specially qualified to supply. In some cases (145c, pp. 300-313), indeed, correct information was apparently given about the contents of books in classical Greek; yet neither Mrs Leonard, nor the sitter, nor the alleged communicator knew classical Greek, while the person who lent the books (Mrs Salter), though she knew Greek, had not properly studied several of the volumes. Neither telepathy with the living, nor communication with the dead, nor yet clairvoyance, would seem to supply us with an adequate explanation here.

I think it would be fair to say this of the book tests:

(a) The fact that in certain cases meaningful reference was made to passages from books to which the communicators had in life had special access cannot be taken as evidence that the surviving memory stores of those communicators were somehow active in the matter. For, as we have just seen, communicators were also able to refer unmistakably to passages in books which it was highly unlikely they had read when alive.

(b) Still, if we grant for the sake of argument that the books were in some sense open to clairvoyant inspection by an agency other than that of the communicator, there remains the problem of how, from this mass of potentially available material, just those passages were so often selected which were particularly appropriate as messages from the communicator to the particular living recipient. *Who selected* for Bim's father the passage about the beetle damaging trees? To select a passage as appropriate as this, the medium would have had e.g. to tap Bim's father's mind, and then in the light of information telepathically gained from it, select that one of the very numerous book passages clairvoyantly accessible to her which would be most likely to impress Bim's family as a message of a kind he might plausibly address to his father. This problem of *selection* will arise again; as will that of the apparent *synthesis* of information extrasensorially acquired from more than one source.

The term 'proxy sitting' is almost self-explanatory. A sitter takes a sitting on behalf of a third party, about whom both he and the medium know as little as possible. If 'evidential' communications are then received, the explanation can hardly be laid at the door of telepathy with persons present. Usually the third party, or absent principal, desires communications from a particular deceased person who has in some way or another to be contacted. To achieve this the proxy sitter may give the medium carefully circumscribed details (e.g. name, identifying phrase) of the desired communicator, or may bring some relic of him to serve as a 'token object'; or he may privately appeal to him, or concentrate upon him, before the sitting; or he may request his own 'spirit guides' to act as intermediaries. The best-known of all proxy sittings are without doubt the numerous sittings with Mrs Leonard at which Miss Nea Walker and the Rev C. Drayton Thomas acted as proxies (157d; 157e; 157f; 167a, 167b; cf. 158). These sittings were usually, although not always, the outcome of letters from bereaved, sometimes despairing, parents, spouses, etc.

Many proxy cases went on for several sittings, and it is hard to convey the 'feel' of them adequately in a brief summary. For instance one of Drayton Thomas's most remarkable cases, the 'Bobbie Newlove' case (157e), extended over eleven sittings. Bobbie was a boy of ten who had died of diphtheria. He proved a fluent communicator, and through Feda made unmistakable references to such matters as a dog-shaped salt-cellar he had owned, a 'Jack of Hearts' costume he had once worn, visits to a chemical laboratory with his grandfather, gymnastic apparatus which he had set up in his room and exercises carried out therewith, a girl skater of whom he was fond, an injury to his nose, and the topography of his home town (including place-names). Most curious of all, he repeatedly insisted that some weeks before his death his constitution had been undermined by contact with poisonous 'pipes', and that this had lowered his resistance to the diphtheria. In connection with the pipes he talked of cattle, a sort of barn, and running water. This meant nothing to his family, but upon investigation some water pipes round which he had played with a friend were discovered. The locality answered the description given and it is possible that Bobbie had drunk bad water there.

In another case, Drayton Thomas was asked by Professor E. R. Dodds, well-known as a critic of the evidence for survival, to attempt to contact a certain Frederic William Macaulay on behalf of the latter's daughter, Mrs Lewis. Thomas had five sittings with Mrs Leonard.

Distinctive references were made to Macaulay's work as an hydraulic engineer. The following passages (157f, pp. 265–269) refer to more personal matters. Mrs Lewis's annotations are in square brackets.

FEDA: There is a John and Harry, both with him. And Race . . . Rice . . . Riss . . . it might be Reece but sounds like Riss, and Francis. These are all names of people who are connected with him or linked up with him in the past, connected with happy times. I get the feeling of an active and busy home in which he was rather happy.

[This is a very curious passage . . . Probably the happiest time of my father's life was in the four or five years before the war, when we, his five children, were all at school, and the home was packed with our friends during the holidays. John, Harry and Francis could be three of these . . . But the most interesting passage is 'It might be Reece but it sounds like Riss' . . . My elder brother was at school at Shrewsbury and there conceived a kind of hero-worship for one of the 'Tweaks' (sixth form boys) whose name was Rees. He wrote home about him several times and always drew attention to the fact that the name was spelt 'Rees' and not 'Reece'. In the holidays my sister and I used to tease him by singing 'Not Reece but Riss' until my father stopped us . . .]

FEDA: I get a funny word now . . . could he be interested in . . . baths of some kind? Ah, he says I have got the right word, baths. He spells it, BATHS. His daughter will understand, he says. It is not something quite ordinary, but feels something special.

[This is, to me, the most interesting thing that has yet emerged. Baths were always a matter of joke in our family – my father being very emphatic that water must not be wasted by our having too big baths or by leaving taps dripping. It is difficult to explain how intimate a detail this seems . . . The mention of baths here also seems to me an indication of my father's quaint humour, a characteristic which has hitherto been missing . . .]

FEDA: . . . Godfrey; will you ask the daughter if she remembers someone called Godfrey. That name is a great link with old times.

[My father's most trusted clerk, one who specially helped in the hydraulic research, was called William Godfrey. He was with my father for years and I remember him from almost my earliest childhood . . .]

FEDA: What is that? . . . Peggy . . . Peggy . . . Puggy . . . he is giving me a little name like Puggy or Peggy. Sounds like a special name, a little special nickname, and I think it is something his daughter would know . . .

[My father sometimes called me 'pug-nose' or 'Puggy'.][113]

Altogether, 124 items of information were given, of which 51 were classified as right, 12 as good, 32 as fair, 2 as poor, 22 as doubtful, and 5 as wrong. Dodds, the instigator of this experiment, remarks: 'It appears to me that the hypotheses of fraud, rational influence from disclosed facts, telepathy from the actual sitter, and coincidence cannot either singly or in combination account for the results obtained.'

Of the more impressive proxy cases, most are, like the Bobbie Newlove and Macaulay cases, too long to be done justice to in a brief summary. The next case (157g) has some very unusual (though not unprecedented) features, the essentials of which can be set forth fairly briefly. We may call it the 'Aitken' case, after the family involved.

At a Leonard sitting on 28 October 1938, Drayton Thomas's regular communicators (his father and his sister) enquired if he had recently received from a middle-aged man a letter about his son. He had not yet received such a letter, and the communicators proceeded to give some further particulars of its contents. The letter would concern an accident to do with a motor car. In this accident the young man was killed outright, or nearly so. There was a connection with 'Morton' or a like-sounding name. The father once lived near where Drayton Thomas lived. Finally another name, sounding like 'Char', was given.

The anticipated letter duly arrived. It was dated eleven days after the sitting, and was from Mr Lionel G. Aitken, a member of the SPR. Mr Aitken told Drayton Thomas that he first thought of writing after hearing him speak at a Queen's Hall meeting on 9 October, i.e. three weeks before the sitting and nearer five before he actually wrote. A sentence of the letter reads, 'Not very long ago I lost my son, a splendid young man, full of the joy of life and success.' After reference to certain London mediums, it continues, 'I think on the whole that we have been most fortunate in the evidential nature of the messages received.' Finally Thomas's advice was asked about other mediums, but there was no word to suggest that he might possibly obtain a message for him through Mrs Leonard.

Drayton Thomas entered into correspondence with Mr Aitken. From this correspondence certain facts emerged concerning the statements made at the sitting of 28 October. In this quotation (157g, pp. 103–104) Drayton Thomas places these facts for comparison beside the items given at the sitting.

1. *I am to expect a letter from a father about his son* . . . On my enquiring when Mr Aitken had first thought of writing he replied, 'I don't think I had thought of mentioning my case to you and asking for advice until I actually wrote the letter. I merely intended to thank you for your address. It appears that you had news of something I was going to write before I wrote it or had consciously thought of it.'

2. *The father is middle aged.* This is correct.

3. *An accident case.* This is also correct.

4. *Connected with a motor car.* Mr Aitken writes, 'Not a motor car accident exactly.'

5. *The young man was killed outright or very nearly so.* He was killed outright.

6. *Morton or a like-sounding name; this father once lived near where you lived.* In correspondence about this statement I learnt that Mr Aitken had resided at the village of Norton and that his son was born there and had been familiar with all the neighbourhood. Norton is but one and a half miles from Baldock where I lived with my parents in 1876–8. Is it too much to suppose that Feda's 'Morton' was misheard by her for Norton?

7. *Another name like Char – is given.* This was unsatisfactory, just possibly an attempt for Charles, the Christian name of Mr Aitken's friend killed at Gallipoli.

Drayton Thomas was entirely convinced that something more than chance was at work here. Several of the items, however, are either commonplace or wrong. The case rests largely on:

(a) the coincidence in time between the prediction of a letter that a man would write about his son, and the fulfilment of that prediction, and

(b) the fairly clear indication of a particular locality.

The former is somewhat hard to assess in the absence of detailed knowledge about the sort of letters Drayton Thomas habitually received; (b) is, however, not easy to discount.

Thomas uses the apparent precognition displayed by his communicators to knock the super-ESP hypothesis. He says (p. 104):

Those who incline to the universal telepathy hypothesis will suggest that the messages originated with Mr Aitken. But this would imply that the medium tapped the Aitken memory before either she or I were aware of his existence and, more incredibly still, that she divined a purpose of which he remained entirely unaware until he was in the act of writing to thank me for remarks he heard me make in public.

Drayton Thomas's criticism of the 'universal telepathy hypothesis' is no doubt entirely justified. One suspects, however, that he wishes to pass from the shortcomings of that hypothesis directly to the validity of the survivalist position. The principle seems to be – and it is, unfortunately, a principle enthusiastically applied in this field by partisans of all persuasions – that if your chief competitors are bankrupt, your own business must be on a sound footing. Many hopeful theorists have tried to persuade themselves of the latter by proving the former to their own satisfaction. But of course the present problem – that of the apparent precognition of Mr Aitken's letter – is not solved simply by attributing the precognition to discarnate spirits. Such a move would be entirely regressive.

The most remarkable aspect of this case, however, still remains to be told. At four later Leonard sittings, for which Drayton Thomas was sitter, and at which Mr Aitken was not present, a good deal of material ostensibly relating to Mr Aitken's son was received. Mr Aitken regarded much of this matter as highly evidential. There were however some passages which he could make little of, but which his other son recognized at once as a message concerning a common friend of his and his brother's, a friend of whom Mr Aitken had never heard. It transpired that the living son had (in thought) deliberately asked his dead brother to try to send a message concerning this friend through some medium.

I give now Mr Aitken's own corroborations of Feda's statements (157g, pp. 122-123):

> In Mr Drayton Thomas's sitting of 20 January 1939, Feda says: 'There was somebody else he was very interested in, that perhaps you don't know . . . a name that starts with the letter B, and I think there is an R in it . . . it's not a long name – very much linked with him . . . it might be a Mr BRICK . . . I feel this is something you could use for building, and is a name much connected with this boy and his interests.'
>
> In Mr Drayton Thomas's sitting of 3 February 1939, Feda says: 'A name starting with BR – rather an important name with him . . . Somebody he was linked up with shortly before his passing . . . there is a link between this BR . . . and the boy's passing. I also want to know if there is anything to do with him like a little ship . . . or a little model of a ship – something he had on earth and was very fond of. He is showing me something like a toy ship – a fancy ship, not a plain one – 'laborate, rather 'laborate – with a good deal of detail shown in it – it seemed to be connected with his earth life – but some time before he passed over, rather early in his earth life, but I think it is something that his people have still got . . .'
>
> A name beginning with BR – like the name Feda says 'might be Mr BRICK' – had been mentioned by other mediums, but we had been unable to place it, nor was the reference to a 'model ship' understood; but my son, on seeing the Leonard script, recognised its meaning.
>
> He and his deceased brother had been friends at an RAF Station with a young officer called BRIDGEN – whom we had not heard of – and who had been killed about a year after my son.
>
> This young man, before joining the RAF, had worked for a firm which made *scale models of ships* for shipping companies, and he had shown my son a photograph of one of these models which he had made himself and which he said his people still had at home. My son had felt sure that this matter of the model ship would be given as a sign if they were unable to get the name through correctly.

These corroborations were accompanied by the following letter from Mr Aitken's surviving son:

The Editor,
Journal of the Society for Psychical Research.
Dear Sir,

I have read my father's account of the 'Leonard–Aitken' proxy sittings, and I testify to its correctness.

I was the only living member of the family who knew of 'Bridgen', and I had never had any communication with Mr Drayton Thomas or Mrs Leonard.

My 'thought-message' was not directed to Mr Drayton Thomas or to Mrs Leonard – but to my 'dead' brother – and to me, the reply was unmistakable.

Yours sincerely,
LIONEL AITKEN,
Flying-Officer, RAF

14 November 1939

I shall not at this point attempt to work out the full implications which successful proxy sittings may have for the problem of survival. But the following points are worth bearing in mind for future discussion:

1.   It seems rather unlikely that all or even most of the information transmitted at these sittings could have come in a large part from clairvoyance by the medium. Many of the details given could be verified only by consulting the memories of friends and relatives of the deceased persons; there were, so far as we know, no pictures, no records, written or printed, and no other physical state of affairs which, clairvoyantly perceived, might have yielded such pieces of information as that Bobbie Newlove had an affection for a girl skater a little older than him, that F. W. Macaulay had an obsession about baths, and that he used unfeelingly to call his daughter 'pug-nose', and so on. And even if there had been such clairvoyantly accessible sources of information, the sources for each case would almost certainly have been scattered, so that the medium would have had to locate them, read them and synthesize them into a coherent and plausible story. Telepathy with some living person possessed of all the relevant scraps of information sounds a far more hopeful proposition.

2.   However it appears that in at any rate two of the proxy cases cited in this chapter there was no one living person who possessed all the information. This is most obvious in the Aitken case just described, in which Feda produced some distinctive pieces of information not known to Mrs Leonard, to Drayton Thomas, or to Mr Aitken, but only to the latter's still living son. In the Bobbie Newlove case some of the

relevant information (about the pipes and their location) was not known to any member of the communicator's family. We are forced to attribute its production either to telepathy between Mrs Leonard and one of Bobbie's friends (the one who played with him around the pipes), or to clairvoyant scanning of the neighbourhood plus skilful guessing about Bobbie's likely habits, or to a clairvoyant monitoring *prior to Bobbie's death* of his pastimes and activities, and a subsequent storing up of a record of them in the medium's unconscious mind. (This last possibility, implying as it does continual monitoring of the lives of an indefinitely large number of potential communicators who are as yet still living, seems to me more fantastic than any version of the survival hypothesis.) For both of these cases, therefore, we would on the ESP (or super-ESP) hypothesis have to postulate that Mrs Leonard located (telepathically or clairvoyantly) two separate sources of information, tapped them, and collated and synthesized the results.

In the remaining case cited, the Macaulay case, Drayton Thomas listed three correct items given by Feda which were not known to Mrs Lewis, the presumed principal source of telepathically obtained information. However Dodds found these items too vague and general to be convincing; and I agree with Dodds's estimate of them.

3. An obvious underlying problem which successful proxy sittings present for the ESP hypothesis is of course that of how the medium manages to locate (telepathically or clairvoyantly) sources of information appropriate to the case in hand. These sources are, in a number of different senses, remote from the sitting and the sitter, to whom the very existence of some of them is likely to be unknown. We might propose that the medium learns from the sitter's mind the identity of his principal (i.e. of the person for whom he is acting as proxy), and that this somehow enables her to home in on the mind of the principal; from the mind of the principal further clues to other sources of information may be obtained; and so on. One has only to ask oneself in detail what would be involved here to see that the proposed process is grotesquely implausible. Proper names, addresses, dates, and so forth – details which identify a person *uniquely* – are notoriously among the most difficult of all items for sensitives to obtain; and yet such uniquely identifying details (or their equivalents) would have to be obtained in a proxy case before the medium could pinpoint the right source of information to tap; and in some cases they would have to be obtained from several sources as the medium's mind so to speak moved along the chain of clues.

It must be added, of course, that the survivalist theory too must cope with the problem of how Feda managed to locate Bobby Newlove, F. W. Macaulay, etc., on the 'other side' in order to extract evidential messages from them. Did she do it by ESP? Certainly she often speaks as though her awareness of communicators were of a fluctuating and uncertain kind. However, if there is 'another world' to which our spirits pass at death, it is perhaps reasonable to suppose that it contains some form of established communication network or heavenly post office directory.

4. Finally it should be noted that in some proxy cases the principals have felt the messages received contained not just correct information, but hints of the personal characteristics (humour, interests, turns of phrase, and so forth) of the ostensible communicators. If they are correct in this, we have additionally to attribute to the medium the power to glean the relevant facts and then, instead of presenting them in statement form ('he had a dry sense of humour'), so to speak to enact them in dramatic form by reproducing the communicator's characteristic dry humour (or whatever it may be). Certainly, the more numerous the unusual gifts we have to attribute to mediums in order to support the super-ESP hypothesis, the more cumbersome that hypothesis becomes.

5 'Drop-In' Communicators

In successful proxy sittings, such as those described in the last chapter, there is still, it is often, however implausibly, argued, some kind of link between the medium and some absent person or persons possessing the relevant information. If necessary an upholder of the super-ESP hypothesis will propose a series of such links, ending up, naturally, with someone who knows whatever it was that the medium came out with. In the class of cases which I shall now discuss even those tenuous and exceedingly ill-defined links are absent. The class concerned is that labelled by Professor Ian Stevenson (153d) 'drop-in' communicators. 'Drop-in' communicators are, as the name implies, communicators who arrive uninvited, and are ostensibly unknown to medium and sitters. We have on record a number of cases in which 'drop-in' communicators have made statements about themselves and their careers which it has subsequently proved possible to verify. Such cases are of obvious theoretical interest and, before proceeding to some actual examples, I shall briefly explore their potential theoretical implications. These implications are, in general, hostile to the super-ESP hypothesis, and favourable to some form of survival theory. The difficulties for the super-ESP hypothesis may be spelled out under two headings, viz. selection of communicator and locating of materials.

The first of these sets of problems becomes apparent if one asks why, in any verified drop-in case, the medium's supposed ESP should have lit upon facts about that particular deceased person. The facts about the great majority of 'drop-in' communicators are not in any way especially eye-catching. They would not, for instance, be enshrined in unusually striking obituary notices or letters of condolence such as might be supposed to attract the medium's clairvoyance more than would other such notices or letters. Nor, so far as one can tell, would they stand out with such prominence in the minds of grief-stricken relatives as particularly to arrest her telepathic attention. Nor have medium and sitters any special motive for desiring information about that particular deceased person. Some very broad constraints do seem to be imposed on the selection of 'drop-in' communicators, in that most of them (that is most of the ones whose statements about themselves have been verified) come from the medium's own country and speak her own language. But these constraints aside, we seem reduced, on the super-ESP hypothesis, to supposing that selection of communicator depends upon the random operation of wholly unknown factors.

The second set of difficulties which verified 'drop-in' cases may raise for the super-ESP hypothesis, that to do with the location of materials, is much more complex and difficult. In most 'drop-in' cases there is, no doubt, some single possible source, such as a printed record, or the organized memory system of a living person, from which the medium could through her supposed extrasensory powers have obtained the whole of her information. But what if (and some cases may at least approximate to this type) the requisite information could have been assembled only through the tapping of a number of discrete sources, e.g. the memory systems of several different living persons or a variety of different printed records? How is the medium, having selected the deceased person she will present to her sitters, to discriminate from amongst all the innumerable items of information telepathically and clairvoyantly available to her, those and only those which are relevant to that person? I do not think that it is possible to give an account of this matter that is even remotely plausible.

Consider first the case where the different items are locked in the memories of a number of different people. The most obvious hypothesis is probably that the various relevant memory-sets in different peoples' minds are all flagged or marked out by similar quasi-perceptible features, for instance recognisably similar images of the deceased communicator. But even if we set aside for the moment the logical difficulties involved in the suggestion that one person can inspect another person's images by a kind of quasi-perception, the image-theory remains grossly implausible. It would force one to predict that mediums should be prone to confuse with each other persons who simply happened in life to look alike, and even perhaps confuse real people with fictional characters. It would force one further to maintain that each person's memory-images are, when not in use, stored away in some internal filing cabinet accessible to the medium's telepathic rummagings. This is a remarkably implausible idea. Yet if one replaces it with the notion that memories are stored up in the form of subtle structural or functional changes in the brain, one must attribute to the medium the ability to read the neural code in which the memories are represented, a skill which no neurophysiologist is currently anywhere near attaining (or, as I shall later argue, ever could attain). Finally, it is in any case quite clear that it is not any quasi-perceptible features of an image which make that image an image *of* some particular person, but the reference or intentionality with which the imager invests it. An image of a round and jolly face – the same face – can serve as an image of one's late Uncle Nat, as an image of John Bull, as an image of Mr Pickwick, as an image of a brand of breakfast cereal, as an image of Jupiter, the bringer of jollity, as an image of jollity in general, and so forth. Psychological processes outside the image determine what the image is an image of.

It might seem as though the case where the different items of information exist in the form of written or other records presents less difficulty than the case just discussed. For obituary notices, letters of condolence, and so forth, commonly carry distinctive headings or addresses which, clairvoyantly perceived, would at once indicate that the same person was involved. Perhaps this does simplify the problem; but it is far from making it simple. Consider the case where a number of newspaper notices have to be clairvoyantly collated. Let us assume that (as is commonly the case) the newspapers concerned are old ones, and not current issues lying on breakfast tables throughout the country. Then it has to be supposed that the medium, in the course of her incessant clairvoyant but presumably unconscious browsings among the files of old newspapers, picks out from the enormous number of obituary notices thus accessible to her those and only those relating to a certain person, and then juxtaposes and synthesizes them. In other words she must discriminate these obituaries from all obituaries of persons of the same or similar name, from all obituaries of persons who had similar careers, from all obituaries of persons who had the same dates, and so on and so forth. Anyone who has had (as I have had) occasion to study newspaper obituary notices extensively will realize that this is an exceedingly tall order, and a few examples of obvious confusion between newspaper obituaries would greatly strengthen the clairvoyant explanation – especially in view of the fact that so far as I am aware we do not have, from outside the mediumistic situation, a single properly authenticated example of a clairvoyant managing to read a concealed passage of prose in anything like the necessary detail.

It is thus possible to construct an idealized 'drop-in' case which pushes the super-ESP hypothesis to the verge of unintelligibility; indeed beyond that verge. Such a case would have the following features:

(a) The 'drop-in' communicator in question would have a strong and comprehensible reason for wishing to communicate; a reason clearly stronger than any which the medium might have for wishing to contact him.

(b) The information which he communicates would be such that the medium could not have obtained it all by extrasensory contact with a single living person, obituary notice, etc.

(c) We can be tolerably certain that the medium could not have obtained the information by ordinary means (this is a point to which I shall shortly return).

It is hardly necessary to spell out how great are the advantages of the survivalist theory in respect of cases where the super-ESP hypothesis would have to suppose that the medium had used her extraordinary powers of ESP to locate several disparate sources of information about the communicator and had then put together the information thus gleaned. It also has obvious advantages when it comes to explaining why the medium selects one unknown deceased person rather than another unknown deceased person as the subject for her extrasensory researches. The deceased person selects himself. As Stevenson remarks (153d, p. 63), 'Some "drop-in" communicators have explained their presence very well and their motivation to communicate is an important part of the whole case which has to be explained as well as the provenance of any information communicated.' 'Drop-in' communicators may represent themselves as wishing to assuage the grief of living friends, as brought along by persons in the next world who have previously communicated through the same medium, as lost in a kind of limbo where the medium is their only means of contact with others, as linked through common interest to persons present, as altruistically trying to help, as simply 'dropping in' for a chat. It is difficult indeed to decide how seriously communicators' own explanations of their presences ought to be taken; but sometimes at least the professed explanations are 'in character'.

So much for the theoretical implications of 'drop-in' communicators and for the ideal (and hence imaginary) case. We must now get to grips with some actual cases and see to what extent (if at all) they measure up to the ideal.

Cases of verified 'drop-in' communicators are fairly scarce in the 'reputable' literature of psychical research (for examples see 48; 64b, pp. 97–102; 110a, II, pp. 471–477; 153d; 153e; 162a; 174). How far this reflects an overall scarcity it is hard to say. 'Drop-in' communicators seem to be much more characterisic of the 'home circle', the ouija and planchette boards, and the automatist experimenting out of curiosity and interest, than they are of the professional medium. There could be various reasons for this, one of them being, of course, that there are often pressures on mediums who regularly give sittings to individual clients to exclude communicators other than those with whom the sitter wishes to speak. Since a high proportion of the investigations of mediumship published by the SPR and the ASPR have concerned mediums of this latter sort, cases of 'drop-in' communicators have not often figured (for some cases of this kind with Mrs Piper see 66a, pp. 37–42). Also, of course, the verification of 'drop-in' cases requires a good deal of time, and also, very often, a working knowledge of the country's public records system together with access to a large library. 'Drop-in' communicators of the utmost veridicality could march into and out of the average home circle without its occurring to anyone that it would be feasible to check up on them. And where such checks have been undertaken, they have often fallen far short of the required standard of thoroughness.

I shall illustrate this last point with an example taken from Sir Lawrence Jones's Presidential Address to the SPR (76). In the year 1900 Sir Lawrence had for some time at his house in the South of France a home circle centring around the well-known amateur medium, Miss Kate Wingfield (she is referred to as 'Miss A.' in F. W. H. Myers's *Human Personality*). Communications were received both by raps and by automatic writing. On 8 September 1900 a certain Sarah Willett, of 7 Sydney Street, London, wrote through Miss Wingfield that she had been shot and killed by one Jack Parr, of Green Street, a polisher. On 30 September, Miss Wingfield had a vision of this girl, and on the evening of 2 October saw an ominous 'figure with a black thing like a sack tied over his head and shoulders'. Raps spelled out 'John Parr hanged today'. Miss Willett, whose dallyings with another man had precipitated the murder, expressed terror at the revenge which Jack Parr might exact upon his premature transition to the other side. Shortly afterwards John Parr began to communicate regularly, at first breathing vengeance against the doubly persecuted Sarah. Later on, however, he calmed down and dictated a recipe for furniture polish which proved highly serviceable.

John Parr's execution on 2 October was not mentioned in British newspapers until the following day. However its date could probably have been predicted by any knowledgeable person who had read accounts of the murder and inquest (*Morning Post* 29 August and 1 September) and of John Parr's trial (*The Times*, 14 September). The details given in the 'communications' corresponded closely to the newspaper reports. Sir Lawrence Jones, by all accounts a man of the greatest charm, was happy to accept the assurance of the medium, and of her mother (who was also staying with him), that they had not read these newspaper accounts, and normally did not look at *The Times* and *The Morning Post*. But a cynic would certainly say that Miss Wingfield had fraudulently 'got up' the newspaper accounts and regurgitated them in her automatic writing. A less serious supposition would be that of cryptomnesia; the supposition, that is, that she looked at the reports, forgot them, but retained a latent or hidden memory of them which subsequently found expression in her automatic writing. One or other of these hypotheses would certainly have been suggested if, for instance, the newspaper accounts had proved to contain errors which were reproduced in the communications. Sir Lawrence did not even attempt to discover whether the recipe for furniture polish had been lifted from *Aunt Kate's Home Treasury* or some similar compilation. Nor on the other hand did he enquire whether the two addresses given (Sidney Street and Green Street), which do not appear in the *Times* report of the trial which he quotes, were correct. If they had proved correct, the case for paranormality would have been correspondingly strengthened.

To rule out the fraud and cryptomnesia explanations one would need, not charitably to accept the medium's say-so that she had never come across the relevant information, but to give reasons for supposing that she *could not have* come across it. And this involves proving a negative, a notoriously difficult undertaking. The negative cannot, I think, be proved in the case just discussed; certainly it was not proved. But there are other cases in which it may be not proved exactly, for 'proof' is a word somewhat strong for any non-mathematical demonstration, but at any rate powerfully supported. I shall now proceed to outline and comment upon three such cases.

The first of these cases was received through a well-known Icelandic trance medium, Hafsteinn Bjornsson. Hafsteinn was not a professional medium in the sense of earning his living through his mediumship, but he did accept fees from sitters. He had a regular control named 'Finna', who would relay messages from other communicators; but sometimes the latter would themselves control. The original communications were obtained in 1941, and were investigated shortly afterwards (88). The case was further studied in 1971–2 by Haraldsson and Stevenson, who published their report in 1975 (59b).

On 25 January 1941, Hjalmar Gudjonsson, a visitor from eastern Iceland, had a sitting with Hafstein Bjornsson in Reykjavik, which is in the extreme south-west. (It is perhaps worth noting that at that time communications between Reykjavik and eastern Iceland were poor and mainly by boat.) The sitting was held at the home of Gudrun Jonsdottir, an experienced sitter, who was also present, along with another lady, Hansina Hansdottir. Hjalmar Gudjonsson was anxious to contact various persons he had known, but to his annoyance an intruding communicator, who gave the name Gudni Magnusson, monopolized the sitting. Gudni, who was not known to medium or sitters, stated that he had ties with Eskifjordur, in Hjalmar's part of the world, and addressed himself to Hjalmar for that reason. He said that he had died following internal injuries received while attempting to repair his truck; and he gave various other details about himself which we will come to. Most unfortunately no contemporary notes were made of what was said.

Two days later, Hjalmar's hostess at the sitting, Gudrun Jonsdottir, told a friend, Asmundur Gestsson, about this intrusive communicator. Asmundur had a cousin, Gudrun Gudmundsdottir, who was the wife of a physician practising in Eskifjordur, the place with which Gudni Magnusson had claimed to be linked. He accordingly wrote to this cousin, asking if she knew of anyone corresponding to the supposed communicator. His letter, dated 26 February 1941, survives – it was unearthed by Erlundur Haraldsson – and is the earliest document which gives details of the communications. It antedates, and in fact led to, verification of the communicator's statements.

Asmundur Gestsson's cousin replied on 14 March 1941 confirming that a Gudni Magnusson answering the description given had lived in Eskifjordur and had died in circumstances resembling those given. This letter, which is quite detailed, will be referred to below as the 'Gudmundsdottir letter'.

At this point Asmundur Gestsson realized that he had an interesting case on his hands and got Hjalmar Gudjonsson and Gudrun Jonsdottir to write out independently their recollections of the sitting and sign them. Hjalmar's account is dated 30 March 1941, and Gudrun's, which is fairly full, 6 June 1941. The third sitter, Hansina Hansdottir, signed Gudrun's statement. There do not seem to be any serious discrepancies between these statements, or between them and our earliest document, Asmundur Gestsson's letter of 26 February 1941. I think that, despite the absence of contemporary notes, we may safely accept the statements as accurately reflecting what passed at the sitting, especially since they are confirmed by the Asmundur Gestsson letter written before the verifications were received.

In his investigations of 1971–2, Erlundur Haraldsson found further sources of verification for some of the statements made. He interviewed Hjalmar Gudjonsson, and Gudni Magnusson's brother and sister, Otto Magnusson and Rosa Magnusdottir; he obtained a copy of Gudni's death certificate (such certificates are not obtainable by the general public in Iceland); he found an obituary notice of Gudni in the issue of *Morgunbladid* for 7 November 1940; and he interviewed the author of this obituary notice. Putting together all the information thus obtained we can, following Haraldsson and Stevenson, tabulate the communicator's statements and the verifications as follows:

Communicator's Statement	*Verification from*
1. His name was Gudni or Gudni Magnusson.	Gudmundsdottir letter
2. He was between 20 and 30 years old when he died.	Gudni's death certificate; obituary
3. He was of average height.	Otto Magnusson
4. He had blond hair.	Obituary notice; Otto Magnusson
5. His hair was thin on top.	Otto Magnusson
6. He had died about four or five months before the seance.	Death certificate; obituary
7. He had been a truck driver.	Gudmundsdottir letter; Otto Magnusson
8. He had a connection with Herad (a district).	Unverified; but there were reasons for thinking Gudni might have known Herad
9. His parents were living.	Gudmundsdottir letter; Rosa Magnusdottir
10. He was crossing a mountain pass when his truck broke down.	Gudmundsdottir letter; Otto Magnusson

11. He was alone in his truck prior to his death.	Gudmunsdottir letter
12. He had been repairing his truck and had crawled under it.	Verification not satisfactory
13. He had torn or ruptured something inside himself.	Death certificate; Gudmunds-dottir letter; Otto Magnusson. (He died of peritonitis almost certainly due to the stated cause)
14. He had not died immediately, but managed to get home.	Gudmundsdottir letter; Otto Magnusson
15. He had been brought by boat between fjords to medical care.	Gudmundsdottir letter; Otto Magnusson
16. He had died on the way.	Gudmundsdottir letter; Otto Magnusson
17. He was brought to a doctor	Gudmundsdottir letter. (He was with two doctors when he died, but was on his way to hospital)
18. He had Eskifjordur 'on his mind'.	Gudmundsdottir letter; Otto Magnusson. (He was on his way home to Eskifjordur)
19. There was a connection also with Reydarfjordur.	Gudmundsdottir letter. (He was driving from Reydarfjordur to Eskifjordur)
20. He had known some relatives of Hjalmar Gudjonsson.	Incorrect so far as Hjalmar Gudjonsson could ascertain

We now come to the question of whether this material could have been known to the medium or sitters through ordinary channels. In their article on the case Haraldsson and Stevenson give much attention to this issue. They summarize their conclusions about it as follows (59b, pp. 260-261):

The communicator came from a part of Iceland which the medium had never even visited. The sitters, even including the one person present (Hjalmar Gudjonsson) who was from eastern Iceland, had no connection whatever with Gudni or his family. The newspaper obituary could not have furnished the medium with all the correctly communicated details, nor could the writer of the obituary, who then lived in eastern Iceland, which the medium had never visited. The communicator had an uncle in Reykjavik, but as far as we can learn, he had no connection with the medium. Thus despite extensive enquiries we have not been able to find any channel for normal communication to the medium of the correct information he had about Gudni Magnusson and expressed at the seance under consideration.

Haraldsson and Stevenson are here considering, and rejecting, primarily the cryptomnesia hypothesis, that is, that Hafsteinn Bjornsson might have somewhere come across the relevant information, and have retained a latent memory of it which came to the fore only in his trance state. They do not take seriously the hypothesis of outright fraud by Hafsteinn, and there do indeed seem to be quite strong reasons for dismissing it. Hafsteinn's reputation throughout some forty years of mediumship was generally good; he had no known connection with Eskifjordur, yet to have obtained all the information about Gudni he would have needed not just an agent in Eskifjordur (a remote and sparsely populated place), but an agent who knew Gudni personally; and it was certainly not Hafsteinn who pushed or promoted the investigation of the Gudni communicator – it was in fact a person (Asmundur Gestsson) who was not even present at the sitting. I agree, therefore, with the cautious assessment of Haraldsson and Stevenson: 'We conclude . . . that despite its obvious weaknesses [the absence of seance notes], the case justifies an interpretation that includes some paranormal process.'

But what kind of paranormal process? We can rule out clairvoyance at once, because the only relevant record of events which might be supposed to have been clairvoyantly accessible (the obituary notice) contained by no means all of the items given, and would in any case have had to be cognized *precognitively*. (One cannot, I think, take seriously the idea that by some sort of unconscious clairvoyance Hafsteinn monitored the events at the time when they occurred, and stored up a record of them for future regurgitation; how many other such sets of events must he have been simultaneously monitoring?) The hypothesis of telepathy from the living is more plausible, provided, at least, that one is prepared to believe (despite lack of substantial evidence) that telepathy of such a range and extent can occur; there must at the time of the sitting have been several persons alive who possessed all the requisite information. Thus the case of Gudni Magnusson is not one which strains the super-ESP hypothesis in the way that I indicated when constructing my 'ideal' drop in case earlier in the chapter. It does not require one to suppose that the medium extrasensorially located and then collated relevant information from several different sources. Gudni does, however, offer an intelligible motive for communicating – the desire to talk to someone from his own part of the world – whereas neither medium nor sitters had, so far as can be ascertained, any reason at all for picking out that particular deceased person as a target for super-ESP.

I shall next give a case from a series which I investigated myself (44c). They occurred in the context of a ouija board circle operated by a small group of people in Cambridge during and after the Second World War. Altogether more than two hundred deceased persons (and one living one) communicated through this circle. Most were friends and relations of the sitters. There were, however, eleven instances of verified 'drop-in' communicators, plus a rather larger number of unverified ones. Most of the verified cases were first verified by me, from thirteen to twenty-eight years after the original communications. This constitutes, I think, a strong argument against the likelihood of deliberate fraud. No one, however devious, would be likely to cast so much bread upon the waters, without eventually dropping some hints which might facilitate a return. The sitters, it should be noticed, made no attempts to promote the cases, or to obtain publicity, and had themselves not much idea of how one might set about checking them. I shall briefly summarize one of the more interesting cases.

At a number of sittings between 1950 and 1952 a communicator calling himself 'Harry Stockbridge' (not the real name) spelled out the following items of information about himself:

> Second Loot attached Northumberland Fusiliers. Died Fourteen July sixteen.
> Tyneside Scottish.
> Tall, dark, thin. Special features large brown eyes.
> I hung out in Leicester . . . Leicester hold[s] a record.
> [Asked what were his likes and dislikes] Problems any. Pepys reading. Water colouring.
> [Asked if he knew a 'Powis Street' about which two sitters had dreamed] I know it well. My association took my memory there.
> [Asked if his mother was with him] Yes.

The sitters made one – unsuccessful – attempt to check up on these statements. The matter then rested until 1965, when I began to investigate the Stockbridge case. In an HMSO publication entitled *Officers died in the Great War of 1914–19* I found it stated that a Second Lieutenant H. Stockbridge of the Northumberland Fusiliers was killed on 19 (not 14) July 1916. I then sent for Stockbridge's death certificate. This gives his date of death as 14 July 1916 (as in the scripts) and not 19

July (as in the official list). To resolve the issue, I wrote to the Army Records Centre, and received official confirmation that the death was 14 July.

Stockbridge's death certificate shows that he was born in Leicester in 1896. This information is also contained in Joseph Keating's *Tyneside Irish Brigade* (London, 1896), the only military history I have found which mentions Stockbridge (it does not, however, give the date of his death). This book states that Stockbridge was in one of the Tyneside Irish battalions of the Northumberland Fusiliers. However a record card in the War Office Library, kindly consulted for me by a friend, states that before his death he had been transferred to a Tyneside Scottish battalion.

That Stockbridge was tall, dark and thin, and had large brown eyes, was confirmed by his surviving brothers, and also by a photograph of him preserved in the archives of his old school. Whether he read Pepys or enjoyed water-colouring no-one could say. We may presume that he enjoyed 'problems any', since school records show that he won form prizes in mathematics and physics. He later enrolled for a university science course. His mother had died before the period of the communications.

The sitters thought that 'Leicester hold a record' meant that Stockbridge's name might be on a War Memorial in Leicester. They asked a friend who was passing through Leicester to investigate, but she found nothing. His name is in fact on a War Memorial in his old school in Leicester.

There was a 'Powis Street' near the house in which Stockbridge was born, although the family left the district within a few years.

So much, then, for the verifications of what the Stockbridge communicator said about himself. We have now to ask whether all these correct statements could have originated from a latent memory in the mind of one of the operators of the ouija board. During all the relevant sittings the ouija board was worked by a married couple, whom I shall call Mr and Mrs L.G. (it was quite clear that Mrs G. was the medium). Other persons were present, but did not operate the board. Neither Mr nor Mrs L.G. had any contacts in Leicester or had ever visited it, and I could trace no likely line of contact between either of them and any member of the Stockbridge family. Mr L.G. served in the First World War, but not in Stockbridge's regiment. Furthermore he did not join up until after Stockbridge had been killed (I have seen his pay book).

Could the relevant information have been hoarded up

subconsciously ('cryptomnesia'), following a glance at some obituary notice of Stockbridge? I was unable to trace a contemporary death notice of Stockbridge in any national newspaper, nor did 'In Memoriam' notices appear in later years. Two Leicester newspapers printed an obituary notice of him on 19 July 1916. This obituary notice (which it is highly unlikely that any of the sitters would have seen) gives the correct date of death, but the wrong rank (Lieutenant instead of Second Lieutenant), and makes no reference to the 'Tyneside Scottish' battalion. It give none of the details about Stockbridge's appearance and interests (there is no photograph), and of course says nothing about Powis Street. Keating's *Tyneside Irish Brigade* contains several of the items of information which the Stockbridge communicator produced. It is, however, a very out-of-the-way book, and it gives no death date, makes no reference to 'Tyneside Scottish', and contains no photograph or description of Stockbridge. Stockbridge's appearance, and his Tyneside Scottish connections are, in fact, not mentioned, so far as I can discover, in any publicly available source. It does not seem to me that the hypothesis of cryptomnesia can possibly suffice to explain away the correct statements made by the Stockbridge communicator.

If, as I have argued, we can rule out the fraud and the cryptomnesia explanations in this case, we seem left to weigh up the respective merits of some form of survival hypothesis and of some version of the super-ESP hypothesis. The Stockbridge case does appear to stretch the super-ESP hypothesis in some of the ways which I indicated earlier in the chapter when discussing an 'ideal' 'drop-in' case. Stockbridge advances as his reason for coming that he is to help one of the other sitters (another ex-serviceman). This may not be an especially powerful reason, but it at any rate gives him a stronger reason for communicating than any of the sitters had for singling out facts about him as targets for super-ESP. If we suppose that the medium obtained information about him by clairvoyant apprehension of existing records, we must face the fact that she must have located, and synthesized the contents of, at least four separate sources, including the archives of his old school and the War Office Library. Could there at the time of the communications have been a living person or persons whose minds, telepathically tapped by the medium, might have provided all the requisite items? It is extremely difficult to say. His parents were by that time dead. It was nearly twenty years later that I made contact with two living brothers, and through them with a third brother and a sister. They had only the vaguest recollections of the brother who had died over fifty years before, and it was quite apparent that as a result of following up the seance data I knew more details about his life than they did. My own guess is that the situation would not have been substantially different at the time of the sittings. But in this slippery field a guess is not good enough.

It seems therefore that even the very curious Stockbridge case does not fully measure up to the ideal 'drop-in' case for which I suggested criteria earlier in the chapter. Had it been investigated in 1952 it might have done so. There is in the literature, however, at least one carefully investigated case in which a 'drop-in' communicator made a series of correct statements, the totality of which could not have been obtained either clairvoyantly from a single document, obituary, etc., or telephathically, from the mind of a single living person. I refer to the case of Runolfur Runolfsson ('Runki'), for which the medium was once again Hafsteinn Bjornsson, and the investigators were once again Haraldsson and Stevenson (59a). The case is a complex and singular one, but it is unfortunately too long to be fully presented here. In outline the story is this. During the years 1937–8, Hafsteinn was acting as medium for what seems to have been a home circle in Reykjavik. In this period a highly eccentric communicator began to manifest through the entranced medium. He showed a yearning for snuff, coffee and alcohol, refused to give his name, and kept reiterating that he was looking for his leg. Asked where his leg was, he replied 'in the sea'. In short he must have appeared at this time to be one of those comic-relief characters who so frequently brighten up the otherwise sober proceedings at home circles.

In January 1939 the circle was joined by Ludvik Gudmundsson, the owner of a fish factory in the village of Sandgerdi, about 36 miles from Reykjavik. The unknown communicator showed great interest in this new sitter, and eventually stated that his missing leg was in the latter's house at Sandgerdi. After a good deal of further pressure from the sitters, he made the following statement (59a, p. 39):

My name is Runolfur Runolfsson, and I was 52 years old when I died. I lived with my wife at Kolga or Klappakot, near Sandgerdi. I was on a journey from Keflavik [about six miles from Sandgerdi] in the latter part of the day and I was drunk. I stopped at the house of Sveinbjorn Thordarson in Sandgerdi and accepted some refreshments there. When I went to go, the weather was so bad that they did not wish me to leave unless accompanied by someone else. I became angry and said I would not go at all if I could not go alone. My house was only about 15 minutes' walk away. So I left by myself, but I was wet and tired. I walked over the kambuin [pebbles] and reached the rock known as Flankastadaklettur which has almost disappeared now. There I sat down, took my bottle, and drank some more. Then I fell asleep. The tide came in and carried me away. This happened in October, 1879. I was not found until January, 1880. I was carried in by the tide, but then dogs and ravens came and tore me to pieces. The remnants [of my body] were found and buried in Utskalar graveyard [about four miles from Sandgerdi]. But then the thigh bone was missing. It was carried out again to sea, but was later washed up again at Sandgerdi. There it was passed around and now it is in Ludvik's house.

On another occasion the communicator stated that he had been a very tall man. To cut a long story short, Runki's extraordinary tale was subsequently verified in considerable detail, although it did not appear that he had in fact stopped at the house of Sveinbjorn Thordarson. Ludvik Gudmundsson knew nothing about any thigh bone in his house, but after enquiries among older local inhabitants, he found that sometime in the 1920s such a bone, believed to have been washed up by the sea, had been placed in an interior wall. It was recovered, and turned out to be the femur of a very tall man. No one knew whose bone it was, and there was no record which indicated whether or not the thigh bone was missing from Runki's remains. One wonders, indeed, why, even if the deceased Runki were the source of the communications, and even if the thigh bone were actually his, he should have had any special knowledge of the matter.

The remaining statements were nearly all verifiable from entries distributed between two manuscript sources, the Church books of Utskalar (in the National Archives at Reykjavik), and the Rev Sigidur Severtsen's *Annals of Sudurnes*, which at the time of the sitting rested unpublished and little known in the National Library at Reykjavik. That Runki had been tall was confirmed by his grandson, who, however, had not known him, and was not aware of the bone and of other relevant facts. He could therefore not have been, either through telepathy or through normal channels, a source for all the information communicated. It is possible that the Rev Jon Thorarensen, who in 1953 edited *Annals of Sudurnes* for publication, was even in 1939 aware of the major details of the story, but he did not know about the bone. Nor did he meet Hafsteinn before 1940.

Haraldsson and Stevenson consider in great detail the possibility that Hafsteinn could have obtained by normal means information from these and other less important sources – it seems extremely unlikely that he would have heard of the *Annals of Sudurnes* – and sum up the possibilities as follows (59a, p. 57):

. . . for the medium to have acquired all the correctly communicated information, it does not seem feasible to attribute all of this information to any single person or any single written source. And this would be true, we believe, whether the medium acquired the information normally or by extrasensory perception. We think, therefore, that some process of integration of details derived from different persons or other sources must be supposed in the interpretation of the case. It may be simplest to explain this integration as due to Runki's survival after his physical death with the retention of many memories and their subsequent communication through the mediumship of Hafsteinn. On the other hand, sensitives have been known to achieve remarkable feats of deriving and integrating information without the participation of any purported discarnate personality.

The last remark brings us to the crux of the matter. If sensitives operating in a non-mediumistic context can perform feats of location and integration of detailed information from discrete sources which, duplicated in the mediumistic sphere, would permit the construction of such communicators as Runki, Harry Stockbridge, Mr Aitken's son, or Lodge's Uncle Jerry, then the super-ESP hypothesis, fantastic though this is, will be rendered more plausible. To this issue I shall return in later chapters. With regard to the survivalist hypothesis, the following observation may be made. If communication between the living and the dead is possible, and can be carried on through the agency of mediums, we should expect to meet with 'drop-in' communicators, for there must be many recently deceased persons who earnestly desire to send messages of comfort, reassurance and advice to their bereaved relations. Had there been *no records at all* of verified 'drop-in' communicators, the survivalist position would necessarily have been seriously weakened. As it is, the onus is still on the survivalist either to explain away, or else to present reasons for denying, the supposed fact that such cases are relatively rare. I briefly discussed this matter earlier in the chapter.

6 Manifestations of Purpose

The 'evidence for survival' discussed in the previous three chapters has been for the most part what might be called evidence for the survival of memories. Deceased persons, ostensibly communicating through mediums, have produced about their supposed earthly lives facts, not easily accessible to others, which they themselves, if they are indeed the persons they purport to be, might be expected to remember. It is quite reasonable to concentrate on this sort of evidence; for, as I pointed out in Chapter Five above, nothing – not even fingerprints – differentiates one person from another with greater certainty than his own individual set of memories. Still, the mere survival of memories, however detailed and characteristic they were, would not constitute survival of a person. One might imagine, for instance, that the magical arts of Cagliostro, who summoned back from beyond the grave so many of the sages of the Enlightenment, had created a life-like simulacrum of Dr Johnson. Suppose that this simulacrum sat in a coffee-house chair, exhibited the sort of range of information that Johnson had possessed, and readily gave correct answers to questions about Johnson's life; the whole tallying exactly with data contained in Boswell's *Life*, Mrs Thrale's *Anecdotes*, and as yet unpublished manuscript sources. None the less this Johnson-simulacrum did nothing but sit and inflict a ceaseless flow of factual reminiscence upon its hearers. It exhibited none of Johnson's individual and peculiar goals, purposes, intellectual skills, and personality characteristics; none indeed of *anybody's* purposes and personality characteristics, etc. It did not, for example, engage in intellectual argument upon every occasion; strive energetically for victory in debate; squash any Scotsman present; censure laxity of expression; support Tory and Anglican principles; or in any way try to do anything except prose endlessly about its own past history. Under these circumstances we should have to say of Cagliostro's creation that whatever it was it was not Dr Johnson, or at least was Johnson suffering from some advanced and highly selective form of mental decay, which had destroyed many of those capacities which made him most truly a human being. To switch to a more modern metaphor – a memory bank is not a person.

It is correspondingly important in investigating the problem of survival to look not just at the evidence for the survival of memory, but also at such evidence as we have for the survival of these other individual characteristics. In this chapter I shall consider some of the evidence that certain deceased persons have after their deaths continued to attempt to pursue goals and purposes that were characteristic of them in life, or have begun to pursue goals that might be thought a natural development of these. (Any totally new goals that they might develop would of course help one to regard them as persons, but would not constitute evidence for survival.) In the next chapter I shall take up some of the evidence for the survival of personality characteristics, intellectual skills, and so forth. It is to be observed, however, that none of these kinds of evidence can be sharply separated from one another.

To carry much weight as evidence for survival, a case of ostensible post-mortem manifestation of purpose would of course have to come in the context of related evidence for surviving memory. That said, however, it can readily be seen that such a case might put strain upon the super-ESP hypothesis in two respects:

1.   Different people pursue their purposes – even the same purpose – in very different ways. Butcher Cumberland, for instance, might have had a very different idea of how to squash a Scotsman from that entertained by Johnson. A medium who wished to work the pursuit of a certain characteristic purpose into her personation of a particular deceased person (I am not talking here of conscious deception), would have to select not just an appropriate purpose, but an appropriate way of carrying it out. This would involve her (assuming, of course, for the sake of argument that she has no ordinary access to the relevant information) in discovering by ESP a goal or purpose which the diseased person in question might plausibly be regarded as pursuing; and it would further involve her in rummaging around telepathically in the memories of those persons who knew him well, or clairvoyantly in the files of newspapers which printed obituary notices of him, in order to *infer* from the material thus gathered in what way he would most likely have attempted to implement his purpose. The inference would then have to be worked up into dramatic form for presentation at the sitting. It is, I think one may unhesitatingly say, a pretty tall order.

2. The purpose in question may very possibly be one which the medium herself has no cause to support; conceivably, indeed, it could be one quite opposed to her own conscious desires and interests. In the latter case the problem of motive becomes an urgent one. Why on earth should the medium (play-acting the role of a certain deceased person) endeavour to promote events which (when her normal self) she does not wish to happen? One could, of course, reply that unconsciously, or partly consciously and partly unconsciously, the medium has so great a desire to achieve fame in her chosen profession that no other consideration can stand in its way. This is one of those convenient proposals which it is in principle not possible to refute, and which I suggested in Chapter One, we should whenever possible decline to entertain.

Cases in which a deceased person has, through a medium, apparently manifested a clear-cut and characteristic purpose are somewhat uncommon (see 131). There are a few quite dramatic ones, in which, for instance, suicide or starvation have ostensibly been averted by discarnate intervention through a medium; but these tend not to be among the best-evidenced cases. The following, exceedingly odd, case, was reported in detail by a Russian corresponding member of the SPR, Alexander Aksakov, an Imperial Councillor to the Czar.

In January 1885, Mrs A. von Wiesler (Aksakov's sister-in-law), and her daughter Sophie, began to experiment with a planchette board. The board was soon monopolized by an exceptionally forceful communicator, who claimed to be 'Schura' (Alexandrine) the deceased daughter of somewhat distant acquaintances. Schura, who had adopted revolutionary political views, had committed suicide at the age of seventeen, following the death while escaping from prison of a like-minded male cousin. Schura demanded, in no hesitant tone, that another cousin, Nikolaus, should be brought to a sitting. According to Schura, Nikolaus was in danger of compromising himself politically. Sophie hesitated for reasons of social propriety. Schura's demands became more and more vehement at successive sittings, until on 26 February 1885 she wrote, 'It is too late . . . expect his arrest.' The von Wieslers then contacted Nikolaus's parents, who were, however, quite satisfied in respect of his conduct.

Two years later Nikolaus was arrested and exiled because of political assemblies which he had attended in January and February 1885. 'The notes which Mrs von Wiesler had made were read again and again by the families both of 'Schura' and of Nikolaus. "Schura's" identity in all these manifestations was recognized as incontestably demonstrated, in the first place by the main fact in relation to Nikolaus, by other intimate particulars, and also by the totality of features which characterized her personality' (110a, II, p. 181).

This case exhibits to some degree both of the characteristics which I noted above as constituting especial difficulties for the super-ESP hypothesis: 'Schura' pursued her characteristic purpose in the direct and forceful way which had clearly been typical of her in life; and this purpose was quite definitely not that of the operators of the planchette board, to whom the thought of contacting Nikolaus's family caused considerable embarrassment.

Among the purposes frequently professed and pursued by mediumistic communicators is that of proving their own survival and thus bringing consolation to their bereaved relatives. This purpose is one which a considerable percentage of deceased persons might, if they indeed survive, be thought likely to entertain. That a particular communicator exhibits it will therefore hardly constitute part of the ostensible evidence for survival. There have been, however, some people who, when alive, exhibited an intense, even a passionate, interest in the problem of survival itself, and the methods by which it may be investigated. We might expect that if such persons in some form survive the dissolution of their bodies, they will make some special, ingenious, and above all *planned*, attempt to prove that fact to those still on earth. And this brings me straightaway to a discussion of what is undoubtedly the most extensive, the most complex, and the most puzzling of all ostensible attempts by deceased persons to manifest purpose, and in so doing to fulfil their overriding purpose of proving their survival. I refer to the celebrated 'cross-correspondences'.

Cross-correspondences

A 'cross-correspondence' occurs when what is written or spoken by or through one medium or automatist corresponds to an extent that cannot be normally explained with what is written or spoken by or through another, and independent, medium or automatist. *The* cross-correspondences are the extensive and complexly interlinked series of cross-correspondences which appeared between 1901 and 1932 in the automatic writings (and sometimes speech) of a group of automatists associated with the British SPR. The automatists were all ladies, and the principal ones were Mrs M. de G. Verrall, wife of Professor A. W. Verrall, a well-known classical scholar, and her daughter Helen (later Mrs W. H. Salter, the only member of the group whom I myself met); Mrs 'Willett' (Mrs Winifred Coombe-Tennant, of whom more will be said in the next chapter); Mrs 'Holland' (Mrs Fleming, the sister of Rudyard Kipling), and Mrs Piper, the only professional medium among them.

The communicators ostensibly responsible for the cross-correspondences were at first three early leaders of the SPR, F. W. H. Myers (died 1901), Henry Sidgwick (died 1900) and Edmund Gurney (died 1888), all three of whom had of course been deeply concerned with the problem of survival. Other deceased persons later appeared as members. The cross-correspondences were not instigated or asked for by the communicators' still living colleagues; they simply began to appear in the scripts, and were, indeed, not noticed for some time. The idea thus came ostensibly from the 'other side'. The scripts and utterances were principally studied and collated on 'this side' by five leading members of the SPR, Miss Alice Johnson, J. G. Piddington, and G. W. Balfour (later the second Earl Balfour), and to a lesser but still noteworthy extent by Sir Oliver Lodge and Mrs E. M. Sidgwick. Their task proved an extraordinarily difficult one. This was partly because of the sheer quantity of material they had to scrutinize – there were several quite busy automatists over and above the ones I have already named. Partly also it was because of the content of the writings. Those of Mrs Verrall and her daughter, both of whom were accomplished classical scholars, contained many Greek and Latin phrases, and other literary allusions. All the writings tended to be fragmentary, allusive, and disjointed, and to operate at a symbolic rather than a straightforward level. This may have been because automatisms originate from an unconscious or dissociated level of the mind (the 'subliminal self', 'primary process thought') which tends to function in symbolic terms. But it was also, as we shall see in a moment, part of the plan of the supposed communicators that messages should be transmitted in an obscure and disguised fashion, so that their true significance should not be at first appreciated. Both the communicators and those who attempted to decipher the communications were exceptionally well-read and literate persons. The whole enterprise reminds me sometimes of that old radio favourite 'Transatlantic Quiz', in which devious and obscure questions are put to particularly well-informed people, who had often to work their way towards the right answers. In the present case, the gulf between the teams seems vastly harder to overcome than the Atlantic Ocean.

The cross-correspondence materials are exceedingly voluminous, and publication of them marks out a kind of epoch in the history of the SPR. In his valuable short introduction to the subject, H. F. Saltmarsh (140) lists fifty-two papers about them (many of them book length) from the *Proceedings of the SPR*. Even so a substantial quantity of material remains unpublished. Obviously I shall not, in the brief space which I have at my disposal, be able to do anything like justice either to the strengths or to the weaknesses of the cross-correspondences considered as evidence for survival.

Saltmarsh distinguishes between 'simple', 'complex' and 'ideal' cross-correspondences. Simple cross-correspondences 'are those where in the scripts of two or more [independent] automatists there occurs the same word or phrase, or else two phrases so similar as to be clearly interconnected.' An obvious explanation of simple cross-correspondence would be that one automatist gains extrasensory knowledge of what the other is writing, and writes something similar herself. Complex cross-correspondences 'are cases where the topic or topics are not directly mentioned, but referred to in an indirect and allusive way'. An 'ideal' complex cross-correspondence would be one in which two independent automatists each wrote apparently unconnected meaningless messages. 'Now, if a third automatist were [independently] to produce a script which, while meaningless taken by itself, acts as a clue to the other two, so that the whole set would be brought together into one whole, and then show a single purpose and meaning, we should have good evidence that they all originated from a single source.' If these conditions were fulfilled one might propound the following argument. Call the first two automatists A and B, and the third one, who gives the key that unlocks the whole, C. B will not be able to discover what he should write by paranormally cognizing A's script, and A's mind; nor will C be able to discover the 'key' by paranormally cognizing the scripts or minds of A and B; for in this 'ideal' case (to which perhaps no actual case has done more than approximate) there is nothing in A's script or B's script, or in the minds of A or B, to indicate what must be written to complete the cross-correspondence.

There is in my view no doubt that the scripts of the SPR automatists do contain numerous cross-correspondences, for the occurrence of which no ordinary explanation will suffice. Conspiracy to deceive by the principal automatists seems extraordinarily unlikely. They were all persons of excellent reputation, and no indications of fraud ever came to light; besides, at important periods one (Mrs Holland) was in India, another (Mrs Piper) was in the United States, while the rest were in Great Britain. Chance-coincidence is another explanation which can, I think, be very quickly ruled out. It is true that the scripts are full of cryptic literary and other allusions, so full that one might expect occasional coincidences of theme and reference. But Piddington, who counted such references on a large scale, found that allusions pertinent to a given cross-correspondence did not wax and wane haphazardly, but arose during the appropriate period, and then largely died out again (modern techniques of computer analysis would have immensely helped him in this arduous task). Furthermore various attempts to generate artificial cross-correspondences by collating pseudo-scripts written by outsiders were largely unsuccessful (134b; 164b).

One can readily imagine in the abstract that some of at any rate the simpler cross-correspondences might have arisen because two or more of the automatists had simultaneously been exposed to the same external source of stimulation, e.g. the same issue of a daily newspaper. This seems particularly likely in the case of Mrs Verrall and her daughter Helen, who at this time lived together, though they produced their scripts independently. If both these ladies had on a given morning noticed a quotation from Aristotle's *Politics* in *The Times*'s leading article, or had come across a copy of Lemprière's Classical Dictionary lying open at a certain entry, their minds, and subsequently their automatic writings, would, so this theory goes, have been set racing off along similar tracks. One has, however, only to read a few pages of the cross-correspondence records to see that this sort of explanation will not get one very far. In any case, of course, the really interesting correspondences are not those between the scripts of Mrs Verrall and her daughter, but (say) between the scripts of Mrs Verrall and those of the very distant and very different Mrs Holland or Mrs Piper. To explain such correspondences as these we shall be forced towards some very odd hypotheses indeed.

I shall now give a much abridged outline of a not excessively complex 'complex' cross-correspondence. It is the case commonly called the 'Hope, Star and Browning' case (120b, pp. 59–77; 75d, pp. 28–49). Some idea of just how complex these cases can be will be given if I point out that the 'Hope, Star and Browning' case is in effect a cross-correspondence within a cross-correspondence. It forms part of the case known as the 'Latin Message' case.

The Hope, Star and Browning case was triggered off on 16 January, 1907, when J. G. Piddington suggested to 'Myers', who was communicating through Mrs Piper, that he should indicate when a cross-correspondence was being attempted by, for instance, drawing on the script a circle with a triangle inside.

This notion was apparently taken up by the 'Myers' who influenced Mrs Verrall's automatic writing. He wrote on 23 January 1907: 'an anagram would be better. Tell him that – rats, star, tars and so on . . .' (Myers was in life greatly addicted to anagrams).

Mrs Verrall's Myers toyed further with the anagram idea in her script of 28 January 1907. He wrote 'Aster' (Greek for 'Star') and 'Teras' (Greek for 'Wonder'). He then apparently proceeded to free associate on the themes of wonder and star, producing a jumble of quotations from the poetry of Robert Browning, together with some related Greek phrases, as follows:

> The world's wonder
> And all a wonder and a wild desire –
> The very wings of her
> A WINGED DESIRE
> *hupopteros eros* [Greek for 'winged love']
> Then there is Blake
> and mocked my loss of liberty
> But it is all the same – the winged desire
> *eros potheinos* [Greek for 'passion']
> The earth for the sky – Abt Vogler for earth
> too hard that found itself or lost itself – in the sky.
> That is what I want
> On the earth the broken sounds threads
> In the sky the perfect arc
> The C major of this life
> But your recollection is at fault

There followed drawings of a triangle inside a circle and of a triangle within a semi-circle, a clear response to the proposal Piddington had made to Mrs Piper's communicator.

On 3 February 1907, a supposed 'Myers' influence upon Helen Verrall's script drew a monogram, a star and a crescent, and wrote, 'A monogram, the crescent moon, remember that, and the star.' This shows a knowledge of what Mrs Verrall's Myers communicator had written, and perhaps, in the reference to a monogram, hints at a knowledge of Piddington's original proposal to the Piper–Myers.

On 11 February 1907 Mrs Piper's Myers communicator showed undoubted knowledge of what Mrs Verrall's Myers had recently written. He wrote: 'Did she [Mrs Verrall] receive the word evangelical [later corrected to Evelyn Hope, the title of a poem by Browning]? I referred also to Browning again. I referred to Hope and Browning . . . I also said star . . . look out for Hope, Star and Browning.'

Next the Myers influence on Helen Verrall's script picked up the Browning theme. On 17 February 1907 he drew a star, and then wrote: 'That was the sign she will understand when she sees it . . . No arts avail . . . and a star above it all *rats* everywhere in Hamelin town [reference to Browning's poem on the Pied Piper of Hamelin].'

Lastly came three scripts from Mrs Piper's Myers communicator, the second of which supplied the supposed 'key' to the whole.

On 6 March 1907, the Piper–Myers told Piddington that he had given Mrs Verrall a circle and a triangle, but doubted that the latter had appeared. (In fact it had.)

On 13 March 1907 the Piper–Myers claimed that he had drawn a circle and a triangle for Mrs Verrall, and then said, 'But it suggested a poem to my mind, hence BHS' (i.e. Browning, Hope, Star). Myers here offers an outright explanation of the obscure references that had appeared in the scripts of the other two automatists. He says, in effect, that Piddington's original proposal about drawing a triangle within a circle suggested certain anagrams (rats, star, etc.) to his mind, and these in turn suggested certain passages of Browning. He developed all these themes (triangle, circle, rats, star, Browning, etc.) in the scripts of the other two automatists, and then returned to Mrs Piper to give an explanation of what he had done.

On 8 April 1907 the Piper–Myers said he had drawn a circle, and added that he had drawn a star and also a crescent moon.

It is at first sight tempting to conclude that the cross-correspondences between these three sets of writings were brought about by a purposive intelligence external to the conscious minds of the automatists concerned. Whether this intelligence belonged to the deceased F. W. H. Myers is an issue that one could properly assess only in the light of the numerous other communications allegedly received from him at that time through these and other automatists. It is, however, not difficult to think up possible alternative explanations.

One might suppose, for instance, that the various automatists were by now aware of each other's identities, and of the principle underlying the attempts at cross-correspondence. One might suppose further that Mrs Verrall, the central figure in the Hope, Star and Browning case, maintained an unconscious, extrasensory scrutiny of the scripts and related mental processes of the other automatists. By this means she learned of Piddington's suggestion to the Piper–Myers that he should indicate a cross-correspondence by drawing a triangle within a circle. She took up the idea in her own scripts, introduced the alternative proposal of anagrams (being an old friend of Myers', she knew his fondness for anagrams), and in her subsequent scripts unconsciously gave free rein to her own associations relating to rats, stars, etc. The result was a series of Browning quotations interspersed with Greek phrases. The other automatists exercised their ESP upon Mrs Verrall's scripts, 'saw' the drawings and references to 'star', picked up the not very obscure Browning quotations, and began to elaborate these themes in their own writings. After the ball had been thrown to and fro for a few weeks, Mrs Piper brought the game to an artistic conclusion by making her Myers communicator state that the Browning quotations and other material represented his own associations to Piddington's original proposal.

Mrs Piper was, however, a lady of somewhat limited education, and perhaps did not possess the requisite literary knowledge. One might therefore instead propose that Mrs Verrall (or rather her unconscious mind or subliminal self) played a more active role, and somehow injected her own associations and Myers-fantasies into the depths of the other automatists' minds. Thence they found their way out in the scripts.

This is very much the position taken by Frank Podmore in his able early critique of the cross-correspondences (122e, pp. 225–276). Podmore could 'see no evidence whatever to justify the assumption, even provisionally, of a directing intelligence other than those of the automatists concerned.' He has two sorts of reasons for saying this. The first (which some people would probably dispute) is that although Myers was the purported instigator of these cross-correspondences, the Piper–Myers, who played a leading role in several of the cases, was never able unequivocally to state the principle of the cross-correspondences.

Podmore's second line of argument is as follows. There is at least one case, the 'Sevens' case (75b, pp. 222–258), in which it seems likely that Mrs Verrall (or rather some part of Mrs Verrall's mind) was 'behind' a complex and absolutely characteristic cross-correspondence. Between April and July 1908 the scripts of several automatists, including Mrs Verrall, contained numerous allusions to the number seven. Certain of these allusions were, additionally, clear references to passages from Dante. It turned out that Piddington (who, as we have seen, was much involved in the study of the cross-correspondences) had deposited with the SPR a sealed package, the contents of which he hoped to communicate after his death. The package contained a statement referring to his life-long obsession with the number seven. The statement did not mention Dante. Mrs Verrall, however, had lately been reading Dante. Podmore puts his case as follows: 'Mr Piddington had for years been repeating *Seven* for all the world – that is, all the world within the range of his telepathic influence – to hear. His is a voice crying in the wilderness, however, until it happens that Mrs Verrall reads the "Divine Comedy", and the idea of *Seven*, already latent in her mind, is reinforced by a series of Dante images. Mrs Verrall then . . . swells the stream of telepathic influence, and the effects, in the five remaining automatists, rise to the surface of the dream consciousness.'

There are further considerations which might be thought to point to Mrs Verrall as the probable source of these cross-correspondences. Hints and foreshadowings of the cross-correspondences appeared first of all in her scripts; many of the individual cases began there; she possessed much of the necessary classical and literary knowledge. No other member of the group of automatists would have filled the bill. None the less Podmore's theory, according to which Mrs Verrall's unconscious mind was, unknown to her conscious mind, a telepathic broadcasting station of formidable power, sending out, furthermore, signals of whose import she was frequently unaware, faces what appear to be intolerable difficulties.

An initial and obvious difficulty is that, as I have already pointed out, we have not much clear evidence for the sort of active telepathic 'sending' or intrusion into other peoples' minds which Podmore postulates. This is an important issue which I shall mention again when talking about communications from the living. Podmore seeks to bolster the notion by invoking the 'Sevens' case (see above), but his account of this case is somewhat over-simplified. He fails to point out that the Verrall–Myers claimed to have 'read' Piddington's message at the time when it was written, and to have spread its theme around the various automatists. Piddington himself asserted that he was quite unsuccessful as a sender of telepathic messages; certainly he did not succeed in sending one when he served as an agent for some experiments in the generation of pseudo-correspondences (139b).

A second difficulty for Podmore's proposal is this. Mrs Verrall was centrally involved in several cross-correspondences in which the ostensible communicator conveyed literary information apparently possessed neither by Mrs Verrall nor by any other automatist involved. An example which merits a brief discussion is the *autos ouranos akumon* incident (120b, pp. 107-172). At a sitting with Mrs Piper on 29 January 1907, Mrs Verrall, who had given much previous thought to this test, spelled out to the Piper–Myers (in Piddington's presence) the Greek words *autos ouranos akumon* and suggested to him that he might either translate them, or tell her of what they made him think. (Myers, of course, was a considerable classical scholar, whilst Mrs Piper knew no Greek.) These words may be translated as 'the very heaven waveless'. They come from a passage by the neoplatonist philosopher Plotinus, and form part of a description of the conditions necessary for the attainment of ecstasy or connection with the divine. This passage states that the soul must be 'free from deception and every kind of beguilement, and be in a state of peace, also that the earth must be calm, the sea calm, and the air, and the very heaven waveless.' It should be noted that Myers had used the words *autos ouranos akumon* (untranslated) as a motto for his poem on Tennyson, and that he gives them in translation (without the original Greek) in his *Human Personality* (110a, p. 291).

During the next six weeks Mrs Verrall's own automatic scripts were filled with references to Tennyson, and especially to passages which concern calm seas, calm air, and serene and calm spaces. The poem which cropped up most frequently was *In Memoriam*, and there were also some insistent allusions to *Crossing the Bar*. The constant references to *In Memoriam* led Mrs Verrall to suspect a special link between that peom and the *Enneads* of Plotinus (the general similarities of thought had of course been commented on before). After some investigations Mrs Verrall unearthed certain parallel phrases on which she wrote a paper in the *Modern Language Review* for July, 1907 (165).

It seems quite likely that F. W. H. Myers (the communicator) had known of these parallels. He was himself well read in Plotinus; in his essay on 'Tennyson as Prophet' he mentions the influence of Plotinus on Tennyson; and he tells us elsewhere that he learned this in conversation with Tennyson, whom he knew well.

Now we come to Mrs Piper's side of the cross-correspondence. On 6 March, 1907, the Piper–Myers wrote: 'A cloudless sky beyond the horizon'. In the waking stage of her trance Mrs Piper said 'moaning at the bar when I put out to sea' (A quotation from *Crossing the Bar*). She also mentioned Arthur Hallam (whose early death inspired Tennyson to write *In Memoriam*).

On 29 April 1907, Mrs Verrall had a sitting with Mrs Piper. The words 'Azure a blue sea' were spelled out. Mrs Verrall took them to relate to the idea of halcyon days (i.e. days when the sea is especially calm), which had been alluded to in her own scripts. At the end of the sitting came some incoherent references to Swedenborg, St Paul and Dante.

The next day, the Piper–Myers claimed to have answered the question about *autos ouranos akumon*, adding that it reminded him of Socrates and of Homer's *Iliad*. Neither of these references nor the preceding ones made sense at the time.

On 1 May 1907, Mrs Verrall's scripts contained the words 'Eagle soaring over the tomb of Plato', a well-known description of Plotinus which is quoted in Myers' *Human Personality* (110a, p. 261). This led her to delve further into Myers' book. She found that the Epilogue to this book, in which occurs a passage concerning the 'vision of Plotinus', is prefixed by a Greek quotation from Plato's *Crito* mentioning Socrates and quoting a line from the *Iliad*. It thus appears that in life Myers could well have associated Plotinus with Socrates and the *Iliad*. On page 261 of Volume II is a list of persons who, like Plotinus, underwent moments of mystical ecstasy or union with the divine. This list includes Plotinus, Tennyson, Swedenborg, Dante and St Paul. The Piper–Myers' references on 29 April 1907 can thus be seen to have reflected Myers' own associations.

Finally, on 6 May 1907, when Mrs Sidgwick was sitting with Mrs Piper, the Piper–Myers wrote, 'Will you say to Mrs Verrall – Plotinus'. Mrs Sidgwick said, 'What is that?' The Piper–Myers replied, '*My answer* to *autos ouranos okumen* [sic].'

It was quite clear that J. G. Piddington, the principal sitter with Mrs Piper did not know enough of Mrs Verrall's scripts, and of Plotinus and his relation to Tennyson, to have been the source of Mrs Piper's 'hits'. Nor was Mrs Piper sufficiently well educated to have caught the drift of the allusions in Mrs Verrall's scripts even had she been able to read these scripts in detail by means of ESP. The important question is, did Mrs Verrall herself possess the requisite knowledge to have engineered the whole thing, always supposing that we grant to her unconscious mind the somewhat sinister ability to direct the course of Mrs Piper's automatisms? I think we may safely assume that she was not consciously aware of the *detailed* links between Plotinus and *In Memoriam* until the script intelligence (purportedly Myers) led her to them. But could she have known of them unconsciously? It is hard to know what to make of this proposal. What is being suggested is *not* cryptomnesia (the re-emergence of a latent memory), a possibility for which we have some evidence. Mrs Verrall's article on the Plotinus–*In Memoriam* links was considered sufficiently original for publication, and so presumably could not have been based on a latent memory of a previous similar article. Presumably also Mrs Verrall could not have noticed the links herself before, and subsequently forgotten about them; for she would surely have written her article when she first thought of them. The proposal must therefore be that having separately read Tennyson's *In Memoriam* and Plotinus's *Enneads*, and retained fairly detailed, but perhaps largely latent, memories of both, she unconsciously grasped the connection between them. This unconscious insight then began to work its way into the light through her own automatic writing, and also through that of Mrs Piper, over which she exercised a continual but unconscious influence.

Mrs Verrall claimed, too, that she did not discover the relevance of the Socrates, Homer, Dante, Swedenborg, and St Paul allusions given by the Piper–Myers until her own Myers-communicator provided the clue 'Eagle soaring over the tomb of Plato', which made her turn again to Myers' *Human Personality*. Now we can hardly deny here that Mrs Verrall, who had certainly read this book, might have retained a latent memory of the relevant allusions. The problem, however, is that the allusions were given not through her own automatic writing, but by the Piper–Myers. On the theory we are considering Mrs Verrall's unconscious mind must have reasoned as follows: 'I remember now that Myers' book contains a series of names close to that phrase about Plotinus. If I produce these names as if from Myers, it will look as though these are Myers' associations, not mine, which will be very striking. But hang on – I see a snag! I knew Myers quite well, and everyone is aware that I have read his book. Therefore if I produce these names myself it will not make much impression. Suppose, however, I were to infiltrate them into Mrs Piper's scripts. Then it will look as though they really are Myers' associations. Good! I will do it!'

I simply do not know what to say about these tortuous and quite unverifiable hypotheses, which seem, it should be noted, to follow inevitably from Podmore's proposal that Mrs Verrall brought about the cross-correspondences through her unconscious ability to direct and infiltrate the writings of the other automatists under a false name. I know of no independent evidence to suggest that such happenings are possible, and it is hard to see what evidence there could be, since the postulated events go on unconsciously and unobserved by anyone. The only reason for adopting Podmore's hypothesis seems to be the antecedent implausibility of its main alternative, the survival theory, which, implausibility apart, can on the face of it give a much simpler account of the case we have just been considering. But the implausibility of one theory is never by itself a satisfactory reason for adopting some other theory; the other theory may be quite as implausible.

There are still further reasons for abandoning Podmore's proposal. By no means all of the cross-correspondences began in Mrs Verrall's scripts; in some she was not involved at all; one particularly famous example – the 'Palm Sunday' case (6) – began in her scripts, but continued for many years after her death in the scripts of other automatists; some cases were wholly initiated after her death. It is indeed sometimes stated that the cross-correspondences at any rate declined after Mrs Verrall's death. I think it is more nearly true to say that the scripts had begun to change character before her death, with cross-correspondences playing a less prominent part. It seems clear that the cross-correspondences canot be wholly or even largely laid at Mrs Verrall's door. At early as 1911, Alice Johnson was able to write (75c, p. 291):

> . . . we have now reached a point where, on the supposition that the whole of the cross-correspondences are worked exclusively by the automatists, we should have to assume that several of them, besides Mrs Verrall, are capable of the task. Or else we should have to assume a sort of telepathic committee meeting of the subliminal selves of the automatists, at which they scheme together and settle on their different parts.

The idea of a telepathic committee meeting of subliminal selves is one that we shall meet again in Chapter Fifteen. It is essentially what has been proposed to account for the fact that the different aspects of a collectively perceived apparition seen by the various percipients seem to be in correct perspective.

We have no independent evidence that telepathy of such detail and complexity ever takes place. One might add, too, that we have no evidence for unconsciously hatched, telepathically co-ordinated, plots or conspiracies. It is, indeed, hard to see what such evidence might consist in.

Alice Johnson herself did not believe in the telepathic committee meetings of subliminal selves. Like the other principal investigators of the cross-correspondences she ultimately came to believe that Myers and the other deceased SPR leaders were behind them. I too find it hard to believe in telepathic committee meetings, nor can I deny that an intelligence, or rather intelligences, seem to have inspired the cross-correspondences. But was the intelligence of F. W. H. Myers among them? This is an altogether larger question. To answer it one would need to take into account the style and intellectual and personal characteristics of the Myers-scripts, and any correct information given about Myers which could not have been known to the automatist in question. There was very little of the latter sort of evidence (several of the more important automatists knew the living Myers well), but the investigators seem in the end to have found the former satisfactory. Thus J. G. Piddington wrote (120b, pp. 242–243):

> On the problem of the real identity of this directing mind – whether it was a spirit or group of co-operating spirits, or the subconsciousness of one of the automatists, or the consciousness or unconsciousness of some other living person – the only opinion which I hold with confidence is this: that if it was not the mind of Frederic Myers it was one which deliberately and artistically imitated his mental characteristics.

I can at this point offer no useful comment on Piddington's views; but in the next chapter I shall take up the question of how far manifestations of ostensibly surviving personal characteristics and ostensibly surviving intellectual skills may constitute evidence for survival.

7 Manifestations of Other Personal Characteristics

It is not uncommon for persons who have had successful sittings with mental mediums to say afterwards something like this: 'Here is a transcript of the tape recording (or stenographer's notes), with my comments. There were a good many excellent 'hits'. But simply reading the record can give you no idea of just how convincing the communicator really was. So much of the impression he made was due not to what he said, but to the way he said it, to his turn of phrase, tone of voice, characteristic humour, to his mannerisms and gestures. They were so completely right!'

Lest I be thought to exaggerate, I shall quote the comments of a very experienced sitter, Una Lady Troubridge (161, pp. 362-363), on communicators who 'controlled' Mrs Leonard (i.e. displaced Feda as the personality speaking through Mrs Leonard's vocal apparatus):

> . . . on the other hand, a totally different faculty is demonstrated [in personal control], sometimes to a startling degree, that of the reproduction with varying success of intonations, vocal mannerisms and general characteristics pertaining to deceased persons whom the medium had never known. It is difficult to convey an accurate impression of these personal controls to anyone who has never witnessed the production, through the agency of a really fine medium, of phenomena of this description. Any assertion regarding these impersonations is naturally open to the suspicion that the imagination and expectation of a witness may play a very considerable part in the impression received . . . nevertheless, in my own experience these objections have been countered to a great extent by the fact that the purported personal control with which I am most familiar . . . has in the majority of cases been witnessed both by myself and by Miss Radclyffe-Hall.

In the published Piper and Leonard records (I single out these mediums because of their SPR affiliations) one finds various controls who achieved remarkable verisimilitude in mannerisms, turns of speech, etc. One might instance, in the case of Mrs Piper, GP and

Bennie Junot, and, in that of Mrs Leonard, 'AVB' (a deceased lady to whom Lady Troubridge is especially referring in the passage just quoted), John and Etta Thomas and Ernest White (on whom see 167b). In none of these instances had the mediums any such knowledge of the communicators in life as would account for the accuracy of the dramatizations. But as Lady Troubridge indicates it is exceedingly difficult to pin down these 'characteristic touches' in terms that would carry conviction to outsiders. I shall confine myself for the moment to making one preliminary and obvious point about such cases, namely that in addition to crediting the medium concerned with whatever powers of ESP she may have required to collect factual information about the characteristic mannerisms, turns of phrase, tone of voice, etc., of the deceased person concerned, we have now to credit her with the ability to incorporate this assembly of facts into a convincing dramatic representation of the so-called communicator. And this is to credit her with a further kind of unusual gift.

Somewhat more amenable to independent assessment are claims that a given communicator can still exhibit a particular and somewhat distinctive competence or skill which he possessed in life. Suppose, for example, that a certain deceased person (call him Professor Sharp) was in his life particularly adept at the game of bridge. He now purports to control a medium who knows nothing at all about the game. The medium proceeds to play several hands of bridge competently, even well. This must surely count as evidence of Sharp's survival. For not everyone can play bridge, and only a few can play it really well. The fact that the medium's 'Sharp' control can play it well, whilst she cannot play it at all, would seem on the face of it

(a) to show that the 'Sharp' influence cannot be the normal personality of the medium, and

(b) to narrow down the influences it could be to a range including the deceased Sharp.

Other facets of the Sharp control might serve to narrow this range down still further, perhaps even just to Sharp himself. If, on the other hand, the 'Sharp' influence had been quite ignorant of bridge, or a hopeless duffer at it, this would have given us strong grounds for thinking that the 'control' could not possibly have been the late Professor Sharp.

Let us assume next that evidence that the medium knows nothing of bridge is absolutely cast-iron. Then we can ask, what explanation is possible of her sudden access of skill at bridge other than the proposal that she is controlled or overshadowed by the deceased Sharp or one of his deceased fellow players? We could suggest instead that the medium learns the rules of bridge clairvoyantly by cognizing the printed rule-book, or telepathically by reading the minds of those who regularly play bridge. She might even look clairvoyantly at a text-book on the subject, or telepathically glean a handy list of dos and don'ts from the mind of an accomplished player. But would all this extrasensory study enable her to play a competent hand as soon as she was 'controlled' by the soi-disant Professor Sharp? Surely not; for there is much more to learning to play bridge competently than merely getting the rules off by heart and mugging up a list of hints for the helpless. The fundamental requisite is hours and hours of intelligent and attentive practice against good opponents. And nobody is going to suggest that that can be obtained by ESP.

It seems to me, therefore, that even if we allow that the rules of bridge might be adequately learned by ESP (and I do not know a particle of evidence that ESP of such a degree ever occurs), the super-ESP theory would still fall far short of giving any plausible account of the Sharp-control's ability to take a hand at bridge.

The example is of course an hypothetical one, but the point has wider applicability. It does not seem likely that skills and competences, intellectual, and for that matter physical, could be acquired by ESP. If a mediumistic communicator unmistakably exhibits an unusual skill or competence which he possessed in life, and which the medium is known not to possess, this fact may in some circumstances be very difficult for the super-ESP theory to digest. It is time to inquire whether any actual case will carry us as far as our hypothetical example.

I shall not attempt to deal with cases of the apparent post-mortem manifestation of such skills as piano-playing or painting, because it is in most cases so difficult to decide whether or not the medium could have herself reached the level of competence displayed. In a few cases (see, e.g., 41, pp 431–438; 110a, II, pp. 231–234; 120a, pp. 235–243), the hand-writing of a particular deceased person has been closely imitated: the problem, however, is in most cases to ascertain with certainty whether the medium could not at some time or another have seen the handwriting of the individual concerned.

Literary Puzzles

I shall begin, therefore, by considering certain cases which do not, perhaps, exactly qualify as examples of the apparent post-mortem exercise of an intellectual skill, but which without doubt constitute examples of the ostensible post-mortem display of a high level of a rather unusual intellectual attainment (an attainment which had been characteristic of the alleged communicator in life). I refer to the cases – closely interlinked with the cross-correspondences – generally known as the 'literary puzzles'. In these cases attempts were ostensibly made by communicators who were in life particularly well-read in classical literature to manifest their knowledge through mediums largely ignorant of classical languages and literature. I shall briefly outline two such cases – the 'Lethe' case and the 'Ear of Dionysius' case – and shall consider how far each of them may be brought into line with the super-ESP hypothesis.

In the 'Lethe' case (120c, pp. 86–144), the principal medium was Mrs Piper and the sitter was Mr G. B. Dorr, a Vice-President of the ASPR. Dorr was in touch through Mrs Piper with a communicator who claimed to be F. W. H. Myers. Myers had in life been a profound classical scholar. Dorr had dropped Latin and Greek at eighteen, had scarcely looked at any since, while 'translations from the classics I have hardly read at all.' Mrs Piper knew virtually nothing of classical literature. In order to test the memory of the Myers communicator, Dorr began to obtain and put to him various questions on classical subjects. On 23 March 1908 he posed the question: 'What does the word LETHE suggest to you?' He clearly expected a reply making reference to forgetfulness and the waters of oblivion. Instead he got the following:

> MYERS [i.e. Mrs Piper's communicator]: Do you refer to one of my poems, Lethe? [This is not an inappropriate answer, since Lethe is referred to in one of Myers' verse translations of Virgil.]

The Myers' communicator, egged on by questions and remarks from Dorr, then wrote some disjointed words, including 'Winds', 'Greece', and 'Olympus', and went on:

> . . . It is all clear. Do you remember Cave?
>
> GBD: I think you are confused about this. It was a water, not a wind, and it was in Hades, where the Styx was and the Elysian fields. Do you recall it now?

MYERS : Lethe. Shore – of course I do. Lethe Hades beautiful river –
Lethe. Underground.

Shortly afterwards Dorr closed the sitting. As Mrs Piper came out of
trance (the 'waking-stage') she spoke the following words:

Pavia [later conjecturally emended by Piddington to *papavera*, the Latin for
'poppies'].
. . .
Lethe – delighted – sad – lovely – mate –
Put them all together . . .
Entwined love – beautiful shores . . .
Warm – sunlit – love.
Lime leaf – heart – sword – arrow
    I shot an arrow through the air
    And it fell I know not where

Mrs Piper then described a vision of someone with a bow and arrow.
   On 24 March 1908, the Myers communicator wrote as follows (the
deceased Richard Hodgson is, apparently, acting as intermediary, and
sometimes refers to Myers as 'he' and 'him'):

          I wrote in reply to your last inquiry Cave – Lethe
GBD: I asked him [*i.e.* Myers] whether the word Lethe recalled any-
          thing to him.
MYERS : He replied Cave – Banks – Shore . . . He drew the form – a picture
          of Iris with an arrow.
GBD: But he spoke of words.
MYERS : Yes, clouds – arrow – Iris – Cave – Mor MOR Latin for sleep
          Morpheus – *Cave*. Sticks in my mind can't you help me?
GBD: Good. I understand what you are after now. But can't you make it
          clearer what there was peculiar about the waters of Lethe?
MYERS : Yes, I suppose you think I am affected in the same way *but I am not.*

After this some of the above words were repeated in conversation with
Dorr, and the words 'Clouds' and 'Flower Banks' were introduced. As
the medium came out of trance she again murmured the word 'pavia'
(*papavera?*), and went on:

Mr Myers is writing on the wall . . . C [a pause] YX. I walked in the garden
of the gods – entranced I stood along its banks – like one entranced I saw her
at last . . . Elysian shores.

On 30 March 1908, after an erroneous translation of CYX as 'chariot', the Piper–Myers spelled out CYNX. Then, after some confused passages, he continued:

> We walk together, our loves entwined, along the shores. In beauty beyond comparison with Lethe. Sorry it is all so fragmentary but suppose it cannot all get through.

On 7 April 1908 the letters SCYX and CSYX were written, and in the waking stage Mrs Piper gave, 'Mr Myers says, "No poppies ever grew on Elysian shores".' (This seems to be an oblique way of denying that there is forgetfulness in the after-life.)

The records of these sittings, which I have considerably abridged, were carefully examined first by Mrs Verrall, and then by G. W. Balfour, both of whom were accomplished classical scholars. To neither did they make sense. They were then sent to J. G. Piddington, who previously located a passage (previously unknown to him) in the eleventh book of Ovid's *Metamorphoses* which seems to provide the key to Myers' 'Lethe' associations. It tells the story of Ceyx and Alcyone, of which I give the following summary, adapted from Podmore (122e). The correspondence with the scripts are indicated by capital letters:

> CEYX, King of Trachin, was drowned at sea, and Juno sent IRIS, goddess of the rainbow, to Somnus (SLEEP), to bid him carry the news in a dream to Alcyone, Ceyx's beLOVED Queen, daughter of Aeolus, ruler of the WINDS. Iris points her BOW upon the sky, and glides down to the CAVE of Sleep, which was surrounded and hidden by dark CLOUDS. From the foot of the rock flows the river of LETHE, and on its BANKS are POPPIES and innumerable FLOWERS, from whose juice Night distils Sleep. Somnus sends his son MORPHEUS to impersonate in a dream the dead Ceyx. Going down to the SHORE, Alcyone finds Ceyx's body, and in despair throws herself into the sea. The gods take pity on her SADness, and transform her into a halcyon. Later her LOVED Ceyx is restored to her as her MATE in the form of a kingfisher. Her nest floats on the sea; and every winter her father Aeolus confines the WINDS for seven days to secure a calm surface for her brood.

The correspondences, I think it is fair to say, are absolutely unmistakable. Now Myers had certainly read Ovid in detail (110b, p. 10), whereas none of the SPR investigators had studied the *Metamorphoses*, nor, of course, had Mrs Piper. (I should add, perhaps, that reading Ovid in the original is not so light an undertaking that one is likely to forget it!) On the face of it, therefore, the Myers-communicator's associations to 'Lethe' accord with the supposition that they came from Myers' own mind; they do not fit the hypothesis of telepathy from any of his living colleagues. But of course the story of Ceyx and Alcyone has often been told in the English language. Perhaps Mrs Piper, or else G. B. Dorr, had read an English version of it. Despite considerable search, Piddington could only locate two popular works which gave the story in the requisite detail, viz Bulfinch's *Age of Fable*, and Gayley's *The Classic Myths in English Literature*, which is based on Bulfinch. Mrs Piper, of whose honesty there was never any serious question, said that she had never read any such books, and this was borne out by close questioning of herself and her daughters, and by examination of her bookshelves. Dorr had as a boy read at least some parts of Bulfinch. No recollection of the story, however, stirred in his mind when he saw the scripts or read Piddington's interpretation of them. His own association to 'Lethe' was the obvious one, waters of forgetfulness.

There seem in fact to be reasons for denying that the script intelligence reflected Bulfinch's version of the story. Scripts immediately following the 'Lethe' ones make apparent references to other passages of Ovid which are not paraphrased by Bulfinch; and the scripts introduce at a certain point the word 'Olympus' which is in the text of Ovid Myers would probably have had, but is not in Bulfinch (120d).

It appears, therefore, highly unlikely that Mrs Piper could have obtained her information about the story of Ceyx and Alcyone telepathically from anyone in the circle of those who were investigating her. Nor, incidentally, could she have read it up in a library after the first sitting – too much undeniably relevant information was given straight away.

Could Mrs Piper have obtained knowledge of Ovid's version of the story by ESP, by, for instance, clairvoyantly reading a translation of Ovid, or telepathically tapping the mind of a classical scholar? Even if one were prepared to admit that such a degree of ESP is possible (for which there is very little evidence), there still remains the problem of how this material was located. For what had to be located was not Ovid, or the story of Ceyx and Alcyone, but associations which Myers might plausibly be expected to give to the name 'Lethe'. Did Mrs Piper first track down the passage in Ovid by clairvoyantly (and *instantaneously*) reading about Lethe in some reference work? Piddington could not find one which mentioned Ovid under the heading *Lethe*. Or did she with lightning speed pick out from the minds telepathically accessible to her one well furnished with classical knowledge (a Harvard professor no doubt), and flicking straightway through his subconscious, much as she might have done through a reference work, unearth the word 'Lethe' and a string of obscure associations to it? These suggestions are totally preposterous; and later on we shall have to try to put a finger on just why they are preposterous.

The next 'literary puzzle' which I shall outline is one of two obtained through the mediumship of Mrs 'Willett' (Mrs Coombe-Tennant). The other Willett puzzle is known as the 'Statius' case (5a). Mrs Willett was not a professional medium, but a British 'Society' lady active in national politics and in the League of Nations. She began automatic writing in 1908, but in 1909 it was suggested to her, ostensibly by the deceased Myers and Gurney (she was related to Myers by marriage), that she should instead try to apprehend ideas and images which they would insinuate into her mind, and should then record them by writing or speaking. The principal investigator of the Statius and Ear of Dionysius cases was G. W. Balfour, and the communicators were two recently deceased classical scholars, A. W. Verrall (the husband of Mrs M. de G. Verrall) and S. H. Butcher. They had been close friends. Butcher was not known in life to Mrs Willett, and Verrall only slightly.

The Ear of Dionysius case (5b) is long and complicated, and once again I can only give a bare outline. In a number of Willett scripts, the majority dating from 1914, with G. W. Balfour as sitter, the following topics are mentioned or alluded to:

The Ear of Dionysius. [A cave from which Dionysius the Elder, Tyrant of Syracuse 405–367 BC, was wont to listen to possibly seditious conversations among prisoners. It opened from certain stone quarries in Sicily. A Willett script of 1910 had referred to it, and Mrs Verrall had in consequence asked her husband about it.]

The stone quarries of Syracuse, in Sicily.

Enna, in Sicily.

The heel of Italy.

Ulysses and Polyphemus. [Polyphemus, the one-eyed giant, imprisoned Ulysses in his cave.]

Acis and Galatea. [Acis, a shepherd, loved the nymph Galatea, and was murdered by the jealous Polyphemus.]

Jealousy.

Music.
A Zither.
Aristotle's *Poetics*.
Satire.

These references did not 'add up' to anything so far as Balfour and Mrs Verrall were concerned. The key was provided by the Butcher-communicator in a script of 2 August 1915, Mrs Verrall being the sitter, in which the following was written:

> The Aural instruction was I think understood *Aural* appertaining to the Ear and now he asks HAS the *Satire* satire been identified . . .
> The man clung to the fleece of a Ram & so passed out surely that is plain [i.e. Ulysses escaping from Polyphemus' cave]
> well conjoin that with Cythera & the Ear-man . . .
> There is a satire
> write Cyclopean Masonry, why do you say masonry I said Cyclopean
> Philox He laboured in the stone quarries and drew upon the earlier writer for his Satire Jealously
> The story is quite clear to me & I think it should be identified
> a musical instrument comes in something like a mandoline thrumming . . .
> He wrote in these stone quarries belonging to the tyrant

This script links together the previous cryptic references. Philoxenus of Cythera (436–380 BC) was an obscure Greek poet who lived under the protection of Dionysius the elder, tyrant of Syracuse. Philoxenus fell into disfavour with Dionysius, and was imprisoned in the stone quarries of Syracuse, because he seduced the tyrant's mistress, Galateia. After his release (or, according to some accounts, while still in prison) Philoxenus wrote a satirical poem entitled either *Cyclops* or *Galateia*. In this he represents himself as Ulysses, and Dionysius, who was blind in one eye, as Polyphemus. It was poetry of a kind usually recited to the accompaniment of a zither. Philoxenus's *Cyclops* is mentioned in Aristotle's *Poetics* (II, 4), which Butcher had translated.

Neither Mrs Willett nor the investigators had ever heard of Philoxenus, of whose works only a few fragments remain. The classical knowledge displayed in constructing this puzzle was far beyond that possessed by Mrs Willett, who had no acquaintaince with classical languages and little if any with classical literature in translation. Articles on Philoxenus in various standard classical reference books current at that time did not contain all the details given in the scripts. Many (but not all) of these details are, however, to be found in a moderately obscure American book (H. W. Smyth's *Greek Melic Poets*), a presentation copy of which Professor Verrall, the ostensible communicator, had used in the preparation of some lectures.

Now there is no doubt that if Mrs Willett was consciously and deliberately dishonest, we can readily account for the material ostensibly communicated in this case. Any reasonably intelligent person could have put together a puzzle like this after a moderate period of hard research in a large library, or after a piece of luck in a second-hand bookshop (such as finding Smyth's book and following up the leads contained therein). No test phrase to which the communicator had to respond was presented to Mrs Willett at the outset; she was free to introduce whatever subject-matter came readiest to hand. There is, however, no evidence of Mrs Willett's dishonesty in this or any other case, so that the hypothesis has no ground in established fact, but is instead an assumption based only upon the supposed antecedent implausibility of the alternatives. This, as I have pointed out before, is never a satisfactory reason for adopting a theory.

If we reject the theory of deliberate deception by Mrs Willett, we seem forced towards some form of ESP theory; for cryptomnesia (latent memory) concerning obscure points of classical scholarship hardly seems a likely possibility in a person of Mrs Willett's known reading habits. We might try supposing that Mrs Willett, scanning clairvoyantly around for likely material, happened upon the relevant page of Smyth's *Greek Melic Poets*, or that in her telepathic investigations of the contents of suitable minds, she chanced upon that of a classical scholar who had read and assimilated this work. She extracted the juice from her chosen source, and (at a purely unconscious level) concocted the 'literary puzzle'. We have reached this point so often before that it grows wearisome. There is no independent evidence for such 'super-ESP'. Clairvoyance, indeed, we can rule out immediately, because Smyth's book, though in derivative accounts of this case often represented as containing all the relevant facts on a single page, does not in reality do so. The information which it gives on page 461 would need to be supplemented by an informed classical scholar before the Ear of Dionysius puzzle could be constructed from it. There remains the possibility that the information was extracted telepathically from the mind of a classical scholar. But the communicating intelligences did not just present a package of facts; despite the apparent difficulties of communication, they deployed their facts intelligently in the manner of persons who were masters of their subject – the extract given above from the sitting of 2 August 1915 will perhaps convey something of what I mean. We come back to the fundamental point that I raised earlier – to acquire a set of facts about, from or related to a certain topic or area is not by itself to become a master of that topic or an adept in that area. Mastery is achieved by use and intelligent practice, not by swallowing and regurgitating facts.

Shortly after G. W. Balfour's paper on the Ear of Dionysius case was published came a brief but incisive critical note by a classical scholar, Miss F. Melian Stawell (150). Miss Stawell pointed out that Mrs Willett, though not a classical scholar, no doubt had *some* relevant knowledge latent in her mind. She probably knew the story of Ulysses and Polyphemus, and may have heard that S. H. Butcher had written on Aristotle's *Poetics*. Perhaps this latent knowledge could have been first stimulated and then augmented by the external influence of (this will not come as a surprise!) Mrs Verrall's subsconscious mind. Probably Mrs Verrall had at some time or another come across all the necessary information. There are quite a few scattered references to Philoxenus in classical literature, and students commonly follow such things up when they come across them. Miss Stawell herself had run into much of the relevant material. None the less it did not spring to her mind when she heard Balfour's paper. It is reasonable to assume that Mrs Verrall had similarly come across it and forgotten it. And surely she could have had a look (subsequently forgotten) at her husband's presentation copy of Smyth's *Greek Melic Poets*? And the 'Sevens' case (mentioned in the previous chapter) shows that Mrs Verrall's subconscious was capable of influencing the productions of other automatists.

Miss Stawell added that Smyth's book had now been adopted as a standard textbook at Cambridge. Hers is a persuasive case, and Balfour's reply to it (5c) does not seem to me to be effective. Still, we must beware of constantly treating the supposed prodigious powers of Mrs Verrall's subliminal self as a universal solvent for disposing of cases which might otherwise endanger the super-ESP hypothesis. There is little clear evidence that she (or anyone else) possessed the powers for the imagined use of which she has so often been incriminated. Let us spell out what these putative powers must have been: Mrs Verrall must have been:

(a) An immense repository of information which she could not consciously call to mind.

(b)   A successful automatist in her own right.

(c)   Capable of telepathically but unconsciously controlling in some detail the writings of other automatists, including Mrs Willett; of being, in effect, an unconscious 'living communicator' operating by means of 'active' telepathy.

(d)   Capable of deciding at an unconscious level what material she might appropriately incorporate in her own scripts, and what material would (like classical knowledge) be more convincing if palmed off on other automatists.

(e)   Capable of acting as a living communicator under false names, her real identity and indeed her 'presence' remaining unknown to the automatists she influenced.

(f)   (In some cases) capable of telepathically or clairvoyantly apprehending (again unconsciously) what was said to the distant automatist and of unconsciously inducing in that automatist a relevant reply quickly enough to conduct a conversation with that automatist's sitter.

In a later chapter I shall say a little on the important topic of living communicators; but I do not know of any case of ostensible communication from the living which would justify us by analogy in attributing all these extraordinary powers to Mrs Verrall.

Xenoglossy

Interest in the apparent post-mortem exhibition of characteristic skills has in recent years focused especially on cases of ostensible xenoglossy; on cases, that is, in which persons (usually mediums, or the subjects of reincarnation cases) have spoken a real language (not an imaginary one, as in 'glossalalia'), of which they have ordinarily no knowledge (see especially 153f). (Comparable cases in which the language is written are called 'xenography', but I shall neglect this distinction.) Such cases are obviously of crucial importance to the present discussion. Imagine, for instance, that a mediumistic communicator, who has, for preference, given some factual 'proofs of identity', purports to speak through a medium in his own native language. He does so fluently, maintaining long and grammatical conversations with detailed understanding on both sides. Yet the language is one which the medium quite certainly does not know. Could we plausibly argue that the medium acquired her transient linguistic skill by ESP?

Several decades of fairly intensive laboratory investigations of ESP have not enabled us to fix any clear limits to its possible scope. If there are distances too great for ESP to transcend, or 'targets' too complex for it to grasp, we have not discovered what they are. There seems no reason to suppose that linguistic facts would not be as much within its reach as any other kind of fact. Or at any rate we should be ill-advised to deny the possibility if the alternative is so difficult an hypothesis as survival. There are in fact some experimental findings (128a), together with a few anecdotes, which suggest that subjects may grasp through ESP the meaning of individual words in a language unknown to them. And if word-meanings can be thus learned, why not grammatical rules?

We are now, of course, back again with the point which I raised when discussing the imaginary example of the mediumistic communicator whose bridge-playing skills had not deserted him at death. The ability to play bridge well is not simply a matter of learning (whether normally or by ESP) the rules (considered as a set of facts) together with the precepts given in some manual. It can only be acquired by practising intelligently until things fall into place. And it is the same with learning a language. I might study (say) a textbook of German, and learn innumerable word-meanings (such as that *Fehler* is the German for 'mistake', and *Pfote* the German for 'paw'), together with all sorts of tricky grammatical rules about the formation of passive tenses, the word-order in subordinate clauses, and so on and so on. Perhaps I could even learn these things by ESP directed upon the textbook or upon the mind of a teacher of German (there is no evidence whatsoever that ESP of this degree occurs, but that is not the present point). But knowledge of *facts* to do with word-meanings and grammatical rules (knowledge *that*), while it might *help* me to become a fluent German-speaker, would not immediately transform me into one, would not by itself give me the skill (knowledge *how*) of speaking German. Every schoolchild who has had to learn the grammar and vocabulary of a foreign language by rote is well aware of this gap – a gap that can only be crossed by intelligent practice, preferably with accomplished speakers of the language in question. The gap would exist whether or not one's factual knowledge of the elements of the language were acquired ordinarily or by ESP. Thus cases of fluent xenoglossy – were such to occur – might in the right circumstances constitute strong evidence against the super-ESP hypothesis. For we have (so far as I am aware) no clear evidence, e.g. from spontaneous cases, to suggest that complex skills may be suddenly acquired by a process of extrasensory induction from persons already possessing them, and then as suddenly vanish again. I have not heard, for example, of any English traveller in darkest Wales who has unexpectedly found himself able to speak and understand Welsh, and has then lost the ability on recrossing into England.

What evidence, then, do we actually have for xenoglossy in a mediumistic or related context? The answer, I think, is not a great deal, or rather not a great deal that has been satisfactorily recorded and analysed. What evidence there is may be conveniently taken under four headings, of which the first three may be treated very briefly.

1. In some cases a mediumistic communicator, though unable to speak a foreign language known to him in life, has shown some understanding of words or phrases spoken in that language. Thus Mrs Piper's supposed French control, Dr Phinuit, was occasionally able to understand bits of spoken French, even though himself able to speak only occasional clichés. Another control of Mrs Piper's was able to translate the first few words of the Lord's Prayer in Greek (112, pp. 45-48), but the similarity of the first words (*pater hemon*) to the first words of the better known Latin *Pater Noster* may have provided the clue.

2. In a number of cases a communicator has correctly used single words or very short phrases of a language unknown to the medium. For instance, some Italian and Hawaiian words were on occasion spoken through Mrs Piper (66b, pp. 416-418, 480-482), and Dutch words (36) through Mrs Rosalie Thompson (b. 1868), a British medium studied by Myers and Piddington.

3. We have a few examples of what Ducasse (34b) calls 'recitative xenoglossy' in a mediumistic or similar context. In 'recitative xenoglossy' the subject repeats, as it were by rote, fragments of a strange language which he does not necessarily understand. In most such cases cryptomnesia (latent memory) is difficult to rule out (see, e.g., 130). There are in the literature one or two curious cases of adult or elderly persons in a state of illness or delirium repeating phrases, sentences or passages from languages they had known or heard as children, but had subsequently forgotten (e.g. 43). I shall describe a case of recitative xenoglossy in Chapter Twelve.

Where cases of categories 1 to 3 are not due to cryptomnesia, it does not seem impossible (though it may be implausible) to frame an explanation of them in terms of ESP. Understanding of phrases in foreign languages might be gained by telepathically or clairvoyantly grasping the intention of the speaker. Isolated words, phrases or sentences might be telepathically or clairvoyantly cognized, with or without their meanings, or, if 'active agent' telepathy is possible, might be injected into the sensitive's mind by the endeavours of another person. It is with cases of the remaining category that the sort of difficulties for the super-ESP hypothesis which I described above become acute.

4.   Lastly we have cases of what Ducasse (34b) calls responsive xenoglossy, cases in which the subject converses intelligently in the foreign language. Quite a few accounts of such cases are to be found in the literature of Spiritualism, but the standards of recording and investigation are rarely such as to carry weight. An apparently remarkable case is that of the automatist 'Rosemary', studied by Wood and Hulme (70; 173a; 173b) Rosemary's guide 'Nona' claimed that she had been a Babylonian princess who had married the Pharaoh Amenhotep III (c. 1410–1375 BC). In addition to giving some highly circumstantial accounts of her life in Egypt, and of her relationship with 'Vola', a previous incarnation of Rosemary, Nona communicated over a period of years a very large number of apparently correct phrases and short sentences in the ancient Egyptian language. Rosemary heard these phrases 'clairaudiently' and then spoke them out loud. They were taken down phonetically by Dr Wood, who submitted them for study to a scholar interested in the ancient Egyptian language, A. J. Hulme. Wood later studied this language himself. The late Professor C. J. Ducasse, who submitted the case to a close analysis, concludes (34a, p. 256): 'The xenoglossy . . . does provide strong evidence that the capacity once possessed by some person to converse extensively, purposefully, intelligently, and intelligibly in the Egyptian language of three thousand years ago, or anyway in a language closely related to it, have survived by many centuries the death of that person's body.' I think, however, that Ducasse's positive verdict is premature, and that one should suspend judgement concerning this case until such time (if ever) as it has been independently examined by an acknowledged authority on the ancient Egyptian language. For it is far from clear how acceptable were Hulme's qualifications.

Many of the alleged cases of responsive xenoglossy have involved 'direct voice' mediums, and have taken place in the darkness which the spirits seem to find essential for manipulating the speaking trumpets and for constructing 'voice boxes' out of ectoplasm. In a volume (103) concerning the American direct voice medium, Mrs Etta Wriedt (I quoted in Chapter Five above Sir William Barrett's account of an experience with her) we are told that there were occasions on which the deceased friends and relations of Norwegian-, Spanish-, Croatian-, Dutch-, Italian-, German-, French-, Hindustani-, Welsh-, Serbian-, and Gaelic-speaking sitters conversed with them on appropriate topics in their own languages. Many of these sitters supplied signed and dated statements.

Unfortunately we do not have gramophone or stenographic recordings of these voices, and it is extremely difficult to know what to say about them. A similar diversity of languages was allegedly heard at the seances of another American direct voice medium, George Valiantine (15a; 156b, 68). A Welsh sitter, Mr Caradoc Evans, spoke at a sitting on 27 February 1924 to the soi-disant spirit of his father. Asked in Welsh for the location of the house in which he died, Mr Evans' father replied (15a, pp. 210–211): 'Uch ben yr avon. Mae steps – lawer iawn – rhwng y ty ar rheol. Pa bath yr ydych yn gofyn? Y chwi yn mynd i weled a ty bob tro yr rydych yn y dre', which means, we are told, 'Above the river. There are steps – many steps – between the house and the road. Why do you ask? You go to see the house every time you are in the town.' At a Valiantine sitting in New York, an expert in oriental languages, Dr N. Whymant, conversed in an archaic Chinese with an alleged K'ung-fu-tzu upon points of textual scholarship. Whymant prints (170) what appear to be contemporary notes in English of this voice's Chinese pronouncements.

Unfortunately our assessment of these exciting claims is bound to be affected by the fact that Valiantine was several times detected in fraud of the grossest kind (15c; 138c). A recording of his 'Chinese' voice had the appropriate intonation, but could not be understood by Chinese speakers, including Dr Whymant. Valiantine had undoubtedly the gift of catching the intonation and rhythm of various foreign languages, and it was also his habit to repeat the last phrase spoken to him by his interlocutor. The probability seems to be that expectant sitters heard much more in his 'foreign language' utterances than was actually there. Few people realize, perhaps, how prone is the human ear to hear articulate words in all sorts of murmurings and stray sounds with the right kind of periodicity; at least as prone as is the eye to see faces in inkblots. This point is clearly brought out in David Ellis's (39) recent investigations of the 'Raudive voices' (the voices, allegedly of deceased persons, picked up by tape recorders under certain conditions). In one 'Raudive voice' case that I observed personally the sitters were interpreting as comprehensible whispered words sounds made by their own fingers unconsciously rubbing the case of a small tape recorder (the microphone was integral with the case).

The most detailed studies so far of instances of responsive xenoglossy are those by Professor Ian Stevenson of the cases of 'Jensen', 'Gretchen', and 'Sharada'. All three of these cases have what is apparently a reincarnationist rather than a mediumistic setting, but in none has the communicating personality been identified with some person known once to have lived. By far the most remarkable is that of Sharada, which I discuss in Chapter Eleven below. Of the other two the case of Jensen (153f) is the more interesting. 'Jensen' is the name of the Swedish speaking personality that emerged spontaneously in 1955–6 during hypnotic age regression experiments with T. E., the 37-year-old English-speaking wife of a Philadelphia doctor. The hypnotist was the lady's husband, K. E. The language spoken by Jensen, and the details he gave of his life, were consistent with a previous existence in seventeenth century Sweden. Three Swedish speakers who conversed with Jensen, and four who have subsequently listened to the tape recordings, agreed that he conversed sensibly, grammatically and with good pronunciation in Swedish, though his remarks were usually short. An analysis of four tape-recorded sessions showed that, if doubtful words, and words which sound alike in Swedish and in English were excluded, Jensen introduced into one conversation at least sixty Swedish words not previously used in his presence by his interviewers.

Stevenson considers in great detail the possibility that Mrs T. E. might have acquired a knowledge of Swedish by normal means. His conclusions are entirely negative. Some years after the Jensen experiments, however, T. E. developed a more conventional kind of mediumship, with a control and various communicators. During this period, evidence came to hand that on two occasions she had 'got up' in advance the material for some 'scientific' messages which were delivered at her sittings. Stevenson advances reasons for supposing that she did so in a dissociated state for which she was afterwards amnesic. There was nothing to suggest that she had ever entered such states prior to the Jensen experiments.

Mr Ian Wilson has lately argued (172, p. 113) that this case may be entirely rejected. He quotes part of Stevenson's remarks on the 'scientific message' imbroglio just mentioned, and goes on: 'The identities of the doctor and his wife have become known to me, and suffice it to say that the case does not merit the serious consideration which Stevenson advances for it.' Of course it will *not* 'suffice' to say this. I cannot imagine why any reasonable person should attach more weight to Mr Wilson's one dismissive sentence than to the twenty pages which Stevenson devotes to the question of whether or not T. E. could have learned her Swedish by normal means.

A curious point to do with responsive xenoglossy is the following. If I am right in proposing that skills, linguistic or other, cannot be acquired by ESP, then they obviously cannot be acquired by telepathy with deceased persons (if such a thing be conceivable). Hence we should not expect a mental medium whose gifts are essentially those of telepathy with the living or with the dead to exhibit a fluent responsive xenoglossy (as distinct perhaps from the ability to understand or hesitatingly utter the odd phrase or word of a foreign language unknown to her). This might be thought by some to accord with the fact that most apparent cases of responsive xenoglossy come either from direct voice⁄mediums or from persons ostensibly reincarnated.

I began this chapter by mentioning cases in which mediumistic communicators have so exactly reproduced the mannerisms, gestures, intonations, humour, etc., characteristic of them in life, that friends and relations were overwhelmingly impressed. I went on to describe examples of the apparent post-mortem manifestation of characteristic skills and accomplishments. And in previous chapters I described at some length evidence for the survival of memories and characteristic purposes. But (and this is a point almost impossible to put over in so brief a space) in certain rather striking cases – the GP case, say, or the AVB case, or the Myers communicator of the cross-correspondences – these various elements were, according to those best qualified to judge, *blended together* in a characteristic and recognizable way. Something that is almost a whole personality had been built up.

Now the ability to construct, or dramatize, or imitate a whole personality out of these elements is itself a skill which cannot be reduced to mere knowledge of facts concerning the various elements. Let me illustrate what I mean. At one period of my life I spent a good deal of time studying the correspondence, diaries, papers, etc., of Henry Sidgwick and F. W. H. Myers. I learned a great many facts about their private lives, their friends, their habits and their domestic arrangements; far more facts than it is remotely plausible to suppose that the greatest sensitive could have obtained by ESP. But no amount of such factual knowledge (knowledge *that*) would *per se* have enabled me to imitate them (a skill, knowledge *how*) in a way that their close friends would have found anything other than absurd or pathetic. My performance would have been infinitely less impressive than those of Mrs Piper or Mrs Leonard at their best – indeed at their worst! It might be pointed out that I am not exactly the sort of person who gives impersonations at parties to the accompaniment of loud applause. I am not talented in that direction. But could even a skilled impressionist, of whom we have seen so many on stage and television, have done much better? Such a person would presumably have generalized skills related to his profession, and would no doubt attempt *something* if pressed. But impersonating, say, Mr Edward Heath, is none the less a *different skill* from impersonating Sir Harold Wilson. Some impersonators might be able to 'do' one but not the other. And the skills of doing a Heath-impersonation and of doing a Wilson-impersonation have to be acquired separately by listening to tape and video recordings, practising, recording the practice attempts, practising again, and so on. They don't arise directly from knowing *facts about* Heath's and Wilson's lives, mannerisms, voices, habits of thought, turns of phrase, etc. Even if we grant (which is a rash thing to do) that such mediums as Mrs Piper and Mrs Leonard may have had enormously extended powers of ESP, there still remains an immense problem over how they translated the factual knowledge they were thus able to obtain into convincing impersonations of deceased people well known to their sitters.

8   The Controls of Mediums

In the preceding five chapters, I have placed myself, as it were, on the side of the angels. I have been principally concerned to set forth examples of the ostensible evidence for survival from the phenomena of mediumship. My conclusions have been, on the whole, favourable to this evidence, in that I could find no ready formula for explaining all of it away. The time has now come to change sides and undertake the role of devil's advocate. In this chapter, and in Chapters Ten and Thirteen below, I shall introduce and evaluate various considerations which may be thought either to undermine large chunks of the evidence for survival, or else more directly to prove that survival is impossible. (Perhaps 'devil's advocate' is the wrong phrase, since the devil might be supposed to have his own reasons for favouring survival.)

An initial problem with this enterprise is that of finding a starting point. Many of those who have inveighed most strongly against survivalistic views and the alleged evidence for survival display a readiness to accept inadequate evidence quite as marked as that which they so freely (and often so rightly) attribute to their opponents (for an example see 44b, pp. 361–363). (It can, I think, be no freak fact that one of the worst pro-parapsychology books of recent years, and one of the worst anti-parapsychology books, are both written by the same individual.) The most succinct, and the best informed, statement of the case against survival is still the late Professor E. R. Dodds' classic paper 'Why I do not believe in survival', published in the *Proceedings of the SPR* about fifty years ago (33). I shall base my own statement of that case primarily upon Dodds' paper, without, however, giving detailed references to it. The present and succeeding chapters will attempt a critique and assessment of the ostensible evidence for survival provided by the phenomena of mental mediumship.

As a classical scholar and historian of Neoplatonism, Dodds was very impressed by certain historical considerations. If the departed can indeed communicate with the living through the agency of mental mediums, why did they show so little sign of doing so prior to the start of the modern Spiritualist movement in 1848? There was no lack of the necessary machinery or the necessary interest on the part of the living, for

> ... the evidence collected in Oesterreich's book on Possession shows that the mediumistic trance is a fairly constant phenomenon in all ages and among all peoples; and curiosity about the state of the dead has left its mark alike on the literature of Greek and Rome, of the Middle Ages, and of the Renaissance. But there is something more singular still. The two groups of pre-nineteenth century mediums about whom we have most information, the *katochoi* of the late Graeco-Roman period and the witches of the sixteenth and seventeenth centuries [or rather the 'victims' of the witches], while performing a number of the feats performed by modern mediums, perversely attributed them in the one case to the agency of non-human gods or demons, in the other to the agency of the devil. Once again, why? (33, pp. 152–153)

It seems to me that Dodds is here exaggerating somewhat. His remarks hold true mainly of Western Europe, where untypical constraints have operated, and even in Western Europe there have been notable exceptions (for a sixteenth century example see 45, pp. 23–27). There is every reason to suppose that in many non-European cultures mediumistic communication with the dead has been practised for centuries in the forms touched upon in Chapter Two above. It seems to be, and to have been, a very widespread practice indeed. It is true, of course, that little in the way of 'evidence for survival' has come down to us from these cultures, but that could well be because, for totally different reasons, neither the members of the culture, nor visiting travellers, anthropologists, etc., have felt called upon to record it.

Still, even if Dodds's point is not proved, there is a related point which carries some weight. If most people survive the transition of death with their memories, purposes, affections and intellectual skills more or less intact, we might expect them, or at least a substantial number of them, to try as hard as they can to communicate with loved ones left behind should communication be possible. Why are drop in communicators not all the time insinuating messages for friends and relations through whatever mediums may be available? Drop in communicators are apparently rather rare, and I do not know of a single instance in which a drop in communicator has tried to put the same message through two different mediums. Yet surely we might expect that some of them would try. In fact cases in which any kind of communicator has convincingly manifested through more than one medium without the presence of the same sitter are fairly uncommon, though we have some examples. The Myers and Gurney communicators of the cross-correspondences did so, but they were of course well-known personalities; so did Mrs Piper's GP control (I have not, however, seen any useful comparative analysis of the communications). In short: visit a good medium, and there is a reasonable chance that you will hear from the deceased person you desire to contact. That deceased person is, however, rather unlikely to send you a message out of the blue. Other things being equal, this might be held to suggest that whatever may be involved in mediumistic communication, it is factors in this world that are crucial rather than factors in the next.

A reply to this argument might, for instance, explore other possible reasons for the seeming scarcity of drop-in communicators (compare Chapter Five above), or contrast mediumistic communicators with apparitions of the dead. Apparitions of the dead very often come as unwanted intruders upon the peace of mind of perfect strangers, yet refuse to appear for those who deliberately seek them out – especially if they happen to be parapsychologists.

> . . . when the glum Researchers come
> The brutes of bogeys – go.

An issue of more substantial importance, and one which has excited a great deal of argument, is that of the status of the 'controls' of trance mediums. Leading trance mediums, such as Mrs Piper, Mrs Leonard, Mrs Soule and Mrs Garrett, have provided what must surely be the most impressive of all the mediumistic evidence for survival. Trance mediums tend to have one or a few regular controls (that is spirits who ostensibly 'take over' the medium's body for extended periods, and communicate through it) amongst whom will be the medium's own 'guide' (spirits who, like Mrs Piper's Phinuit or Mrs Leonard's Feda, look after the medium's interests, and act as interviewers or masters of ceremonies on 'the other side'). It has often been suggested that the controls of trance mediums are simply secondary personalities, to be compared with the different phases of the various well-known cases of hysterical multiple personality (for an illuminating history of this idea see 81). This tactic might well be objected to as explaining one phenomenon of doubtful status in terms of another; but one implication is fairly clear. Psychiatrists these days tend to argue that earlier investigators greatly exaggerated, and sometimes by their own probings greatly increased, the differences between the various personalities which manifest in such cases. At root there is only one personality, undergoing sudden and rather sharp changes (no doubt of pathological origin). If this is the correct way of looking at the controls of trance mediums, these controls – even though they may exhibit flashes of paranormal knowledge – are not entities independent of the medium.

It is possible to pile up arguments on both sides of this question. Thus in favour of the multiple personality theory we may say:

1.   It is possible to construct a whole series of intermediate cases which so to speak bridge the gap between, say, Mrs Piper's and Mrs Leonard's most realistic controls and instances of undoubted multiple personality. (See for instance 110a, I, pp. 34–70, 298–368.)

2.   There are obvious similarities between the somewhat childish guides of certain mediums (Mrs Leonard's Feda for example – see 161, pp. 348–359) and the rather mischievous and capricious secondary personalities which have emerged in some cases of hysterical multiple personality.

3.   In at least one case (Doris Fischer – see 71b; 125a; 125b; 125f) the subject of a classic case of multiple personality afterwards developed into a versatile medium. (However it must be added that this happened after she had been relieved of hysterical symptoms, and had become for the time being apparently a normal person.)

Against the multiple personality theory we can advance the following considerations.

1.   The number of distinct personalities which may control a trance medium during the course of her career greatly exceeds anything for which the annals of multiple personality provide a parallel; nor do I know of a complete parallel for the simultaneous and apparently quite full manifestation of two personalities (one through the hand and one through the voice), which occurred quite commonly during one period of Mrs Piper's mediumship.

2.   There does not seem to have been anything disturbed about the normal personalities of Mrs Piper, Mrs Leonard, and other leading trance mediums. (In Chapter Five I made a similar point about the

shamans and witchdoctors who fulfil analogous roles in other societies.)

3. The comings and goings of most mediumistic controls, unlike those of secondary personalities, are strictly circumscribed.

I cannot see much hope of reaching a decision on the basis of these general observations. Attempts have been made, with Mrs Garrett and Mrs Leonard, to throw light on the issue by administering various psychological tests to the medium in her normal state, and when controlled by her guide. Certain differences emerged, but the work has been criticized, and it is unclear how the results should be interpreted (22a; 22b; 22c; 23; 159a). To get any further we must look at in-depth psychological studies of individual trance mediums. Unfortunately these are not numerous. By far the most important is Mrs E. M. Sidgwick's very lengthy investigation of the phenomenology of Mrs Piper's mediumship (145b; cf. 145a).

Mrs Sidgwick discusses in considerable detail what the Piper controls and communicators say about themselves, their situations, and the process of communication. Much of this is in line with the general traditions of Western Spiritualism. They one and all represent themselves as autonomous beings quite separate from the medium. They have bodies of a substance more subtle than that of our earthly ones, so that they can change shape and size and transport themselves great distances very rapidly. They say that to them the medium appears as, or surrounded by, a ball of light, to which they are attracted. They have to 'enter the light' in order to communicate. The light seems to be regarded as a sort of energy or power which makes communication possible. Sometimes it seems to be thought of in terms of the notion of a luminiferous ether which was utilized in the physics of the day, at other times we get such absurd suggestions as that the light is made of 'air, light and hydrogen' or of 'vacium' (*sic*).

When a spirit enters the light he is able, by means that are not made altogether clear, to operate the medium's organism more or less effectively, and to become aware of the sitter and the medium's surroundings through her sense organs, especially her ears (her eyes being usually shut). Sometimes, however, controls speak as if they could directly see the seance room, or for that matter other and more distant earth scenes; and they regularly speak as if they could both see and hear and so transmit messages from other deceased persons in the hereafter.

An obvious question that arises at this point is that of what happens to Mrs Piper, or to the spirit of Mrs Piper, when her body is being operated by deceased persons. The story told by her controls is that as a spirit moves into her organism, she herself moves out of it, and into the spirit world. She is frequently said to remain connected to her body by a slender cord, perhaps made of the mysterious 'light' referred to above. If this cord were broken, she would not be able to return to her body and it would die. The cord is sometimes assigned other functions. Controls are occasionally represented as sliding down it in order to enter the medium's organism, and it is also more than once said to function as a sort of telphone line by which non-controlling communicators can speak to controls occupying the body.

Mrs Piper herself, on awakening from her trance, would sometimes for a short while retain an apparent memory of what had befallen her in the spirit world, and even seem to have some lingering awareness of that world. In this 'waking stage' she would sometimes repeat (correct) names given to her while 'in' the spirit world, and on a number of occasions she was able to pick out from photographs deceased persons whom she had ostensibly met there.

Mrs Piper's controls thus apparently regard themselves as entities completely separate from the medium, and in support of their contention they present a detailed picture of their own activities whilst controlling and communicating. Can we accept their own estimate of themselves? Mrs Sidgwick argues that we can not. There are many points which weigh against it.

To begin with, there are a number of controls who are quite certainly fictitious. Phinuit is one. Chlorine is another. Among others are, for instance, a Julius Caezar (*sic*) and a Sir Walter Scott so totally unlike the originals that one can hardly even regard them as impersonations. The 'Imperator' band of controls also belong in this group. They claimed identity with the controls of the same pseudonyms who had manifested through the famous British medium, W. Stainton Moses (see 160). They were never able to establish this identity, but hazarded all kinds of incorrect and contradictory guesses at their own 'real' names. Even the most life-like and realistic controls, such as GP, show signs of being impersonations (not deliberate ones). They break down at just the point where Mrs Piper's own stock of knowledge runs out, viz. when they are required to talk coherently of science, philosophy and literature (which the living GP could readily have done).

Mrs Piper's controls sometimes excuse their shortcomings on the grounds that coming into the medium's 'light' has a confusing effect upon them, or that they cannot manipulate her organism in ways to which it is not accustomed. These excuses are, however, not adequate. The confusion which obliterates the controls' grasp of science and philosophy does not prevent them from spouting reams of pompous nonsense upon religious and philosophical topics and presenting it as profoundest truth, sometimes in the teeth of the sitters' queries; so that we have to attribute to them not just confusion but downright tale-spinning, which was certainly not a habit of the purported communicators in life, nor yet of the normal Mrs Piper.

Similar tale-spinning tendencies are manifested in the way in which controls cover up their mistakes. Controls will, generally speaking, not admit their blunders. They will rationalize, explain away, concoct any excuse, however tenuous and childish. All other considerations seem subordinated to an overwhelming urge to keep the drama flowing without pause or hiccup.

That the trance drama of communication with the departed really is only a piece of play-acting by the medium (not a deliberate piece of play-acting – call it rather the enactment of a dream) is strongly suggested by the following further consideration. Some controls, like GP, or Bennie Junot, are very life-like, and in fact convinced many people of their authenticity. Others, however, like Julius Caezar, Sir Walter Scott, and the George Eliot who claimed she had met Adam Bede in the next world, are so implausible, and so stilted and stylized in their diction and sentiments, that no one could possibly regard them as anything other than fictions. Yet the most plausible communicators will in the firmest tones guarantee the authenticity of the least plausible ones, so that the authenticity of the former is inextricably and disadvantageously tied up with the authenticity of the latter, and it becomes abundantly clear that the maintenance of the drama is all-important and that every one of the controls, from GP down to Julius Caezar, is part and parcel of the playwright's creative fantasy.

If further proof were wanted that the controls and communicators are simply aspects of Mrs Piper herself, it can perhaps be found in features of the diction and wording of the communications. It may be found for instance in the waxing and waning of the use by the Imperator Band and others of archaic forms of speech. Although members of the Band claimed to be (behind their pseudonyms) Homer and Ulysses, Mrs Piper (a New England Protestant) would naturally have expected religious leaders to use Old Testament forms of speech, and the mistakes made in the handling of the archaic diction would have been in accordance with her somewhat limited education.

Again, there was evidence that the various ostensibly separate controls possessed a common stock of associations, which could hardly have been the case if they had really been separate personalities. Thus Imperator once called Lodge 'Captain', which was Phinuit's nickname for him; yet Phinuit never overlapped with the Imperator regime. Several communicators showed a somewhat marked interest in clothes and hats, which would not have been characteristic of them in life, but *was* characteristic of Mrs Piper. For my part I do not see how it is possible to dissent from Mrs Sidgwick's conclusion that the Piper controls were one and all aspects of Mrs Piper's own personality.

Mrs Piper was without doubt one of the most remarkable and the most successful mental mediums of all time, and it seems highly likely that if Mrs Sidgwick's conclusions about the status of the Piper-controls are correct, they will also hold true of the controls of other trance mediums. Unfortunately we do not have any investigation of the status of Mrs Leonard's controls comparable in scope and detail to Mrs Sidgwick's massive study of the Piper controls. A number of papers on the *modus operandi* of trance communication through Mrs Leonard, together with relevant observations from other papers, are summarized and critically discussed in a valuable chapter of C. D. Broad's *Lectures on Psychical Research* (1962). Mrs Leonard's controls seem to have been fewer in number than Mrs Piper's (Feda stuck to her post throughout Mrs Leonard's career), and I have the impression that they were rather less prone to engage in fishing, covering up mistakes, giving each other spurious testimonials, and the other sorts of activities which, carried out by the Piper controls, encouraged Mrs Sidgwick to regard them as stage characters in a drama created by the medium. The Leonard controls also give a somewhat more coherent account of the process of communication, though I can by no means reconcile with each other, or fully make sense of, their various statements as to how they operate the medium's organism. None the less there are certain hints that in the Leonard mediumship, as in that of Mrs Piper, a dramatic construct is being built around events which, whatever their real nature, are not as they are made to appear. For instance, Feda often talks as though she can directly see and hear the communicators from whom she relays messages. But there is much to show that these claims cannot be taken at face value. Thus Mrs W. H.

Salter says (138b, pp. 309, 312) of a series of statements made by Feda concerning a communicator subsequently said to be her mother (Mrs Verrall), 'Many of these statements . . . are true; they contain, however, an admixture of such errors as could hardly have arisen had Feda's knowledge been derived from any clearly apprehended image or series of images.' And again, 'The general inference which I should draw . . . is that a certain amount of veridical information about my mother was woven by Feda into an imaginary picture of an elderly widow, based on preconceived ideas of the appearance such a picture might be expected to present.'

Of course if we leave the top end of the scale and descend to the bottom we find trance mediums in whom the element of 'veridical information' is largely missing, and imagination reigns supreme. Such a medium was the Genevese 'Hélène Smith' (Catherine Elise Muller), of whom the Swiss psychologist, Theodore Flournoy wrote a remarkable study, *From India to the Planet Mars.* Flournoy's conclusion is that all Hélène's controls are constructs of a somewhat childish dream stratum of her personality, and are, indeed, not separated from her own consciousness 'by an impenetrable barrier, but that osmotic changes are effected from the one to the other'. It would, I think, be possible to produce a graduated series of cases, from those in which there is no element of veridicality (say the shamans or witchdoctors who are controlled by animals or godlings), through cases, like that of Hélène Smith, in which there is a small admixture of veridicality, up to cases like those of Mrs Piper and Mrs Leonard in which there is a good deal of veridicality, and argue that there is no discontinuity marking a changeover from mediums who in trance exercise their own dramatic gifts, eked out perhaps by ESP, to those who are 'possessed' by alien and intrusive spirits which operate their bodies directly. The psychological processes are in all cases at root the same.

It would seem, therefore, that we have to abandon the idea that the controls of trance mediums are the spirits of deceased persons temporarily controlling a living body. Are we then forced to adopt some form of the super-ESP hypothesis, to suppose that Mrs Piper and Mrs Leonard were able to inject into their dramatic representations of various deceased persons correct and appropriate information obtained telepathically from the minds of living persons or clairvoyantly from existing records? Mrs Sidgwick did not think so. She eventually came to believe that behind Mrs Piper's dramatic rendering of communication from the dead, overshadowing it and somehow directing its course, there might sometimes lie those same deceased persons who figure as characters in the drama. The medium writes many of the speeches, and ensures continuity in the plot; but some of the lines (perhaps the most important ones) are filled in by outside authors. Let us call this theory the theory of 'overshadowing'. It seems to be a version of it towards which William James moves at the end of his report on Mrs Piper's Hodgson-control (74, p. 117):

> Extraneous 'wills to communicate' may contribute to the results as well as a 'will to personate', and the two kinds of will may be distinct in entity, though capable of helping each other out. The will to communicate, in our present instance, would be, on the *prima facie* view of it, the will of Hodgson's surviving spirit, and a natural way of representing the process would be to suppose the spirit to have found that by pressing, so to speak, against 'the light', it can make fragmentary gleams and flashes of what it wishes to say mix with the rubbish of the trance-talk on this side. The wills might thus strike up a sort of partnership and reinforce each other. It might even be that the 'will to personate' would be comparatively inert unless it were aroused to activity by the other will.

9 'Overshadowing' and the Super-ESP Hypothesis – Theoretical Considerations

If we hold, as I certainly do, that fraud and chance-coincidence will not suffice to explain away the successes of such mediums as Mrs Piper and Mrs Leonard, and if we agree that Mrs Sidgwick is correct in regarding the 'personalities' which communicate through mediums as being facets of the medium herself, we appear to have left on our hands not a theory of 'possession' or direct control by deceased persons, to which is opposed some kind of super-ESP hypothesis, but two forms of ESP theory, namely the super-ESP theory, aforementioned, and the theory of 'overshadowing' which I have just touched upon. 'Overshadowing', if it takes place, would appear by definition to involve telepathic interaction between the deceased person and the medium. In so far as mediums who are 'overshadowed' may instead or in addition have a 'clairvoyant' or 'clairaudient' awareness of deceased persons, we may need to enlarge the theory of overshadowing to accommodate it.

Since ESP is thus a keystone both of the survivalist and of the anti-survivalist positions, I shall begin by raising the question of how ESP is itself to be conceived. For it may be that the super-ESP theory and the theory of overshadowing do not harmonize equally well with the conception of ESP towards which we are forced. My remarks will necessarily be brief to the verge of total inadequacy, but it is important that I raise certain issues even though I can hardly pretend to resolve them. (For further discussion of these and related issues see 17 and 128b.)

In a recent Presidential address to the Parapsychological Association, Palmer (118c) distinguishes two 'paradigms' (models or patterns of thought) which parapsychologists have applied to psi phenomena (ESP and PK). The first of these is what he calls the *transmission paradigm*. This paradigm, which has until recently been the received one, 'assumes that psi involves the transmission of information across some kind of channel from a source to a receiver, at least one of which is a mind (or, according to a few diehards, a brain).' Palmer's second paradigm, the *correspondence paradigm*, is, he thinks, harder to define. 'In fact, it might be fair to say that it is simply a negation of the transmission paradigm. About the best I can do to define it positively is to say that it postulates some principle which causes events in nature to coincide to a greater than chance degree, given certain preconditions.'

The Transmission Paradigm

I shall begin by looking at the transmission paradigm. This paradigm clearly encounters its greatest difficulty when one attempts to extend it to cover the phenomena of clairvoyance (precognition is too vast an issue for me to raise at this point). In terms of the transmission paradigm clairvoyance must involve the receipt, through some sort of surrogate sense-perception, of a distinctive emanation (kind unknown) from the object that is clairvoyantly perceived.

It seems to me that the implications of this theory have only to be set forth for it to be decisively rejected. We should have to suppose that an object may emit a kind of emanation that passes round or through all obstacles; that is emitted by all the sorts of objects that have been targets in successful clairvoyance experiments; that supplies information about colour and shape, regardless of whether the target objects are edge-on or in a light-tight box; that is not confused or obliterated by, but can be distinguished from, the emanations emitted by all surrounding objects; that yields indifferently the information normally provided by sight, hearing, etc.; and that gives rise to no characteristic sensory experience of its own, but is accurately translated into the terms of any other sense-modality. It is impossible not to agree with the late Professor C. D. Broad when he says in a classic paper (186, pp. 27–67) on this theme that such theories involve a 'very heavy draft on the bank of possibility.'

One might at first think that telepathy, so often conceived as 'mental radio', would accord more happily with the transmission paradigm than does clairvoyance. But this is not the case. Consider the following points.

1. If we regard the 'transmission' as mediated by any form of physical energy transfer, we confront the problem that the energy concerned appears able to pass through all material barriers. But then it should pass through the brain too, and not be stoppped as, for example, radio waves are stopped by aerials.

2. If (again thinking in physical terms) we suppose that the end

result of the supposed process of energy transfer is to produce in the receiver's brain a pattern of brain cell activity similar to that which obtains in the sender's brain, we run upon the following difficulty. There does not seem, as we shall see in Chapter Thirteen, much reason for supposing that the same spatio-temporal pattern of brain cell activity will necessarily give rise to the same experience in two different people, or even in the same person on two different occasions.

3. Let us waive the preceding objection, and assume that, following upon some process of transmission from sender to receiver, the latter becomes aware of what the former is experiencing. For example, a friend of mine had one night a distressing dream of his father (69). He felt that his father was about to die, and he himself underwent the pain of his father's heart attack. His father was not known to have a weak heart; yet the dream turned out to be veridical (it was actually precognitive by about twenty-four hours, a point which I shall here neglect). Now one can just about imagine that by some unknown process of transmission and induction he might have been brought to feel a heart-pain resembling his father's. But how did he know that the pain reflected *his father's pain* rather than that of any other of the numerous persons who would at that time have been undergoing heart attacks? He had no previous experience of the quality of his father's heart-pains. To his father, of course, the heart-pains had a meaning. They meant 'I am dying'. The son, however, did not pick up the meaning the pains had for this father. He did not think 'I am dying'. He thought 'My father is dying', which was not what his father was thinking. So how did the son know how to interpret the pain? He knew because in a strange way he identified with his father, almost became him. But what signals could be transmitted that could induce this state of mind in him, and how, indeed, could he recognize such a state, given that he had (and could have had) no prior experience of what being his father was like? In short the *meaning* of the heart-pains is something that could not be transmitted.

4. Most cases of ostensible spontaneous telepathy are, however, not of this kind; they are not instances of the receiver undergoing an experience mirroring the experience of the sender. Take the following example of a 'reciprocal dream', quoted by Mrs Sidgwick (145d, pp. 415–417). A mother holding her sick baby sleeps, and dreams that her son of thirteen, away at boarding school and ill with measles, wanted to put his head on her shoulder, but could not because of the baby. On the same night her son dreams that he wants to put his head on her

shoulder but finds the baby in the way. Now the minimum hypothesis here, within the transmission paradigm, is that one of the two dreamers picked up the other's dream, and himself or herself dreamt accordingly. But consider what this hypothesis involves, say from the boy's point of view. His mother, in addition to dreaming, must have been transmitting her dream to him. But he did not dream her dream; he did not dream of being his mother, holding a baby, and having a boy cuddle up to her. Nor, for exactly the sorts of reasons given under 3. above, is it clear how he could have attached any meaning to 'copies' of his mother's sensations had he undergone them. Perhaps, then, some part of his mother's brain was watching her own dream and broadcasting a coded account of it which the equivalent in words would be, 'I, NN, of such and such an address, and mother of FN, am dreaming that . . .' The boy, picking up this message, and decoding it, could initiate a reciprocally corresponding dream. But this idea too is nonsense. Any such telepathic code would have to be the functional equivalent of a language, perhaps of a universal language, would have to be as flexible as a language, and like a language would have to grow continually as the conceptual equipment of its user enlarges. For there does not seem to be any limitation on the sorts of telepathic messages that can be sent and received, other than the limitations imposed by the conceptual equipment of sender and receiver. None the less this code would have to be untaught and, with most people, very rarely used.

I hope that these few remarks will at any rate serve to suggest that any defender of the transmission paradigm is taking on an uphill task. There is, however, a variant of the transmission paradigm that requires brief notice. It may perhaps be called the 'scanning paradigm'. Its central idea is that the percipient or receiver is not a passive recipient of ESP, but actively and continually 'scans' those parts of the environment accessible to him by ESP. Some such idea as this seems essential in connection with clairvoyance to account for the fact that clairvoyance seemingly yields not useless information about a haphazard selection of physical states of affairs, but primarily information relevant to the concerns of the percipient. Dr Louisa Rhine (129) thinks that a similar idea is forced upon us in connection with telepathy, because in certain cases of apparent spontaneous telepathy, namely 'call' cases (cases, that is, in which the telepathic message takes the form of a heard 'call') the supposed 'sender' did not in fact call or even think of the receiver. Telepathy in her view is thought-*reading* rather than thought-*transference*. (It may, however, be that Dr Rhine, whose collection of cases consists mostly of letters just from the percipient, underestimates the possibility of an effect from the agent; cf. Gibson, 49, and Stevenson, 153c, pp. 25–26.)

The notion of scanning is all very well if it is held to involve some active process of selection among competing inputs, where the inputs are conceived in terms of the transmission paradigm. Such a notion is legitimate, but of course mistaken since the transmission paradigm is mistaken. But there is a half-hidden tendency for the idea of scanning to pass into something quite different from this. Scanning seems sometimes implicitly to be regarded as (in the case of telepathy) a direct and immediate cognizing of other people's mental states, or (in the case of clairvoyance) a sort of reaching out of the mind to grasp (or 'prehend') a distant physical state of affairs. It is very hard indeed to make sense of either of these conceptions. Take first this kind of view of clairvoyance. In terms of it the clairvoyant mind seems rather like an amoeba. It can extrude itself round obstacles and seize upon targets beyond them. It can prehend the faces of objects which are edge on to it, presumably by flowing across them. It can filter into sealed boxes or closed houses. Unlike an amoeba, it can operate on any scale; it can prehend playing cards, printed words, even (on some accounts) the state of electronic circuitry or nerve cells in the brain; it can equally readily grasp a portrait, furniture, the front of a house, the view from a hill. It operates usually upon the surfaces of objects, but could no doubt operate equally well upon their insides. It can be functionally equivalent to any sense modality. It can, in short, do anything that is required of it. Hence the idea of prehension is of no explanatory value whatsoever.

The notion of 'telepathic scanning', a direct and selective cognizing of other peoples' minds, is in no better case. For it makes no sense at all to talk of a 'direct awareness' of other peoples' experiences. The only awareness one can have is of one's own experiences – this is a logical rather than a factual point. One cannot, so to speak, break out of the circle of one's own awareness into someone else's; any experience that one has is one's own experience and not another person's. And in any case it is obvious, from what was said above, that in most instances of spontaneous telepathy the experience of the percipient does not directly reflect that of the agent.

Another reason why the 'scanning' concept of telepathy has

surreptitiously gained ground is of course that it seems to be an essential ingredient in the super-ESP hypothesis. For that hypothesis had to suppose that mediums can have access to the memories of distant persons even when those memories are not activated, i.e. are presumably not generating telepathic signals. Since the idea that even an activated memory could be directly scanned by telepathy makes no sense, the idea that unactivated and merely stored memories may be so scanned must be equally unintelligible. Indeed, the proposal that our memory stores contain vast numbers of memory-images through which mediums can telepathically rummage appears so bizarre that most theorists have instead supposed mediums to have clairvoyant access to memories stored in the form of neural charges in the brain. This suggestion seems to me no more helpful than the previous one. I have already proposed that both transmission and prehensive theories of clairvoyance are quite untenable, and they will be no less untenable when the target of the clairvoyance is the state of someone's brain. Furthermore I shall argue in Chapter Thirteen that the notion of a memory store, containing coded representations of our past experiences, is quite incoherent in whatever form it is cast, and cannot possibly explain our ability to remember. If this argument is correct, the thesis that mediums can 'scan' distant memory stores necessarily collapses, whether the scanning is regarded as telepathic or as clairvoyant, and with it collapses all hope of coherently formulating the super-ESP hypothesis in the terms of this offshoot of the transmission paradigm.

The Correspondence Paradigm

We come now to the correspondence paradigm of ESP. This paradigm dispenses with ideas of transmission and proposes that in certain circumstances certain sorts of events in nature come into correspondence with each other. The tendency for such correspondences to occur is, presumably, an ultimate fact about the way things are. The principal theories of this category are the 'conformance' model of Stanford (16; 35; 149a; 149b) and the 'synchronicity' theory of Jung and Koestler (77, 82; I am not sure how the so-called 'observational' theories – see 101 – should be classified). However I do not think it would be profitable at this stage to stick to one specific version, so I shall merely offer some general remarks about the correspondence paradigm. I shall furthermore confine myself to discussing this paradigm in relation to telepathy. Telepathy is, for our immediate purposes, more important than clairvoyance; and I find it extremely hard to think how clairvoyance might be intelligibly handled within the correspondence paradigm.

So far as telepathy is concerned, a 'correspondence' approach might go something like this. Under certain preconditions the mental processes, and also the actions, of two persons may without any explanation of an ordinary kind from time to time come into correspondence in such a way that if, for instance, one of them develops a pain in the knee, the other will likewise feel such a pain; if one feels depressed, the other feels depressed also; if one has a certain tune running through his head, the other will whistle it; and so on. The time relations between the two sets of events might not be exact, but the gap would not be very great. One might suppose that the occurrence of such correspondences is simply a feature of the workings of extraordinarily complex systems (such as brains) and is susceptible of no further explanation (other perhaps than that the apparently separate systems, in some way that we cannot comprehend, are parts of a larger and overriding system or systems). The 'preconditions' mentioned above may include such factors as, for example, the minds of one or both being in a relatively relaxed state (i.e. open to intrusive random thoughts and stray ideas); the two persons concerned already having many associations and habits of thought in common; and the presence of emotional bonds and motivational factors.

I am far from sure that I can make sense of these ideas. But if we are going to entertain them at all, I think we are bound to extend them a little, and suppose that the correspondences concerned will not be just ones of sensory content or of emotional state (which are in fact not very common), but correspondences on what may be called a propositional or conceptual level. This seems to be required to account for the not uncommon instances of apparent dream telepathy in which there is similarity of theme rather than of details dream content (163); and also for cases (such as the boy's dream of wanting to lay his head on his mother's shoulder cited above) in which two people have reciprocal or complementary dreams. E.g. if Jack dreams of kissing Jill, Jill's reciprocal dream will not be that she *is* Jack and is kissing a simulacrum of herself. It will be that she is *in propria persona* and is being kissed by Jack. One would have to say here, I think, that Jack's mind and Jill's correspond (some would say overlap) in point of an underlying idea or conception, which could be expressed as 'Jack-kissing-Jill' (or in more complex cases, perhaps, as 'Jack-kissing-Jill-on-the-hill-and-to-hell-with-the-bucket-of-water), and that the dream consciousness of each elaborates this theme in individually appropriate ways. Elaboration of the theme could, however, only be in terms of the knowledge and conceptual equipment which the dreamers already possess.

Much more might be said both for and against these notions. However, for immediate purposes the important question is how could the super-ESP hypothesis fare within the bounds of the correspondence paradigm as thus conceived? One could not, I think, exactly rule the hypothesis out – all kinds of odd correspondences *might* come into being between the thoughts of any two persons whatsoever, even persons well separated in space and time. None the less it seems to me unlikely that within the correspondence paradigm the super-ESP theory would ever get off the ground. For the correspondence paradigm is not a cognitive paradigm; there is no question of one person scanning, or becoming directly aware of, events in another person's mind or brain; and it is the idea that a medium might as it were look at, riffle through, and make a selection from, another person's memories that more than anything else has led people to take the proposals of the super-ESP theory seriously. For if you can riffle though one person's memory-store, why not through another's and another's, until you come to the information you want? The correspondences of the correspondence paradigm, however, are, and can only be, between actual mental events (even if these are ultimately brain-processes); the correspondences might just conceivably involve events in dissociated or subconscious streams of consciousness, but they could not be between events in one person's mind and inert memories stored away in another person's memory-store. For in the absence of scanning there could be no principle by which one out of the innumerable coded memories in A.'s memory-store is selected to bring about a corresponding effect on current events in B.'s mind. The only possible form of selection would consist in A.'s activating the memory. But why should not the event in B.'s mind conform itself to whatever memory in A.'s memory-store represents the information which B. *needs*. B.'s need then constitutes the principle of selection. To suggest this is to endow B.'s mind with a power of selective discrimination among A.'s memories which is simply scanning in disguise. One could continue debating these issues more or less indefinitely, but I do not see the super-ESP hypothesis becoming any more plausible within the framework of the correspondence paradigm.

To recapitulate: I distinguished two kinds of theory about how mental mediums, and especially trance mediums, achieved their successes. Both involved attributing ESP to them. One theory – the super-ESP theory – suggested that they obtain all their information by telepathically tapping the memory-stores of living persons, clairvoyantly scanning archives, etc. According to the other theory discarnate persons may sometimes influence the course and content of mediumistic 'communications' by a process, presumably telepathic in nature, which I termed 'overshadowing'. I then outlined two approaches to the question of how ESP is to be conceived. Following Palmer, I called these the 'transmission' paradigm and the 'correspondence' paradigm. I argued that the transmission paradigm is incoherent, and that furthermore no sense can be made of the super-ESP hypothesis within either paradigm. It remains for me to ask whether the theory of overshadowing stands in better case.

Overshadowing

It seems to me that this theory could be given some sort of more or less intelligible expression within either the transmission paradigm or the correspondence paradigm. Its most straightforward expression would be in terms of the transmission paradigm. We should have to suppose a largely passive 'receiver' (the medium) whose stream of thought and action is sufficiently labile to be directed and influenced by the endeavours of an active (and generally discarnate) 'sender'. The relationship between events in the sender's mind and events in the receiver's mind might (in favourable cases) be a fairly straightforward one, so that when the sender thought of certain words or of a certain person or scene, similar words, or a similar picture, came into the receiver's mind. It might, however, be less easy to give within the transmission paradigm an account of how the discarnate person becomes aware of, and thus is able to respond to, what is said and done in the medium's vicinity.

Unfortunately the transmission paradigm is, or so I have argued, untenable upon other grounds, and the correspondence paradigm does not generate quite such a simple account of the proposed process of 'overshadowing'. In general terms, of course, we might suppose that a medium's stream of thought and action is so flexible and so quick to 'correspond' with another person's, that a wily and knowledgeable discarnate influence can exploit this fact to 'drive' it. But many problems arise to which no very obvious solutions present themselves.

Earlier in the chapter I suggested that in cases of, for instance, 'reciprocal dreams' we must postulate correspondence in respect of some *general* idea, which each participant elaborates in his or her own way. 'Overshadowing', however, would on the whole require much more specific correspondences. What determines in a given case the level of generality or specificity of the correspondences? What determines, also, which mind 'overshadows' the other? Must we invoke motivation, concentration, attention, need, purpose, personality factors, role-playing, etc? No clear answers are currently available.

These obscurities are, however, less difficulties for the overshadowing hypothesis as such, than symptoms of the undeveloped state of the correspondence paradigm, a paradigm which has only quite recently come to the fore. I do not think that they render the general notion of overshadowing unintelligible. The main problem which confronts the theory of overshadowing is not whether it is intelligible, which it is, at least up to a point, but whether it coheres with the empirical facts concerning ESP. For central to the whole theory is the idea that the sender, or the dominant partner in the 'correspondence' relationship, by some kind of special concentration or endeavour can directly influence the course of the receiver's or medium's thoughts and actions. Some writers, Dr Louisa Rhine for example, tend to deny that in cases of apparent spontaneous telepathy concentration or activity by the supposed sender has any effect; in a substantial number of cases the supposed sender remains unaware that he has sent. A few experiments, however, do suggest that concentration or strong willing by an agent may have a positive effect (see 118a, pp. 96–102). The issue is one that requires further investigation, on the results of which the tenability of the theory of overshadowing will depend. The experiments concerned might well in effect be ones on 'mediumistic communication by the living', a topic which I shall mention again shortly. (By analogy with cases of trance mediumship one might suppose that such 'communication' would be facilitated if the subject were to imagine himself to be the 'sender' and were to speak in that role.)

'Overshadowing' and the
   Super-ESP Hypothesis –
   the Data

My feeling, then – and I deliberately speak of 'feeling' rather than of 'judgement' because of the obscurities and uncertainties which confront one whichever direction one moves in – is that the theory of overshadowing can be expressed within either of the two leading models of or paradigms for ESP, whilst the super-ESP hypothesis makes sense within neither. But one would be ill-advised to let a decision between the super-ESP hypothesis and the theory of overshadowing hang largely upon the abstract issue of their agreement or otherwise with some speculative framework of thought. How far do they fit the facts? That is the decisive question – or rather would be if we could make the theories definite enough for the question to be answerable!

The super-ESP hypothesis is a peculiarly elusive theory, and I am conscious that I have hitherto invoked it and attacked it without any attempt to set it forth systematically. The trouble is that it is not so much a theory as an attitude of mind – an attitude which simply refuses to admit that there is *or ever could be* any evidence for survival which cannot be explained away in terms of the psi faculties, especially the ESP, of living percipients and mediums. The postulated reach of ESP is progressively extended to cover any new evidence, indeed any possible evidence, that may come in. A justification of this elastic way of thought is usually given by appeal to some principle of simplicity or parsimony. We know that ESP takes place, the argument goes, but we have no independent evidence for the spirits of the dead; hence it is more parsimonious to cast our explanations only in terms of the former. By so doing we avoid postulating a wholly new class of entities.

Considerations of parsimony, however, have to be weighed against considerations of factual adequacy. A theory that will not do the job cannot possibly be parsimonious, for it will soon get snared in a hopeless tangle of supplementary assumptions. The central plank of the super-ESP hypothesis must be that ESP of the required degree (required that is to explain away the most striking mediumistic data) takes place; and whether we consider the literature of experimental or of spontaneous ESP we come across little to suggest that it can. The experimental material is indeed very difficult to relate to the question at hand. In what is, I think, by far the best recent survey of it, John Palmer (118a) concludes there is no evidence that ESP is limited by either separation in space, separation in time or the physical characteristics of the target. But the targets used in modern ESP experiments (Zener cards, the outputs of binary random number generators, etc.) are totally unlike, and, so far as one can tell, usually much simpler than, the 'targets' (memory traces in distant brains, printed obituary notices, etc.) upon which mediums must score regular 'hits' if the super-ESP hypothesis is correct. Furthermore, even the most successful subjects in laboratory ESP experiments do not achieve 'hit' rates which suggest that one could 'communicate' messages to them. An outstanding scorer might correctly guess 350 cards in 1000 in tests where one would expect 250 hits anyway, 'just by chance'. It seems to me that if one compares the most successful mental mediums, on the one hand, with the most successful laboratory subjects, or percipients in spontaneous cases, on the other, the former greatly outstrip the latter in at least the following respects, of all of which I have given examples in the preceding chapters.

1. The rapid and occasionally almost non-stop flow of paranormal knowledge sometimes exhibited – in the best instances a flow of knowledge comparable to that which might occur in an ordinary conversation.

2. The detailed knowledge and the knowledge of detail shown by the ostensible communicators, again, of course in the most favourable instances.

3. The retailing of information which, if obtained telepathically from living persons (as, according to the super-ESP hypothesis, it must have been) could only have come from distant persons whose very existence was unknown to the medium, and who had almost certainly not been consciously thinking about the facts concerned at any recent or relevant time.

4. The retailing of information which, if obtained by ESP not involving deceased persons, must have been assembled and put together from several different sources, often including ones which would also fall under 3 above. The problem of how the medium might be supposed, on the super-ESP hypothesis, to locate such sources is (as I

pointed out in Chapters Four and Five) a very considerable one.

5.   The exhibition of intellectual skills and attainments not hitherto characteristic of the medium, but formerly characteristic of a person now dead, skills and characteristics which, on the super-ESP hypothesis, must have been temporarily caught from living persons by some sort of telepathic contagion.

6.   The realistic delineation, sometimes involving impersonation, of the personality characteristics, way of thought, turns of phrase, tone of voice, gestures, etc. of a deceased person; the ability to put on a personation of a given individual being a kind of skill which could not (I argued in Chapter Seven) be caught telepathically from living persons.

7.   Co-ordination of the ESP of several sensitives, so that while the productions of each are individually pointless, taken together they constitute a meaningful pattern (cf. Chapter Six).

Add to these considerations the fact that the mediums who, when purportedly contacting or transmitting messages from the dead, exhibit such unparalleled ESP, are commonly not by any means star subjects in ESP tests, and we would appear to have a formidable case against the super-ESP hypothesis as applied to the best mediumistic material. Nothing that we have so far learned about ESP licences us to claim that ESP can do the job which the super-ESP hypothesis requires of it.

The Evidence for Super-ESP

So can we decisively reject the super-ESP hypotheses? Alas, nothing in parapsychology is ever clear-cut or straightforward. I have omitted to mention two further factors which have a bearing on the issue. The first of these is the performances of certain sensitives who might loosely be described as fortune-tellers. The investigations most frequently cited are those of a French physician, E. Osty, Director from 1926 to 1938 of the Institut Metapsychique of Paris (116). Osty's sensitives, it is alleged, exhibited extrasensory powers amounting to what could justifiably be called 'super-ESP', and did so without any suggestion that the information originated from spirits. Hence, it is argued by Dodds and others, we have undeniable evidence that certain persons indeed possess super-ESP. Furthermore these persons cannot as a class be sharply distinguished from the class of mental mediums. 'Clairvoyant' mediums often talk very much like fortune-tellers, make predictions about their sitters' futures, diagnose their ailments, etc. In fact the guides of trance mediums often act in very much the same way, with respect to sitters and also with respect to other supposed inmates of the next world. It follows that the difference between fortune-tellers and mental mediums is not that the latter tap a source of information that the former do not, viz. deceased persons, but that the latter dramatize the deliverances of their super-ESP as messages from the departed. (Similar arguments have been advanced, e.g. by Andrew Lang (87b), in connection with the achievements of scryers or crystal gazers, but I shall neglect these since the cases appear to be much the same.)

What, then, were the performances of Osty's sensitives like? He seems to have found many such persons – France has a long tradition of them – and his custom was either to arrange sittings for persons known to him, and take notes himself, or else to hand the sensitive an object which has been worn or carried by the person about whom information was desired (Mrs Piper, like many mediums, sometimes made use of such 'token objects' or 'psychometric objects'). The objects seemed in some way to link the sensitive to the absent person but their use was not essential – it was usually sufficient if Osty merely thought of the 'target person' or handed the medium a photograph. I quote verbatim a sensitive's delineation of a certain Mme F., about whom Osty knew next to nothing, but of whom he was thinking (the omissions, represented by dots, are Osty's own):

> This is a woman with auburn hair, good-looking, decidedly good-looking. I think her frank and sincere, but she knows how to be otherwise on occasion. She is gay, amiable, sympathetic, rather depressed sometimes, and then exuberant . . . she is liable to these ups and downs, as if there were two natures in her.
>
> She had a strong will . . . although nervous, she can control herself. She is conscious of the North.
>
> She is fond of music, gaiety, but of work too. Her past has been cloudy, there are things in it that are not clear . . . I think she was illegitimate, there was some secret about her birth . . . some personage is concerned . . . could he have been her father? Her father seems to have been a well-known personage, an important person.
>
> There is a widow . . . her mother was a widow when her daughter was born. She was attended by a very few persons. It was a difficult birth; there was a doctor and a priest. Her mother had two other children. She was a light woman, had lovers . . . not worth much . . . is still coquettish and does not trouble herself to see her daughter.
>
> The poor child lived away from her mother. What changes and travels. I see her with a wicked woman. She must have gone abroad when quite

young . . . There is a woman near her who has been in prison. Oh! Thefts and imprisonment – what surroundings? She has been beaten and roughly treated. No worse people could be found than those among whom she grew up; they were capable of anything, would have made her a lost woman. Happily the child had an honest nature. She has wept much. Many changes from one town to another.

Her mother came back to her. They wrote to each other and met about her marriage. The mother will make a little revelation before she dies. The young woman is married now and very happy. Her husband is good and clever . . . he seems to be a chief over others . . . he wears a uniform and is much at sea – has travelled much and will travel more. (116, pp. 92–93)

To cut a long story short, a large part of the information given was confirmed by two of Mme F.'s close friends. But almost none of it was known to the sitter, Osty. We therefore have here a case in which a sensitive gives detailed, copious and correct information about a distant living person without anyone possessing that information being actually present. In one or two of Osty's cases, furthermore, correct information was given which was probably neither all known to any one distant person, nor contained in any written record, document, etc., which might be supposed accessible to clairvoyance. Extrasensory knowledge as extensive as that displayed by fairly good mediums is here being displayed in a non-mediumistic context. The super-ESP hypothesis, which looked in a poor way only a few paragraphs back, now begins to take on a healthier tinge – or at least it would do if Osty's work were above criticism.

Unfortunately Osty's standards of evidence and presentation (the two are hardly separable) leave a great deal to be desired. It is clear, for example, that the cases he actually gives are only a very limited selection from an indefinitely larger mass of material, much of which represented the errors and confabulations of his sensitives. Even his individual case reports are edited and heavily abridged, and we have no means of knowing what was left out. His verifications of his sensitives' statements are frequently by no means adequate – in the case I quoted, for instance, which is not untypical, the verification was at second-hand. The lady to whom the statements purportedly referred was not herself consulted. I think it is almost certain that were the whole of Osty's materials laid before us, the cases he quotes would appear less rather than more impressive. I could well understand the position of someone who argued that we should reject Osty's findings altogether.

None the less I cannot myself so comprehensively reject them. It would take an immense mass of erroneous material to outweigh Osty's more remarkable cases, and a great deal of misrecording and misverification to undermine them. They receive some support from comparable findings by others (e.g. Pagenstecher, 117; Prince, 125c, 125e). And they have some curious and fascinating features. Consider, for example, the case I have just quoted. Can one possibly attribute the 'hits' to telepathy? The sensitive gave (as often happened) a sort of conspectus or précis of the subject's life. One can hardly suppose that the subject herself was revolving such a précis in her mind and thus broadcasting it to the world. Nor can one plausibly suppose that the sensitive quickly scanned the memory-store of her distant subject and was immediately able to extract therefrom the series of general facts required – especially when one adds that in many cases this sort of conspectus was apparently continued into the future. Clairvoyance is not a possible explanation – it is not stated that the main facts of the subject's life were anywhere recorded in physical form. It seems to me that what we have here does not (in most instances) suggest a telepathic cognizing of the subject's memory-store; it suggests rather the direct acquisition (whatever that may mean) of propositional knowledge about the subject. If I understand Osty's somewhat vague remarks aright, this is the sort of conclusion towards which he too is driven. He points out that the visions and images which pass before the minds of his sensitives cannot be regarded as perceptions of distant persons, scenes, etc. They are often symbolic in form; and the same piece of information can present itself to the same sensitive in numerous different guises. It is as though what the sensitive grasps is on a conceptual level, a level of propositional or factual knowledge, which she then translates into the language of sensory imagery (cf. 162b; also 44d and 44e, pp. 617–618). I am not sure that this sort of knowledge-acquisition fits into the conventional categories of ESP at all. The knowledge is, one may note, knowledge primarily about people and thus differs markedly from the 'knowledge' which it is hoped that e.g. subjects in card-guessing experiments will display.

To return to my main theme: If (and it is a sizable 'if') we accept an appreciable percentage of Osty's findings, there can be little doubt that the super-ESP hypothesis must, so far as mediumistic material is concerned, appear a good deal more plausible. The gap between what mediums can do and what ESP (I call it ESP for lack of a better name) can achieve had been appreciably narrowed. How far it has been narrowed I shall enquire shortly.

I must emphasize at this point that I do *not* think Osty's findings make the super-ESP hypothesis more plausible so far as either the cases of apparitions discussed in later chapters of this book, or the reincarnation cases which will be discussed in Chapter Twelve below, are concerned. For Osty's sensitives were, if we accept his accounts, clearly persons with very unusual abilities; whereas there is much to suggest that both the percipients of veridical apparitions, and the 'reincarnated' personalities in the more striking reincarnation cases, are not on the whole especially endowed with such gifts.

I said a few pages ago that I had left out two factors from my preliminary assessment of the super-ESP hypothesis. The first of these was the performance of sensitives like those studied by Osty. I now come to the second, which is the evidence, such as it is, that mediums actually do incorporate in their representations of deceased persons information obtained by ESP directed upon persons or events in this world. I cited earlier some instances in which Mrs Piper had apparently done this; and there were similar happenings with Mrs Leonard. For instance one evening Mrs Salter heard in conversation a story about a man who wore several pairs of trousers simultaneously. The next day her father, the late Professor A. W. Verrall, communicated through Mrs Leonard and erroneously stated that *he* had once worn two pairs of trousers (138b, p. 320). (Some allowance must however be made in the assessment of such examples for chance; on how many occasions did sitters hear prior to sittings odd stories which were *not* retailed at the next sitting?) The late Dr S. G. Soal claimed to have telepathically foisted a fictitious communicator of his own invention upon Mrs Blanche Cooper, a well-known London medium. Soal would invent 'facts' about this control, 'John Ferguson', prior to a sitting; and these facts would often then be unambiguously communicated to him (147, pp. 523–548).

We have thus:

(a) apparent evidence that persons in many ways indistinguishable from mediums can exercise powers of ESP so marked that they might well be called super-ESP without there being the slightest suggestion that the information concerned is purveyed by spirits; and

(b) evidence that mediums may incorporate in their representations of deceased persons information acquired by telepathy with the living or by clairvoyance of the physical world.

Put (a) and (b) together, and you come up with the possibility that mediums may utilize super-ESP in their portrayals of communication from the dead. And indeed there is at least one case in which this apparently happened.

The case concerned, the 'Gordon Davis' case, is again one recorded by Soal during his sittings with Mrs Blanche Cooper (147, pp. 560–593). In outline it goes as follows. On 4 January 1922 a communicator calling himself 'Gordon Davis' began to speak in a clear and strong voice (Mrs Cooper was a direct voice medium). Gordon Davis was an old school acquaintance whom Soal believed had been killed in the First World War. The communicator did not state that he had been killed, but said, 'My poor wife is my only worry now – and kiddie.' He referred correctly and unmistakably to matters relating to their past acquaintance, and used forms of words characteristic of the real Gordon Davis. At two later sittings, Nada, a regular control of Mrs Cooper's, described in considerable detail certain external features of Gordon Davis's house, and made some quite specific references to the furniture, pictures and ornaments inside it. In 1925 Soal learned that Gordon Davis was still alive, and went to see him. He found that much of what Nada said about the house and its contents was correct; yet Davis, and his 'wife and kiddie', had not moved in until a year after the relevant sittings. Davis's diary showed that at the times of these sittings he had been interviewing clients (he was a house agent).

We seem to have here an instance of the construction of a mediumistic communicator by means of telepathy with the sitter plus *precognitive* telepathy or clairvoyance relating to a distant living person. 'Super-ESP' seems an appropriate term to describe what was going on; and if it could occur in this case, why not in others, indeed in all the others that have been presented as evidence for survival? For the Osty cases, and others like them, show that many persons besides Mrs Cooper can exercise super-ESP.

Do the considerations just advanced suffice to make the super-ESP hypothesis once again seem plausible, and to render the theory of overshadowing, with its survivalistic implications, unnecessary? I think that they do not altogether do so, for the following reasons:

1. Some weight must be allowed to the criticisms of Osty which I detailed above.

2. The performances of even Osty's best sensitives do not, I think,

quite measure up to the achievements of the most remarkable mediums in point of rapidity of information flow, and the level of detail conveyed. The Piper–Sutton sittings, with their mass of identifying detail, including names, will convey something of what I mean (see Chapter Three). Or again: Mrs Piper's Hodgson-control reminded a sitter of the *very words* the living Hodgson had once used in telling him a story.

3. Similar considerations apply with regard to the detailed delineation of personal characteristics, voice, gestures, mannerisms, turns of phrase, etc., and the presentation of a *tout ensemble* of these, in which some trance mediums have, as I pointed out in Chapter Seven, achieved an astonishing verisimilitude, a verisimilitude the attainment of which, I argued, is itself a skill of a kind not to be acquired by the mere gathering of information (whether by ESP or more ordinary means) about the person concerned.

4. More generally, Osty's sensitives give no sign of the paranormal acquisition of skills and attainments (see Chapter Seven above, and Chapters Eleven and Twelve below); rather the sensitives have so to speak their own specialist capacities (medical clairvoyance, depiction of intellectual states, etc.) which determine the type of material they can most successfully obtain.

5. Nor, in general, do Osty's sensitives so co-ordinate their individual deliverances concerning a particular individual or topic that separately those deliverances are meaningless, but together they add up. However to say this is not to say that they could not have done so; for, clearly, their activities were carried on in a context within which such 'cross-correspondences' were not called for.

6. The Gordon Davis case does not quite suffice to undermine some of the more striking mediumistic cases. For in the latter the medium must, according to the super-ESP hypothesis, have assembled the requisite information by telepathically tapping several different sources, none of whom was the alleged communicator. In the Gordon Davis case the principal source must have been Davis (the communicator) himself.

7. It is hard to avoid some degree of suspicion that Soal may have 'improved' the Gordon Davis case. There is now no doubt at all that he manipulated the results of his famous card-guessing experiments (99). The Gordon Davis case has remained for over fifty years without a real parallel, and certain features of it raise doubts – e.g. Soal's claim that he was able to record to medium's statements in detail in the dark using

only his left hand, and the fact that his brother signed a statement that he had read the communications, which took place in February 1922, in the Christmas vacation of 1921.

On balance, then, it seems to me that the super-ESP hypothesis cannot be justifiably extended to cover all the data which were set forth in Chapters Three to Seven above. In so far as the theory of overshadowing seems at present to be the most viable alternative to the super-ESP hypothesis, the former may perhaps draw strength, or at least comfort, from the latter's shortcomings. However, as I have several times emphasized, a theory cannot be adequately established just by undermining its only apparent rival. Its own pros and cons must, so far as possible, be independently scrutinized.

The Case for Overshadowing

It will be best to tackle the pros and cons of the theory of overshadowing in two parts. There is firstly the question of its survivalistic implications. If the theory is correct, somewhere 'behind' the trance and other utterances of certain mediums there sometimes lie the actual deceased persons who purport to be communicating. What evidence can we find telling against this idea, and what for it? Secondly there is the question of the nature of 'overshadowing', which, on the face of it, must be a form of telepathic interaction. Do we have any evidence that this sort of telepathic interaction can occur? I turn first to the theory's survivalistic implications.

   With one standard objection to the survivalistic interpretation of the phenomena of mental mediumship the theory of overshadowing can easily cope. I refer to the complaint so often made that the late so and so (a man of incisive mind and distinguished prose style) could not possibly be responsible for the reams of vapid rubbish he has allegedly written (or spoken) through the agency of such and such a medium or automatist. The obvious answer is that the rubbish comes from the medium; the flashes of knowledge and intelligence (if any) from the communicator. In general we would expect on the theory of overshadowing that the contents of automatic writings, trance utterances, etc., would be limited to matter within the medium's own grasp. For according to the theory of overshadowing, it is her intelligence, not that of the supposed overshadowing entity, that communicates directly with the sitters. One would expect that ideas outside the scope of her own conceptual equipment could be 'got

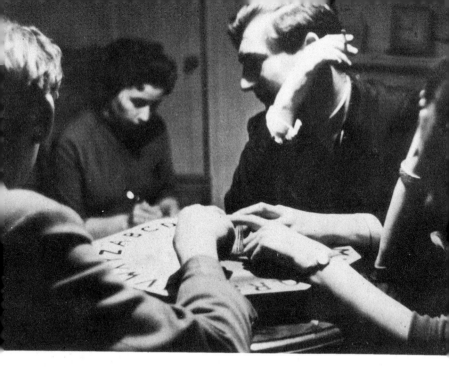

An ouija board sitting. The pointer spells out words letter by letter without conscious intervention by the sitters. (Courtesy of A.D. Cornell).

Mrs Leonora Piper (1857-1950) was the first mental medium to provide substantial evidence for paranormal faculties.

William James (1842-1910), the great American psychologist, was the first person to investigate Mrs Piper's mediumship.

Oliver Lodge (1851-1940) was one of Mrs Piper's sitters; he handed her a watch belonging to a dead uncle and received some appropriate communications.

Richard Hogdson (1855-1905) went to Boston from England to investigate Mrs Piper's mediumship, and after his death became one of her controls.

Mrs Gladys Osborne Leonard (1882-1968) conveyed information which could not have been known to her sitters, through book tests and proxy sittings.

Mrs M. de G. Verrall and below her daughter Helen, later Mrs Salter, were both automatists in the cross-correspondence writings. Mrs Salter also analysed some of Mrs Piper's and Mrs Leonard's communications. (Courtesy of the Mary Evans Picture Library and the S.P.R.)

'Mrs Willett' (Mrs Coombe-Tennant) supposedly received dictation from Dr Verrall and from Myers after their deaths. (Courtesy of John H. Cutten)

F.W.H. Myers (1843-1901) was a founder of the Society for Psychical Research, proposed a theory of apparitions, and was ostensibly one of the deceased people responsible for the cross-correspondences.

Automatic writing by Mrs Willett, supposedly from Myers.

Mrs Eleanor Sidgwick (1845-1936) analysed the material from
the cross-correspondences, and was herself President of the
Society for Psychical Research in 1908-9.

Sketch by Frederic L. Thompson, left with Professor Hyslop
and drawn while he felt he was 'overshadowed' by the
personality of the artist Robert Swain Gifford
(see Chapter 11).

Painting by Gifford (1840-1905) which shows a landscape
with gnarled, windblown trees.

through', if at all, only in a roundabout and circuitous way. Of this there are one or two apparent examples (see 5d; 18c, pp. 308-314).

The other standard objections to the survivalistic interpretation are of a more general kind, and will be discussed in Chapter Thirteen below.

What, then, can be said in favour of the theory of overshadowing in so far as that theory is one which implies survival? What positive indications can we glimpse that the 'overshadowing' is carried out by deceased persons hidden, as it were, from our view, but manifesting themselves through their influence upon a medium's dream life and dramatizing tendencies?

One must tread carefully here. The immediate temptation is to answer this question by citing sample cases in which mediumistic communicators have retailed copious and correct information about their lives on earth, information which the medium could not possibly have acquired by ordinary means. Do not such cases strongly suggest that the deceased persons themselves are somewhere in the background, directing and influencing the communications? The trouble with this line of argument is, of course, as follows. The proposed process of overshadowing, though its nature remains obscure, must be or involve or qualify as a form of telepathic interaction. Hence to the extent that overshadowing is alleged to occur we are invoking a form of ESP. And when the communicators are fluent and successful we are invoking fluent and successful ESP. But as soon as we do this, the theory of overshadowing is in danger of losing any advantages it may have over the super-ESP hypothesis. For if we are going to postulate fluent and successful ESP, why not let it be ESP involving only living persons (the ones who possess the information which confirms the medium's statements)?

Thus it is not so much to the quantity and detail of the material retailed by mediumistic communicators that we might look for indications of an overshadowing discarnate agent, as to the way in which that material is patterned and deployed. The question of the patterning and deployment of material in effect figured prominently among the issues with which, I suggested, the super-ESP hypothesis cannot adequately cope. It is over just these issues that the theory of overshadowing comes into its own. The super-ESP hypothesis has difficulty over cases in which it must assume that the medium integrated into her personation of one communicator information obtained by ESP directed upon a number of different living or contemporary sources (which must furthermore be located); the theory of overshadowing, of course, simply says that since the overshadowing agent already possesses all the information, the need for integration does not arise. The super-ESP hypothesis runs into trouble when communicators exhibit intellectual capacities and skills which the medium does not possess, for acquiring such capacities and skills does not consist simply in learning lists of facts of the kind to which ESP might be supposed to give one access: the theory of overshadowing says that the deceased agent is using his still surviving skill or capacity in directing the medium's activities (if, however, the skill is one, like a linguistic skill, involving a bodily element, the problem is more complex). The super-ESP hypothesis had problems with cases in which a medium's personation of a certain deceased person has been particularly lifelike and convincing, for there is an immense gap between accumulating factual knowledge about a certain deceased person and developing the skill of giving a realistic impersonation of him; the theory of overshadowing holds that the deceased person in question is himself 'behind' the medium's 'impersonation'. The super-ESP hypothesis has great difficulty in accounting for cases of the 'cross-correspondence' kind, in which different and separately meaningless parts of one meaningful communication appear in the productions of different mediums or sensitives; the theory of overshadowing can propose that the same intelligent agency overshadowed them all.

I have already discussed these issues in some detail in earlier parts of this book, and there is no point in elaborating them further now. The overall upshot is this. In certain cases over which the super-ESP hypothesis loses impetus and begins to flounder we can detect hints of the operation of what we may perhaps call 'overshadowing' agencies imposing characteristic, recognizable and appropriate patterns upon the fantasies and personations dreamed up by the medium and fed by her powers of ESP. The patterns are over, above, and beyond anything which can be plausibly accounted for by the medium's own ESP, even if we suppose her to possess unusual dramatic gifts. It therefore looks as though we have here what can reasonably be regarded as positive evidence in favour of the theory of overshadowing.

There are two further groups of cases, not easy to define, which I have not so far mentioned, that seem to me to provide further evidence of the same kind. The first is that of cases in which mediumistic communicators have given their sitters not exactly facts unknown to persons present or outside the knowledge of anyone at all, but what may be called insights into episodes in their own earthly lives, insights which once received can be seen to be valid, but which had not previously been thought of, still less written down, by anyone at all, and which the medium could therefore not have obtained by ESP. Consider the following remarks by Walter Franklin Prince (1863–1934), by far the ablest and most judicious American psychical researcher of his day, upon some sittings which he and his adopted daughter, Theodosia, had with Mrs 'Chenoweth' after the death of his wife.

> . . . It was the peculiar selective character of the details purporting to come from my wife and relating to her last weeks on earth which most impressed me when I realized it . . . in the alleged communications there is no hint of the features of the case which to us stood out so prominently, and in fact she never knew what her malady really was, she never realized that there was an open wound, and she expected, up to her last five minutes, to get better and return to her home. On the contrary, what we do find is a multitude of true little details, her back being rubbed, her head rubbed in a particular way, the trouble with her foot and knee, continuing sensations of hunger, the sensitiveness of her head when her hair was washed or combed, feeling that she would be all right again, trouble with her back towards the last, yet not being permitted to lie on her side, the chicken broth which Theodosia brought her, the trouble her 'store' teeth were to her, a sensation of fulness in the chest and of bad pain in the abdomen, pain stopping all at once (from the opiate), comforting visions of her relatives, sense of rebellion associated with death, etc. It came to me as I scanned this list that it was these details and others like them that had loomed large in my wife's sick mind . . . I, Theodosia, or both of us, knew all the above details, but some were wan and fading images in our minds, luridly overshadowed by the memories I have mentioned and others. (2, pp. 202–3)

The 'insight' in this case is into what might be described as the late Mrs Prince's whole point of view during the last few weeks of her life. The *facts* were known to Prince and his daughter, and probably to them alone, but the *point of view* was not fully appreciated by them. Yet it was the *point of view* that was communicated to them. It was as though the medium's selection and presentation of the facts (facts *perhaps* accessible to her ESP) was shaped and directed by an external overshadowing presence. Prince goes on:

> Nothing that we know or think we know of telepathy would lead us to suppose that it acts otherwise than after the analogy of a mechanical force, gives ground to suppose that it dramatizes, intelligently adopts the

viewpoint of a third person, and selects to suit the characteristics of that person. It appears as though there were the stamp of Mrs Prince's mind upon the details alleged in the text to be connected with her.

The second group of cases is even more difficult to define than the first, yet it contains cases that can be individually and collectively quite impressive. 'Cases' is, however, perhaps the wrong word. What I have in mind are the somewhat numerous small incidents occurring in the course of successful sittings, in which 'communication' seems to encounter a blockage which the communicating intelligence tries by various stratagems to circumvent. Here is an example from an interesting paper by W. F. Prince (a paper in which he is weighing up considerations for and against the super-ESP hypothesis).

Theodosia Prince's mother, controlling Mrs 'Chenoweth', was trying to remind her daughter of a visit to a neighbour's to see a calf (colloquially a 'Bossy'). What came next was (roughly) as follows: 'We went to a neighbour's to see a pet Bunny – pause – pet Bunny BB Bunny – pause – No, it was a pet Bunny BB Bunny B – long pause – (medium moans) Milk – a small cow Bossy.' As Prince remarks:

> Who can doubt that someone or something intended 'Bossy' . . . from the first? Else why did the communicator stop at Bunny every time and begin again, express dissatisfaction, pause as though pondering what was the matter or how to remedy it, experience emotion which extorted moans from the medium, and finally say 'small cow' as though to avoid the word beginning with B? If two minds were engaged in the process, the second receiving from the first, we can see how this second, call it the 'control' or the medium's subsconscious, would, when the 'pet B—' was reached, conceive the picture of a rabbit and cling to the preference for some time despite the efforts of the first mind to dislodge it. (125d, pp. 108–109.)

To explain such incidents in terms of the super-ESP theory we would, I think, have to postulate that the medium was at some level all the time aware of what she wished to communicate, and chose to 'put it through' in this oblique fashion in order to heighten the impression that an external intelligence was indeed present and active in the business. But this is to attribute to the medium not just super-ESP but fantastic skill and subtlety as an impersonator and dramatist, an extra assumption which should clearly be avoided if possible. There is no doubt, as Prince in effect remarks, that an interpretation in terms of the overshadowing hypothesis is far more straightforward and natural.

*   *   *

I turn now to the 'overshadowing' aspect of the theory of overshadowing. The proposed process of 'overshadowing', whatever its precise nature, falls under the general heading of telepathy; and it is a kind of telepathy in which the *active endeavours* of the overshadowing person must play a decisive role in determining the mental processes of the overshadowed person. Without doubt considerable difficulties confront these notions.

The most obvious one is that, as I pointed out before, we have only a little experimental evidence to support the idea that active 'sending' by a telepathic agent makes receipt of the message any more likely. Of course not many relevant experiments have been done; but it must also be remembered that Dr Louisa Rhine's studies of spontaneous cases have (as I said before) led her to a similar (though disputed) conclusion.

Communications from the Living

Of relevance in this connection are the various supposed cases of mediumistic communication from the living. This is a topic which seems to me to be potentially of great interest and importance, and one that has been commonly neglected by English and American parapsychologists. A number of ostensible cases of such communications are scattered through the literature, but only a few attempts have been made to collect them together and analyse them (e.g. 14; 27). For example, Sir Lawrence Jones tells us (76, p. 34) that his youngest daughter, aged nine, alive but asleep, several times purported to communicate from a distance through the automatic writing of Miss Kate Wingfield. On the first occasion she was asked, 'What about the sailor frock?' Those present knew that there was a plan to buy her one but nothing of the outcome. The answer came, 'We went to a shop. Mummie just said, "You get those things out. That is her tallness." And they got them; nothing else to be done, no cutting. They just sent them home. That's what I like.' This turned out to be correct.

The trouble with this case, as with a good many others, is that if there was a deliberate attempt by the 'agent' to send or 'overshadow', we know nothing of it – she was asleep at the time. Furthermore a clairvoyant explanation can hardly be ruled out.

The nearest we can get among cases of 'communications from the living' to a case of overshadowing is perhaps one reported in the *Journal of the SPR* in 1923 by a Dutch member of the Society, Dr J. V. Suringar (155). In this case a Dutch boy of fifteen, who desired to attend a home circle in a neighbouring house, but was not allowed to, apparently spelled through the ouija board operated in the circle substantial parts of a short poem in English which he had passed the time in reading. While the poem was actually communicated, he was dozing. The communication thus did not, so far as one can tell, represent a conscious 'overshadowing'; but the boy's thoughts had been very much oriented upon the sitters and the seance.

In a substantial proportion, though by no means all, of the cases, the purported communicator has been asleep, in a state of dissociation, in a coma, or dying (see, for instance, 157b, pp. 130–131). (In at least one very curious case the ostensible communicator was an elderly lady in an advanced state of senile dementia, which would usually involve extensive degeneration of brain cells. The 'communications', though disjointed, were rational [142].) Some, like Bozzano, have seen in this fact an indication that some part of the communicator's personality 'projects' as in 'astral travelling', and influences the medium directly. Be that as it may, the sad fact is that none of these living communicators was afterwards able to give an account of their endeavours and experiences; so we have little information bearing upon the question of whether or not they could have been deliberately attempting to overshadow the mediums. And, as I said before, there remains the alternative possibility that the medium got her information by her own active ESP, that is by thought-reading or by clairvoyance.

All in all there is at the moment little evidence in favour of overshadowing or agent-active telepathy: this may well, however, be due to the small amount of work done and the difficulty of designing conclusive experiments. It seems to me that studies of attempted communication by the living would be well worth undertaking, and would combine well with the recent growing interest in out-of-the-body experiences. Positive results would lend plausibility to the theory of overshadowing; negative results would weaken it; while certain kinds of results might altogether undermine the survivalist interpretation of mediumistic phenomena – for example if a medium proved able to build up a fictitious communicator from fragments each one of which was in the mind of a different living person. Such results would also reflect back upon the question raised in Chapters Six and Seven, of Mrs Verrall's possible role in bringing about certain of the cross-correspondences and literary puzzles.

A second difficulty which confronts the notion of overshadowing (where overshadowing is regarded as a form of telepathic interaction) is this. In the most impressive cases of trance mediumship veridical communications from the supposedly overshadowing communicators can come with considerable fluency and can convey quite detailed veridical information. The 'fluency' and detail have few if any parallels in the literature of spontaneous and experimental ESP. The telepathy concerned does not (I argued above) have all the characteristics of 'super-ESP' but it is still pretty powerful stuff. It seems inevitable, therefore, that we shall have to add to the theory of overshadowing a postulate to the effect that after one's death one's capacities for telepathically sending or overshadowing, and also for receiving by ESP what may be called the 'return' messages, are greatly enhanced. The most remarkable cases of trance mediumship illustrate what may happen when a telepathic agent, with his powers thus emancipated, works upon a gifted psychic – one, say, at least as remarkable as the best of Osty's sensitives – who adds to these essential gifts the psychological quirk, whatever it may be (a tendency to dissociation, perhaps, or a liability to sink into unstructured reverie), which makes her in addition highly responsive to suggestions conveyed by or implicit in the telepathic influences playing upon her. The proposal that death can unleash a latent power to 'overshadow' may appear wholly fantastic. But it seems to me that any survivalistic interpretation of the phenomena of trance mediumship is bound to involve itself in suppositions about the liberating effect which death may have upon the decedent's powers of ESP. For:

(a)   persons who have in life shown no special gifts of telepathy (either as sender or receiver) seem to have made after death excellent mediumistic controls and communicators.

(b)   Should there be any form of survival of bodily death, we can say for sure that we shall no longer possess our present sense organs. If our post-mortem state is not one of total isolation, locked in the prison of our own dreams and memories, if we can sometimes communicate with friends and relatives on earth, or with other deceased persons, that communication will by definition come under the heading of ESP.

In sum: In Chapter Eight I posed the question of whether or not the 'controls' of trance mediums can indeed sometimes be the deceased persons with whom they claim identity, possessing and operating the medium's nervous machinery much as she does herself. The evidence, I concluded, suggests that they cannot be regarded in this light. They are most probably just phases or aspects of the medium's own personality. However it is possible that these phases of the medium's mental life, in addition to favouring the exercise of 'ordinary' ESP, may sometimes be directed or 'overshadowed' by the deceased persons whom they so to speak represent. There are features of not a few cases upon which it would be very easy to put such an interpretation. Certainly the super-ESP theory, the theory that mediums in all instances simply put on the show by means of their dramatic gifts and powers of ESP, appears for reasons which I detailed most implausible. On the other hand I could not find much evidence for the kind of active-agent telepathy that might be involved in the supposed process of overshadowing, so that overall I feel a good deal more convinced of the shortcomings of the super-ESP hypothesis than I do of the tenability of the theory of overshadowing.

If further investigations fail to yield evidence for such active-agent telepathy we might perhaps instead explore the possibility that a deceased person may sometimes gain some degree of direct control over the medium's neuromuscular apparatus; a control, however, that never fully displaces that of the medium, who continually influences the conjoint output. A theory of this kind was occasionally put forward by Mrs Leonard's controls (18c, pp. 261–286; 157c; 157i). However I do not at the moment find it plausible; for why should the medium's influence so often intervene and override the control's just when the latter is going to exhibit literary and philosophical information greatly exceeding the medium's? And why should it intervene to force the control to appear to give a blessing and a certificate of genuineness to perfectly preposterous 'controls' who can be nothing other than fictions dreamed up by the medium? I shall not attempt to supply answers to these questions, but they bring us conveniently to the topic of the next chapter, viz. ostensible examples of obsessions and possession.

11 Obsession and Possession

I argued in Chapter Eight that the claims so frequently made by the controls of mediums to operate the medium's neuromuscular apparatus directly, much as ordinarily she does herself, cannot (at least in the great majority of cases) be taken at face value. Mediums as it were play at being possessed. I do not mean that they are not in earnest, or that they are conscious deceivers. I mean simply that the whole drama of communication and control, though it may sometimes serve as a vehicle for paranormally acquired information, is a fiction spun from who knows what strange threads within the deeps of the hidden self. Is there ever a reality corresponding to that which the mediumistic trance merely simulates, a possession that is not just play-acting?

In recent years possession, whether considered as a variety of mental illness or as a mode of diabolic mischief-making, has undergone a curious revival – one that, could they know about it, would have saddened and astonished forward-thinking Victorian agnostics. We even have, once again, clergymen who are virtually specialists in exorcism. The form of possession which they have principally to combat, or rather perhaps the form which most often makes headlines, is the diabolic, but cases of ostensible possession by deceased human beings also crop up. Very fortunately it is only the latter which we need, for present purposes, to consider.

Closely related to cases of ostensible possession, and in practice not easy to separate from them, are cases of ostensible obsession. In cases of possession the supposed intruding entity displaces or partly displaces the victim from his body, and obtains direct control of it – the same sort of control, presumably, as the victim himself had. (It will be understood here that I am talking about the 'externals' of the phenomena, not speculating as to their underlying cause.) In cases of obsession, the victim remains in immediate control of his body, but the supposed intruding entity influences his mind. It establishes a sort of parasitic relationship with his mind, whereby it can to an extent see what he sees, feel what he feels, enjoy what he enjoys, etc., and can also change the course of his thoughts and actions to conform with its own desires. The process is commonly, but very vaguely, looked upon as one of reciprocal telepathy. The victim may have a feeling of being 'overshadowed' by another personality, and some writers have seen in obsession a possible explanation for various forms of mental disturbance, including phobias, morbid cravings, sexual perversions, sudden changes of character, paranoid delusions, aggressive outbursts and hallucinations.

Cases both of ostensible possession and of ostensible obsession crop up from time to time in the annals of both Spiritualism and psychical research. Particularly popular with Spiritualists have been the series of cases reported in detail by Dr Carl Wickland of Chicago in his well-known book *Thirty Years among the Dead* (1924). Wickland believed that many cases of mental illness were due to obsession by earth-bound spirits of deceased persons. His method of tackling these cases was to induce the obsessing spirits, if necessary by electric shocks, to leave the victim's body, to enter the body of a medium (to wit Mrs Wickland), and thence finally dislodge them by persuasion, objurgation and the help of spirit guides. Dr Wickland possessed an assertive personality, a commanding voice, and an electric shock machine of terrifying dimensions. His treatment seems often to have been highly effective. Unfortunately he showed insufficient interest in the mundane business of checking out the communicator's statements about themselves. In the great majority of cases he seems simply to have assumed that because the treatment worked, its rationale was fundamentally correct – the psychotherapist's classic error. His copious records provide little solid evidence to support his theories.

None the less one here and there comes across cases of ostensible obsession that are of some parapsychological interest. For instance, some curious examples were reported to the First International Congress of Psychical Research, held at Copenhagen in 1921, by Dr E. Magnin of Geneva (96). Magnin gives, among others, the case of Madame M., aged 52, who suffered from a tendency to undergo spasmodic and violent falls. Her malady had resisted the efforts of four doctors. It chanced that one afternoon, in Magnin's waiting room, this lady encountered a clairvoyant medium whom she had never met before. The clairvoyant afterwards told Magnin that she had seen near Madame M. an authoritarian, brutal and wicked man. Magnin brought the ladies together, and the medium, in trance, was controlled by the purported spirit of the man she had just seen. He claimed to be Madame M.'s father, called her 'Louise', spoke of a quarrel immediately prior to his death (a quarrel brought about by his refusal to put on an overcoat before going out). The father mentioned 'Maurice' (his son-in-law), and 'René' (his grandson). Finally he was brought to a penitent frame of mind, and agreed to leave his daughter. The names and facts given, though unknown to Magnin, were correct. When the medium awoke she gave an accurate description of the old gentleman and of the overcoat which had precipitated the quarrel (and hence the old man's death), and she gave the date of his death as 17 December 1913. The actual date was 19 December 1913. Madame M.'s symptoms disappeared.

The Thompson-Gifford Case

The most voluminously documented, and probably the most extraordinary, of all the obsession cases which have been subjected to serious investigation is that generally known as the Thompson–Gifford case. The principal investigator, Professor J. H. Hyslop (1854–1920), formerly professor of logic and ethics at Columbia University, was secretary and executive head of the ASPR, which he had in effect re-founded in 1907. A dedicated believer in survival, he was none the less a stickler for the recording and publication of all possible details of seances, case investigations, etc., and his report on the Thompson-Gifford case occupies 469 pages of the *Proceedings of the ASPR* for the year 1909 (71a; cf. 71c, pp. 203–230). As a result of his investigations, he became convinced that certain symptoms of apparent mental disturbance may sometimes be due to the influence of obsessing spirits. He subsequently came upon further cases which he thought supported this view, and investigated them by the methods he had tried out in the Thompson–Gifford case. These methods involved consulting several different mediums, sometimes with and sometimes without the presence of the obsessed person. Each of the mediums would clairvoyantly 'see' the obsessing entities, be themselves controlled by them, etc. If the statements made by or through the various mediums agreed with each other, and with the patient's symptoms, Hyslop would diagnose a true obsession, and might instigate a cure on this assumption.

After Hyslop's death, his procedures were taken up by a colleague, Dr Titus Bull, a neurologist practising in New York (86a; 86b). It seems that Bull eventually took the further step of dispensing altogether with any direct contact between patient and medium (134). He would act in effect as a proxy sitter on behalf of the obsessed person. Now if under these conditions:

(a) obsessing entities communicated and gave correct information about themselves.

(b) unknown to the patient these entities were talked or cajoled into quitting; and

(c) the patient thereupon recovered,

we would have a case presenting severe and obvious difficulties for the super-ESP hypothesis.

I do not know whether any of Bull's cases met these criteria. The records which have been published relate mainly to the earlier period. He seems to have had, like Wickland, a good success rate. Unfortunately, and also like Wickland, he tended to accept the mere fact of cure as supporting his theory. He did not go out of his way to verify the communicators' statements about themselves.

To return to the Thompson–Gifford case: The 'obsessed' person here was Frederic L. Thompson, aged 36 at the beginning of the events concerned. Thompson was a goldsmith by profession, and had occasionally exhibited some slight talent for sketching. During the summer and autumn of 1905 he was frequently seized with impulses to sketch and paint in oils. While painting he often felt, and remarked to his wife (she confirmed it), that he was an artist named Robert Swain Gifford (1840–1905), whom he had met briefly a few times, but of whose work he knew virtually nothing.

In January 1906 he went to an exhibition of Gifford's work, and there learned for the first time that Gifford had died a year previously. While looking at one of the pictures he heard a voice say, 'You see what I have done. Can you not take up and finish my work?' After this episode, the urge to paint became stronger, and he began to have frequent visual and auditory hallucinations. He painted some of these visions, and sold two or three of the resultant pictures (their resemblance to Gifford's work was commented upon). The visions were especially of landscapes with windblown trees; and one particular scene – of gnarled oaks on a promontory by raging seas – continually haunted him. He did several sketches of it, and a painting, which he called 'The Battle of the Elements'.

The paintings were done in states of mind which ranged from slight dissociation to more or less complete automatism. Thompson had always been dreamy and prone to reverie. Now he became incapable of attending properly to his work, and his financial position deteriorated. He began to fear he was becoming insane, and on 16 January 1907 called on Hyslop, to whom a mutual acquaintance had recommended he go.

Hyslop was at first inclined to think him mentally disturbed, but decided that it might be interesting to check out the Gifford connection by taking him to a medium. Accordingly he took him on 18 January to visit a non-professional clairvoyant medium, Mrs 'Rathbun'. Mrs Rathbun spoke of a man behind him who was fond of painting, and described this man in terms not incompatible with Gifford. Thompson told her that he was trying to find a certain scene of oak trees by the sea. She described a group of oak trees with fallen branches, and said it was a place near the sea, to which one had to go by boat.

Thompson was encouraged by this sitting to believe that he was not insane and carried on sketching and painting his visions. Meanwhile Hyslop took him to various other mediums (always incognito). The most interesting sitting in this period was one with the trance medium Mrs 'Chenoweth' (Mrs Soule) on 16 March 1907. Full stenographic records were made of what her control said (she also wrote occasionally). Much 'came through' at this sitting to identify Gifford. His characteristic clothes and mannerisms, his fondness for rugs, his love of hills and the ocean and of red and brown leaves, the oil skins he wore when boating and painting, his liking for misty scenes, and the unfinished canvases in his studio, were all unmistakably referred to. Many of the statements made were confirmed by Mrs Gifford. Gifford was represented as saying, 'I will help you, because I want someone who can catch the inspiration of these things as I did, to carry on my work.'

Thompson soon afterwards decided that he would set forth to try to locate the actual scenes of his visions, keeping a day by day diary of his endeavours. On 2 July 1907, before departing, he gave Hyslop a number of the sketches which he had done under the 'Gifford' influence in the summer and autumn of 1905. He went first to Nonquitt, Massachusetts, where Gifford had had his summer home, expecting to locate the scenes in that neighbourhood. He learned here (Mrs Gifford allowed him to see her late husband's studio) that more likely settings were various of the Elizabeth Islands, off Buzzard's Bay, Massachusetts, and especially Naushon Island, on which Gifford had been born. He thereupon set off for these islands. The result of his tour may be summarized as follows:

1. Thompson discovered set up on an easel in Gifford's studio a painting that corresponded in close and unmistakable detail with a sketch of his own, made from a vision, a sketch which was among those he had left behind with Hyslop. Hyslop prints photographs of both in his paper, together with a letter from Mrs Thompson which makes it clear that Thompson could not have seen the painting on any previous occasion. Later on Thompson found the original scene on Nashawena Island, and painted it himself.

Also in Gifford's studio were two other pictures which Hyslop describes as 'identical' with sketches previously made by Thompson, sketches, however, which were not among those deposited with Hyslop. The photographs of the Gifford pictures reproduced as Hyslop's figure XIX are so small and so poor that one cannot properly assess the similarity for oneself.

2. Thompson found actual scenes corresponding to several of the sketches he had left with Hyslop. He photographed these scenes. The photographs (as reproduced by Hyslop) are not of good quality, and some outlines have been inked in. In one instance – that of a group of trees near Nonquitt – the resemblance between the conformation of the trees in the sketch and in the photograph is exceedingly close. In other cases, however, the resemblance is much less close, and I should hesitate to put reliance on it; though it must be said that from all accounts similarities of colouring between sketch and scene, which cannot of course be assessed from a black and white photograph, may have been impressive.

3. Thompson also located, or believed that he had located, other scenes from his visions. He felt that he was led or guided to them. While examining and sketching such a scene, a group of trees on Naushon Island, he heard a voice tell him to look on the other side of the trees. He did so, and found Gifford's initials carved there, with the year 1902. Hyslop later examined the carving (it was not recent) and photographed it.

4. On the same island Thompson located and painted the group of gnarled oaks on a promontory by the seas, the group his earlier pictures of which was termed 'The Battle of the Elements'. An early sketch of this had been left with Hyslop. The painting from the vision and the painting from the reality resemble each other closely. Thompson went back to the island with Hyslop and, after much difficulty, relocated the spot. Hyslop took some photographs which clearly show relevant details of the twisted and fallen branches. Unfortunately he was not

able to take photographs showing the whole of that side of the promontory which is represented in the paintings, but had instead to take close-up shots of the oaks from another angle. Thus the undoubted correspondences between the actual scene and the visionary sketches have to be worked out rather than being instantly obvious to the eye.

It must be pointed out at this juncture that as a lad Thompson had lived for a couple of years in New Bedford, which is within striking distance of the Elizabeth Islands. He maintained (and there was never any serious reason to question his veracity on this or any other aspect of the case) that he had never visited the islands; and the truth of this assertion was attested by his mother, his sister and his wife.

Hyslop decided that in the light of these new, and exceedingly curious developments, he and Thompson (the latter incognito as usual) should have some further sittings, and in April 1908 he once again began to do the rounds of the mediums. Unfortunately they obtained nothing of interest prior to the middle of May, at which point garbled versions of the stories leaked into the press, and could have been picked up and acted upon by the mediums concerned. Still, a lot of material 'came through' which could hardly have been the result of clandestine enquiries. At sittings in June Mrs Chenoweth's controls gave quite a number of small but correct details about Gifford. Mention was made of (for instance) his habit of holding something 'like a cigarette' (a little stick) in his mouth while painting; of the fact that he had illustrated poetry; of his two studios, town and country (identifying details of the latter were given); of his old-fashioned furniture and rush-bottomed chairs; of a bureau with outward-spreading legs; of his habit of keeping large quantities of his old brushes to paint rocks and rough things; of a scene which he had painted near his home; of a white lighthouse there with a steady (i.e. not revolving) light; and of the fact that he had lost a child and tried to put its face into pictures.

At the sitting of 5 June 1908, Gifford himself purported to control Mrs Chenoweth, and asked if Thompson remembered an incident when he had stood on a bridge, and looking down into the water saw there pictures like reflections, which had inspired him with a great desire to paint. Thompson had in fact had such an experience while standing on a bridge on Naushon Island. Gifford again ostensibly controlled, and showed a knowledge of Thompson's hallucinations, at a sitting on 9 December 1908 with another trance medium, Mrs 'Smead'. The purported Gifford wrote 'ocean yes yes yes', drew what looked like a pile of rocks surmounted by a cross, and then wrote 'my name is on it, my name is on it'. Over a month before the sitting, Thompson had come across such a cross beside the sea – it formed part of the wreckage of a ship – and had seen on it Gifford's initials, R. S. G. When he approached the wreck, the initials faded. He was, however, so impressed, that he painted the scene, and described the incident in a letter to his wife, which was in Hyslop's hands *before* the sitting of 9 December. None of the mediums, incidentally, ever gave Gifford's full name, but Mrs Smead produced his initials, first as R. G. S. and then as R. S. G.

It does not seem to me that either the theory of fraud or the theory of chance coincidence can usefully be applied to the Thompson–Gifford case, whether we think just of Thompson's visions, or of the whole complex of other phenomena (the paintings, the mediumistic sittings, etc.) associated with them. Two sorts of accounts of Thompson's visions might be given from the point of view of the super-ESP hypothesis. The first would require us to suppose that, for some appreciable time prior to Gifford's death, Thompson had been in close and frequent (but unconscious) extrasensory contact with him (it will be recalled that the two had met), and had stored up for subsequent use the manifold images thus obtained. Now there is something to suggest that in certain cases of spontaneous ESP there may have been a delay of a few hours between the receipt of an extrasensory impression and its emergence into consciousness. But I know of no case which involves anything like the length of delay and the number of impressions which one finds in the Thompson–Gifford case. I think therefore that one should reject this version of the super-ESP hypothesis.

The second possible version of the super-ESP hypothesis would be the more orthodox one which would postulate that Thompson acquired clairvoyant knowledge of the canvases still in Gifford's studio, learned telepathically (perhaps from Mrs Gifford) of Gifford's favourite hunting grounds, clairvoyantly investigated them, and selected from them, as the themes of recurrent visions, the sort of spots which might appeal to a painter. The only thing I can say in favour of this fantastic hypothesis (for which the annals of ESP provide no parallel) is that it may be less fantastic than its chief competitor, the survival theory. This does not seem to me a sufficient reason for accepting it.

As soon as we pass on to consider other aspects of the case, both forms of the super-ESP hypothesis run upon further difficulties. There is firstly the problem of the style and technique of the paintings. This is perhaps the least serious of the problems. The resemblance of subject-matter between Thompson's paintings and Gifford's was obvious to anyone. As to whether or not there was an underlying similarity of style and technique, expert opinions differed, and it is perhaps safer to say that few experts could believe that the Thompson paintings were the work of a man who had only been painting a short time and had had virtually no formal training. Yet there could be little doubt that this was so. It was clear, however, that Thompson had always had a talent for sketching, and we can hardly define the limits of the possible in respect of a sudden artistic flowering.

A more serious problem is that of motive. Thompson's finances suffered severely because of his overpowering urge to sketch and paint, and he was a married man. No such overpowering urge had previously crossed the threshold of his consciousness. We could say that it had lain simmering in his unconscious for years prior to the death of Gifford, and that the death (of which Thompson remained unaware for a year) had been picked up and unconsciously utilized as an excuse for letting it out. But these proposals about happenings in the unconscious mind are as unverifiable as stories about the other side of nowhere, and seem to me just the sort of barren speculations with which, I argued in Chapter One, we should try to avoid becoming entangled.

Further vistas of complexity unfold if we take into account the statements made by the various mediums. Although several of the sittings were tedious and unsuccessful, it certainly seems to me that at others correct information about Gifford came through, information not infrequently unknown to either of the sitters. Knowledge was also shown of the contents of Thompson's visions. The mediums must, it seems, have telepathically picked the thought of Gifford from Thompson's mind, and then have telepathically and clairvoyantly located other sources of information about him.

There is no doubt that the super-ESP hypothesis, applied to this case (as to others) is *messy* in a way not to be equated with mere complexity. If the survivalist theory were tenable it would immensely simplify things. The trouble with the survivalist theory is not exactly messiness, but rather conflict with other areas of our knowledge, and an underlying vagueness upon certain crucial issues.

Suppose that, purely for the sake of argument, we were to accept a survivalist interpretation of the Thompson–Gifford case. The obvious question would then arise, what sort of relationship might be supposed to exist between the obsessing entity (the deceased Gifford), and his willing victim, Thompson? Thompson's mental state while under the Gifford influence varied from dreaminess and mild dissociation (to which he was in any case liable) to a fairly complete automatism with (probably) a good deal of amnesia, not however quite amounting to a trance. I have seen not a few mediums in what I should guess were states from the same range. It might be proposed, for the sorts of reasons mentioned in previous chapters, that extrasensory influences most readily well up into consciousness or into action when the subject is in a dreamlike and dissociated state of mind, and it might also be proposed (though this is a considerably disputed point) that in some people such a state may be accompanied by a heightened responsiveness to suggestion. Combine these notions with that of reciprocal telepathy between the medium and the discarnate entity – one might suppose that the medium simply picks up whatever the discarnate entity clearly imagines, or one might assign the latter a more active role of somehow injecting material into the former's dream – and we arrive again at a view of the process of communication very like the theory of 'overshadowing' which I outlined in earlier chapters. And it is very easy to see how this theory might be applied in the Thompson–Gifford case – provided always (and it is a big proviso) that we can arrive at a concept of telepathy which will fill the bill. The only difference between the Thompson–Gifford case and many cases of mental mediumship would be first that Thompson was influenced only by one discarnate entity, and second that the influence manifested itself both in sensory hallucination and in motor automatism. If we look upon the Thompson–Gifford case in these terms, there is no question of its being an example of true possession – of the direct control of a living person's neuromuscular apparatus by a discarnate person.

Possession

Are there any cases at all which even suggest a 'true' possession? A case which is often cited as being at any rate a contender is that of Lurancy Vennum, the 'Watseka Wonder'. This case is described in a very rare pamphlet by E. W. Stevens (152), the doctor who was in charge of this young lady. The pamphlet was abridged and excerpted by F. W. H. Myers, who also added details obtained by Richard Hodgson from interviews with some of the principal participants (110a, I, pp. 360–370). I shall draw upon the abridgment in my account of the case.

Lurancy Vennum was born on 16 April 1864, at a place about seven miles from Watseka, Illinois. Her family moved to Watseka on 1 April 1871. They took a house about two hundred yards from that of a Mr A. B. Roff and his family. The two families developed only a formal and distant acquaintance. About the autumn of 1871, the Vennum family moved away from the vicinity of the Roffs, and never again lived nearer to them than the 'extreme opposite limits of the city'.

In July 1877, Lurancy began to have fits or trances. It was generally thought that she had become insane. Mr Roff, whose deceased daughter Mary Roff, had had periods of insanity, persuaded Mr Vennum to let him bring Dr E. W. Stevens to see her. Dr Stevens and Mr Roff visited Lurancy on 31 January 1878.

It appears that various deceased persons now purported to control Lurancy and to speak through her. After being hypnotized by Dr Stevens, she stated that one Mary Roff wished to come. Mr Roff said, 'Yes, let her come, we'll be glad to have her come.' Next morning the girl began to claim to be Mary Roff, who had died, aged eighteen, in July 1865, when Lurancy was just over a year old.

About a week later, Mrs A. B. Roff, and her daughter, Mrs Minerva Alter, Mary's sister, hearing of the remarkable change, went to see the girl. As they came in sight . . . Mary [i.e. Lurancy 'controlled' by Mary Roff] looking out of the window, exclaimed exultingly, 'There comes my ma and sister Nervie!' – the name by which Mary used to call Mrs Alter in girlhood. As they came into the house she caught them around their necks, wept and cried for joy, and seemed so happy to meet them. From this time on she seemed more homesick than before. At times she seemed almost frantic to go home.

On the 11th day of February, 1878, they sent the girl to Mr Roff's, where she met her 'pa and ma', and each member of the family, with the most gratifying expressions of love and affection . . . On being asked how long she would stay, she said, 'The angels will let me stay till some time in May'; and she made it her home there till May 21st, three months and ten days, a happy, contented daughter and sister in a borrowed body.

The girl now in her new home seemed perfectly happy and content, knowing every person and everything that Mary knew when in her original body, . . . recognizing and calling by name those who were friends and neighbours of the family from 1852 to 1865 . . . calling attention to scores, yes, hundreds of incidents that transpired during her natural life. During all the period of her sojourn at Mr Roff's she had no knowledge of, and did not recognize, any of Mr Vennum's family.

One evening, in the latter part of March, Mr Roff was sitting in the room waiting for tea, and reading the paper, 'Mary' being out in the yard. He asked Mrs Roff if she could find a certain velvet head-dress that Mary used to wear the last year before she died. If so to lay it on the stand and say nothing about it, to see if Mary would recognize it. Mrs Roff readily found and laid it on the stand. The girl soon came in, and immediately exclaimed as she approached the stand, 'Oh, there is my head-dress I wore when my hair was short!' She then asked, 'Ma, where is my box of letters? Have you got them yet?' Mrs Roff replied, 'Yes, Mary, I have some of them.' She at once got the box with many letters in it. As Mary began to examine them she said, 'Oh, ma, here is a collar I tatted! Ma, why did you not show to me my letters and things before?' The collar had been preserved among the relics of the lamented child as one of the beautiful things her fingers had wrought before Lurancy was born; and so Mary continually recognized every little thing and remembered every little incident of her girlhood.

. . . Mr Roff asked Mary if she remembered moving to Texas [in 1857] or anything about it. 'Yes, pa, and I remember crossing Red River and of seeing a great many Indians, and I remember Mrs Reeder's girls, who were in our company.' And thus she from time to time made first mention of things that transpired thirteen to twenty-five years ago . . .

After a few brief reappearances, the Lurancy personality returned completely on 21 May 1878, and remained in control thereafter, apart from brief interventions from Mary when Lurancy visited the Roffs. Lurancy's health remained good, and there was no return of the fits.

The simplest explanation of this very curious case is clearly that of impersonation, deliberate or hysterical. Lurancy, it might be suggested, though not living close to the Roffs, might have picked up gossip about them. After she went to live with them she would have had all sorts of opportunities of picking up trivial bits of information. We have no verbatim reports of her conversations with the Roffs, reports in which the hints, leading questions, etc., which probably helped her, could be detected, and from which the numerous mistakes which she probably made could be disinterred instead of left buried and forgotten. All this is very true, and perfectly arguable; yet I do not find it altogether convincing. When Hodgson visited Watseka in April 1890, he obtained from the witnesses (in this case Mary's sister Minerva) such details as the following:

Lurancy, as Mary Roff, stayed at Mrs Alter's home for some time, and almost every hour of the day some trifling incident of Mary Roff's life was recalled by Lurancy. One morning she said, 'Right over there by the currant bushes is where cousin Allie greased the chicken's eye.' Allie was a cousin of Mary Roff, and lived in Peoria, Ill. She visited the Roffs in the lifetime of Mary, with whom she played. This incident happened several years before the death of Mary Roff. Mrs Alter remembered it very well, and recalled their bringing the chicken into the house for treatment.

That does not sound the sort of fact likely to have been elicited by a leading question, or picked up in casual gossip, and it would take quite a lot of forgotten mistakes to counterbalance it.

If the case was not one of impersonation, how might we regard it (speaking still, and simply for the sake of argument, from a survivalistic viewpoint)? Was it an example of unusually sustained 'overshadowing', basically like other cases of mediumship or obsession, or was it a true case of 'possession'? It is quite unlike most cases of mediumship in the length of time for which the apparent control lasted, in the completeness of the control over all aspects of mental and physical functioning, and in the sustained manifestation of what was apparently a whole and recognized personality. Yet there are indications – initial trances, and ostensible control by other deceased persons – that Lurancy was basically of the mediumistic type. Perhaps she had also tendencies towards secondary personality (if that is indeed a different thing). Some combination of these two ideas might suffice to explain the case without resort to the further hypothesis of possession.

Of course if one turns to the super-ESP hypothesis the usual obvious difficulties arise – the extent of the ESP involved and the rapidity with which it must be supposed to operate, together with the length of time for which it would have had to have been almost continuously sustained, and the motive for the charade. But before one rejects this hypothesis as altogether outrunning anything that we know about ESP one must recollect the obvious point that I have in effect made several times before, namely that the 'overshadowing' hypothesis itself postulates a form of telepathy – that between overshadower and overshadowed – which would appear to have *some* of these debatable characteristics.

Some people might be tempted to say that the case of Lurancy Vennum was all a long time ago; and perhaps it didn't happen, and maybe it would be as well if that were so. There is however a very much more recent, and even more remarkable, case which presents certain analogous features, and which has been studied by persons who fully appreciate the standards of evidence which must be applied in investigating such cases. I refer to the case of Uttara Huddar, reported by Stevenson and Pasricha in the *Journal of the ASPR* for July 1980

(154b ; cf. 154a). Uttara is an unmarried lady, born in 1941, and living in Nagpur, Maharashtra, India. She is a part-time lecturer in the Postgraduate Department of Public Administration at Nagpur University. Early in 1974, Uttara's normal personality was quite suddenly replaced by a markedly different one, who called herself Sharada. Sharada remained in control for several weeks, and has reappeared since at least thirty times, for periods ranging from one day to seven weeks.

Sharada appeared ignorant not just of Uttara's family and surroundings, but of all features of modern life post-dating the Industrial Revolution. She dressed, acted and spoke like a married Bengali woman, and spent much of her time in religious exercises. She claimed to be the daughter of a certain Brajanath Chattopadhaya, gave many names and other details of her relatives, and showed a knowledge of various obscure villages and temples in Bengal. Uttara states, and her relatives confirm, that she has never visited Bengal.

Most of the places mentioned by Sharada are in what is now West Bengal, some 500 miles from Nagpur. A town called Bansberia (north of Calcutta) figured prominently in Sharada's statements. It transpired that a family named Chattopadhaya still lives there. The head of this family possesses a genealogy for the period 1810–30 when it seems from other clues that Sharada lived. This genealogy lists five of the men named by Sharada, in relationships to her corresponding to those which, as a daughter of Brajanath Chattopadhaya, she would have had to them. Unfortunately it lists only men, so it cannot directly confirm, or disconfirm Sharada's existence. The relevant part of the genealogy was published in 1907 in a Bengali magazine circulating in the area of Bansberia.

Sharada claims to have 'fainted' after being bitten by a snake at the age of 22, and to have known nothing since then until she 'awoke' to her present intermittent existence.

The oddest aspect of the case remains to be mentioned. Sharada at first showed no knowledge of Marathi, which is Uttara's native language (she has since learned a few phrases), but spoke fluent Bengali, a language with which Uttara denies all acquaintance. There is absolutely no question of Sharada's competence in Bengali. Six different well-educated native speakers of Bengali who have conversed with her, sometimes for long periods, testify on this point. Pasricha has made a tape-recording of Sharada, and the authors also possess another tape-recording with partial transcript.

I have already commented on the importance of cases of responsive xenoglossy and on the difficulties which they present for the super-ESP hypothesis. It is accordingly of the first importance to inquire how far Uttara's claim to have no previous acquaintance with Bengali can be substantiated. While still at school she had had a few lessons in reading the scripts of languages other than Marathi, and these included Bengali. But she was taught to pronounce the letters of the scripts with Marathi sounds rather than Bengali ones. Her father had a few friends from the Bengali community in Nagpur, but none of them ever spoke Bengali with him because he had no knowledge of it himself. Uttara's parents and two of her sisters denied that she had ever had any opportunity to learn Bengali. A brother who had lived in Orissa, and had picked up some Bengali, stated that he had never used it in her presence.

Stevenson and Pasricha spent much time inquiring about and interviewing Bengali-speaking persons who might have communicated a knowledge of Bengali to Uttara. They were not successful.

By way of conclusion I can do no better than quote Stevenson and Pasricha's own conclusions:

> The marked alterations of personality in this case have some resemblance to mediumistic trances, but the differences are greater than the similarities. Mediumistic trances are almost always induced voluntarily, whereas [Uttara's] personality changes occured quite involuntarily. Mediumistic trances usually last an hour or two at the most; Sharada remained 'in control' for days, sometimes for weeks.
>
> The case also has some resemblance to cases of secondary personality, but the usual secondary personality claims to be more or less contemporary and collocal with the primary personality, whereas Sharada described a life in another part of her country and about 150 years earlier. Furthermore, the usual secondary personality has no paranormal powers, although there have been rare exceptions. Sharada's ability to speak fluent Bengali constitutes, in our opinion, a paranormally acquired skill.
>
> The case also resembles in some respects cases suggestive of reincarnation, but in such cases the subject usually begins to speak about the previous life he or she claims to remember between the ages of 2 and 5. Moreover, such a child's ordinary personality is rarely suppressed completely (as was [Uttara's]) during the narration of his or her claimed memories. (154a, p. 1592)

To this I can only add the following. If it is indeed true (as proposed in Chapter Seven) that the linguistic skills required for fluent responsive xenoglossy cannot be transmitted by telepathy, this case (that is, of course, if we accept the paranormal aspects of it) would appear to leave us with a choice only between 'true' possession and reincarnation; for both the super-ESP theory and the theory of 'overshadowing' (which also involves telepathy) would be ruled out.

12 Reincarnation

There can be no issue that more effectively separates optimists from pessimists than that of reincarnation. Will the world of the future be such that a rational man could possibly desire to be reborn into it? I must confess to being a pessimist. Whilst I can endure with fortitude and even curiosity the thought that I may have been incarnated many times in the past, the prospect of future incarnations disturbs me profoundly. I am inclined to apply to reincarnation in particular a remark made by the late Professor C. D. Broad (18d, p. 57) concerning survival in general: 'Having had the luck . . . to draw an eel from a sack full of adders, I do not wish to risk putting my hand into the sack again.' Eels, it seems to me, rare enough now, are likely in the future to be an endangered species.

My pessimism is of no importance to the present discussion, except in so far as my readers need to be warned against it. It seems, indeed, not to be widely shared. In recent decades a growth of interest in oriental thought has brought a greater awareness of reincarnationist philosophies. Opinion surveys suggest that in Europe and America belief in reincarnation is increasing. A Gallup Poll published in *The Daily Telegraph* for 20 April 1981 found that the percentage of Britons expressing a belief in reincarnation had risen from eighteen to twenty-eight per cent since 1969 (cf. 24, p. 10).

What concerns us at the moment, however, is not the extent of belief in reincarnation, but whether that belief can be supported by appeal to empirical facts. For reincarnation is a form of survival, and evidence for reincarnation is therefore evidence for survival. In his *Human Personality and its Survival of Bodily Death*, a massive survey of the materials collected by the SPR in its first twenty years, F. W. H. Myers wrote (110a, II, pp. 134–135), '. . . for reincarnation there is at present no valid evidence; and it must be my duty to show how its assertion in any given instance . . . constitutes in itself a strong argument in favour of self-suggestion . . .' Myers goes on to comment on the reincarnationist form of Spiritualism which, from the mid-nineteenth century onwards, spread in France and Brazil mainly through the influence of 'Allan Kardec' (on Kardec, see 104). Kardec, says Myers (110a, II, p. 135), 'took up reincarnationist tenets, enforced them (as there is reason to believe) by strong suggestion upon the minds of various automatic writers, and set them forth in dogmatic works which have had much influence, especially among Latin nations, from their clarity, symmetry, and intrinsic reasonableness. Yet the data thus collected were absolutely insufficient . . .'

Myer's assessment of the evidence for reincarnation as it stood in his time seems to me largely correct. Nor was there any dramatic upturn in that evidence during the first half of the twentieth century (though see 29; 114; 137). Anglo-American Spiritualism remained generally opposed to the idea, and it received little attention from the SPR and the ASPR prior to the publication of Professor C. J. Ducasse's *A Critical Examination of the Belief in a Life after Death* (1961), and of Professor Ian Stevenson's case investigations, which I shall discuss shortly. (For some reincarnationist communications through Mrs Leonard, however, see 157h.) Today the picture is very different. We have a good deal of apparent evidence for reincarnation, some of which reaches a standard that requires its inclusion in any general survey of the evidence for survival.

The ostensible evidence for reincarnation may be divided into two broad categories. We have, firstly, statements made by sensitives of a certain sort concerning the supposed past incarnations of their clients – the 'life readings' of Edgar Cayce are the most famous examples. Secondly, we have quite numerous cases of persons claiming to have memories, more or less detailed, of their earlier incarnations. I shall not discuss evidence of the former category at all, not because I think that the sensitives concerned never give indications of possessing paranormal faculties, but because searching for and evaluating these indications would require much effort and yield small reward.

Evidence of the latter category – the claimed memories of previous lives – may for our purposes be further subdivided into three classes, namely: evidence from hypnotic 'regression' into past lives; ostensible recollections by (unhypnotized) adults of their supposed previous incarnations; and childrens' ostensible memories of previous incarnations.

Hypnotic Regression

The best-known of these classes is without doubt that of hypnotic regressions into past lives. I do not know who first thought of trying such experiments. They are a fairly obvious development of some of the demonstrations – making hypnotized subjects act the part of Napoleon, act like a child of five, etc., – which had become part of the staple repertoire of itinerant 'magnetizers' and 'electrobiologists' by the middle of the nineteenth century. This trick can be performed with most moderately good hypnotic subjects. Spiritualists of the school of Kardec were certainly attempting hypnotic regression into past lives before the year 1890, and in 1911 the practice received some impetus from the publication of Col. A. de Rochas' *Les vies successives*. Col. de Rochas projected his subjects forward into future incarnations, as well as backwards into past ones, but I have not heard of anyone who, on looking into *Les vies successives*, has found the story of his present life written there. Perhaps this is because the book is very scarce.

The modern vogue – almost craze – for hypnotic regression dates from the publication in 1956 of M. Bernstein's *The Search for Bridey Murphy*. Since then, and especially during the last few years, we have been assailed by numerous books, newspaper articles and TV and radio programmes on the subject. Many of these have contained reports of new cases. A school of fringe hypnotherapy is growing up which approaches behavioural disturbances in this life by seeking out their causes in a previous one. Practitioners of this way of thinking seem often to take a 'cure' as sufficient validation of their patient's story, and, indirectly, of their own theoretical framework. We have here the psychotherapist's classic error in yet another guise.

It will already be apparent that I have strong reservations about the hypnotic regression material. One must, however, at the very least admit that the subjects of these experiments sometimes tell a good story; a much better story than one would ordinarily think them capable of inventing. The hypnotic induction procedure seems to release in them powers of creative imagination that they did not know they possessed. Perhaps this helps to explain the apparent successes of the reincarnationist hypnotherapies which I mentioned a moment ago. But it also lays certain snares for the investigator. The stories are sometimes so dramatic, and so full of human interest, that one can't help wishing them to be true. And then one may be misled into accepting as confirmations of them evidence that would not withstand a really critical scrutiny. For instance one case that has become widely known (72) relates to the supposed massacre in 1190 of a Jewish family which had taken refuge in the crypt of a church identified as St Mary's, Castlegate, York. This church was not at the time of the hypnotic regression known to possess a crypt. Subsequently one was unearthed, and the story was suddenly 'made to seem more likely. The entire regression was now a credible account of what might have happened in York in 1190' (p. 53). The only evidence presented that the crypt really exists is, however, a secondhand statement to the effect that an unknown workman discovered what might have been a crypt below the chancel. It was immediately blocked up again before it could be properly examined.

Cryptomnesia

Still, the creation of a powerful story concerning a previous incarnation, whether fictional or otherwise, requires some quantity of accurate, or at any rate convincing, historical information. In some cases a good many quite recondite historical facts have been incorporated into the story told by an hypnotically regressed subject. Where do these facts come from? The most popular non-reincarnationist explanation has involved cryptomnesia (latent memory). (On cryptomnesia in general see 153j, pp. 345–349; and 153k.) Buried in our mind, this theory proposes, are all sorts of memories not ordinarily accessible to the waking consciousness. Among them will be memories which the subject does not recollect having acquired from another source and is liable to consider his own. The memories concerned may be memories of school history books, of historical films and plays and TV programmes, of historical novels and serials in women's magazines, of historical notes in local newspapers, and so on and so on. This could amount to quite a lot of information. Nowadays the makers of historical films take pains to get the backgrounds right, and historical novelists commonly append bibliographies to their books. All these buried memories may under certain circumstances find their way out. They may break into ordinary waking consciousness with no awareness of their source (various instances of apparent literary plagiarism have almost certainly originated in this way); they may emerge through automatic writing, or in dreams or drug-states; and they may be retrieved and embellished under hypnosis.

Such is the theory, and to some it seems so obviously correct that, given that cryptomnesia occurs, there is no need to worry further about the explanation of cases of hypnotic regression in which verified historical details have been obtained. But this attitude is at best over-simple, and it is over-simple on two counts.

The first is that while there undoubtedly is some evidence for cryptomnesia, that evidence is small in relation to the weight of other material it is being used to support. Many modern workers in the field of hypnotism would simply deny that hypnosis facilitates recall; properly designed experiments reveal no such effect. This is, however, not a denial that cryptomnesia may occasionally be exhibited, but only a denial that hypnosis is particularly conducive to the emergence of memories whose normal source the subject has forgotten. As it happens, the most frequently cited example of undoubted cryptomnesia, the 'Blanche Poynings' case (30), did take place under hypnosis. 'Blanche Poynings' was the name given by a spirit contacted under hypnosis by a young lady referred to as 'Miss C.' Blanche gave a great many exceedingly recondite historical and genealogical details about her life in the time of Richard II and Henry IV. Subsequently it was discovered, through a planchette board which Miss C. operated in the waking state, that almost all these details came from a novel which had been read to her as a child, namely Emily S. Holt's *Countess Maud*. The contents of the novel, in which Blanche Poynings is only a minor character, had, however, been substantially, and one might add creatively, rearranged. One can readily see how, in different circumstances, this material could have emerged as a reincarnationist fantasy. A Finnish psychologist, R. Kampman (79: 80), has obtained some comparable results from a series of experiments with schoolchildren whom he hypnotically 'regressed' into past lives. By the simple technique of taking the children under hypnosis to the occasion on which they obtained the information on which their reincarnationist fantasies were based, he was able to trace several fantasies back to their sources in printed material. But this technique, alas, is by no means universally successful – other hypnotists who have tried the same stratagem have been met by denials that there is any such ordinary source.

The second reason why one must hesitate before accepting the simple cryptomnesia theory is that the reincarnationist theory itself involves cryptomnesia; only, of course, the 'buried memories' retrieved are memories of a previous incarnation rather than of this one. Whatever conditions favour the one sort of cryptomnesia will presumably also favour the other. Hence we cannot argue that because the subject is in a state (hypnosis) believed (by some) to favour cryptomnesia, cryptomnesia for books read, films seen, etc., in this life, must be the explanation of the correct historical details which he gives. Unless we are to rule out the reincarnationist theory (and the other kinds of evidence which ostensibly support it) upon purely *a priori* grounds, we must find support for the cryptomnesia theory (cryptomnesia, that is, directed upon events of this life) from features of the actual regression cases it is intended to explain. This conclusion is reinforced by the fact, just pointed out, that the evidence for cryptomnesia is not so strong as to lead us to regard it as a very frequent occurrence.

The strongest support for the cryptomnesia theory would be provided by a demonstration that in a given case:

(a)   all the information conveyed was to be found in a single source (a book, an article, a film, etc.);

(b)   the subject would have had access to that source; and

(c)   he had actually studied that source.

Of these factors (a) and (b) may not be too difficult to establish – there are various easily accessible indices of historical novels – and any case which falls foul of these two criteria must clearly be set aside as evidence for reincarnation on the grounds that a possible basis for cryptomnesia was demonstrably there. Establishing (c) would be tantamount to establishing the cryptomnesia hypothesis for the case in question, and this has not often been achieved. In some instances the subject has been brought, by hypnosis (as in the Kampman cases mentioned above) or some other stratagem (in the Blanche Poynings case a planchette board), to recollect the source of information himself. Another possibility – one for obvious reasons rarely actualized – is that the source of information should contain an error which the subject repeats. A rather nice example of this has recently been unearthed by Mr Ian Wilson in a case for which Joe Keeton, a leading British exponent of regression, was the hypnotist (105, pp. 7–9; 172, pp. 196–207). One of Keeton's subjects, a young woman, gave under hypnosis copious and consistent details of a trial at which she, as Joan Waterhouse, had been accused of witchcraft. The trial took place at Chelmsford in 1566. Keeton's subject, however, dated it as 1556 – the date mistakenly put upon a Victorian reprint of the very rare original pamphlet describing the trial. The error has been copied by some (though not all) subsequent writers.

Direct support of these kinds for the cryptomnesia hypothesis is relatively uncommon, and it is hardly frequent enough to justify our extending the theory without more ado to cover all the regression cases in which verified information has been produced. There is, however, a substantial block of cases which, though we have no evidence of cryptomnesia in connection with them, cannot be accepted as providing adequate evidence of reincarnation. They must go on that large heap of 'not provens', where, perhaps, the majority of cases belong. I have two sorts of case especially in mind here. The first is that of cases – not so frequent as one might antecedently suppose – in which a subject claims to have been some famous historical figure, e.g. Nell Gwynn, Marie Antoinette or Bonnie Prince Charlie. When the supposed previous incarnation is, like these, a person concerning whom a great deal has been published, it will, save in the most improbable circumstances, be almost impossible to establish with even moderate plausibility that the subject could not somewhere, at some time, have run across a book, magazine article, film, TV documentary, radio programme, or *Reader's Digest* rundown containing the relevant information. Thus it will likewise be almost impossible to reject the cryptomnesia theory with any certainty.

Very similar considerations apply to the second kind of case, that of cases which are thought to be verified (or almost!) by the multiplicity of correct background details given, despite the fact that the central persons in the dramas (the supposed previous incarnations of the subjects) cannot be proved to have existed. Information about interesting places at interesting periods of their history gets very widely disseminated by novels, plays, museums, TV, local newspapers, etc., and it is extremely difficult to be sure that the subject of a regression experiment has never come across it. A significantly high proportion of the published cases (including the celebrated Bridey Murphy case) fall into this category.

Take, for example, another of Joe Keeton's cases (105, pp. 42–74), the fascinating story told under hypnosis by Ann Dowling, a forty-seven-year-old working class housewife from Huyton (Liverpool), of her previous incarnation in the period around 1830–1850 as Sarah Williams, a homeless waif from Everton (Liverpool). Sarah Williams showed some knowledge of the geography of nineteenth century Liverpool; she referred unmistakably to Jenny Lind's visit to Liverpool in 1850; she correctly named a chemist's shop in Byrom Street; she referred to Prince Albert's staying with a Judge in Liverpool in 1846; asked for the name of Victoria and Albert's ship, she replied *The Fairy*, which was the name *not* of the royal yacht but of the tender in which the royal couple made their inspections; she mentioned a demonstration of electric lighting given at Liverpool in 1852; and she referred to Kitty Wilkinson, a social reformer of the time, who advocated setting up wash-houses for the poor. All these verified historical details were given in the context of a very lively rendering of a distinctive personality and of the hardships of poverty in a nineteenth century city. Yet of Sarah herself no trace was found, despite the fact that her death, at least, should by the 1850s have been a matter of public record. A death certificate or obscure newspaper paragraph recording the manner of her murder would at once have made the cryptomnesia hypothesis several orders of magnitude less likely. As it is, many of the facts correctly given concern events which would have found their way into local history books and articles, even into novels or TV programmes, which a local resident, such as Mrs Dowling, could conceivably have come across. To track down all the potential sources and compare them with the statements made by Sarah Williams would be an impracticable task, perhaps an impossible one. The case must be relegated to the 'not proven' category – not proven both from the point of view of reincarnation and from that of cryptomnesia. As for the dramatic force of the Sarah Williams personality – some of the most convincing and dramatically effective personalities to emerge in regression experiments have been without doubt totally fictitious. This at least is a fact of great psychological interest, and one which deserves further study.

When all necessary sacrifices have been made to the cryptomnesia theory, however, there remain one or two cases which it cannot so readily swallow up. These cases have, for the most part, some or all of the following characteristics:

(a)   The existence of the supposed previous personality has been confirmed.

(b)   The personality was an obscure one, not likely to have achieved mention in novels, films, etc.,

(c)   The story is supported by verified background details of the kind we have just been considering.

(d)   There does not appear to be any single source from which all the relevant information could have come.

A case that at first sight fills some of these requirements is described in Jess Stearn's *The Second Life of Susan Ganier*. Joanne MacIver, a girl living in Orillia, Ontario, was hypnotically regressed by her father into a number of supposed previous lives. One of these was as Susan Ganier, allegedly born about 1835 in St Vincent Township, Ontario, about ninety miles from the spot where the MacIvers lived. In 1849 (said Susan) she married Thomas Merrow, a farmer, and lived with him in the town of Massie, Ontario. Thomas was killed in an accident in 1863, but Susan lived on until 1903.

Susan Ganier was born before registration of births was introduced, and no record of her death could be discovered. None the less, she correctly gave various recondite geographical facts about the district where she lived, and some obscure but correct details of the life of that time. She named various persons in Massie whose existence was confirmed from public records. And an elderly gentleman, Mr Arthur Eagles, remembered Susan Merrow, her family, and some of her neighbours, and knew about the death of her husband.

The trouble with this case is that *The Second Life of Susan Ganier* is written like a novel, and it is by no means clear what opportunities the subject might have had to learn relevant facts by normal means. Of such cases one can only say that if there were more of them, and if they were better recorded and investigated than they generally are, they would force us to reject the cryptomnesia hypothesis as totally inadequate. Whether they would force us to accept a reincarnation theory instead, rather than, say, some version of the super-ESP hypothesis, is another question. My own guess would be that further cases fulfilling these criteria will probably come to light; but they will be so small a solid residue from so great a flood of entertaining but inconclusive eyewash, that one would be ill-advised to waste one's lifetime in attempting to induce them.

Non-hypnotic Recollections

We come next to my second class of alleged evidence for reincarnation from claimed memories of past lives, namely ostensible recollections by (unhypnotized) adults of their supposed previous incarnations. This class includes a great assortment of varied spontaneous experiences, ranging from simple 'paramnesias' – feelings that one has 'been here before' – to (in very rare instances) the emergence of complex sets of 'memories' relating to a supposed past existence at a definite period and place. It is only cases at the latter end of the scale that would concern us here. But I do not propose to linger long over them. Mr E. W. Ryall's ostensible memories of his life in seventeenth century Somerset, set forth in a manner reminiscent of a novel (135), have the curious characteristic, on the frequency of which I have already commented, that many of the background details are correct while all the central characters appear to be fictitious. On Dr Arthur Guirdham's recollections of his incarnation as a Cathar in thirteenth century France, together with the correlated past-life recollections of various of his (anonymous) patients and friends, now all reincarnated as a 'group' (53a; 53b), I can offer no useful comments. No one but an independent specialist in the history of that period could properly evaluate the mass of recondite details thus ostensibly retrieved – they include verified names and family relationships, details of Cathar dress, practices, symbols, etc., and events in Cathar history – but such an evaluation would only be profitable if it were based upon Dr Guirdham's original records rather than upon the story as he tells it in his books. In his books he seems more concerned to share his convictions with persons antecedently sympathetic to them, than to dent by signed statements and careful documentation the disbelief of the less romantically inclined.

'Reincarnated' Children

My third, and final, class of claimed memories of past lives, is that of the ostensible past-life recollections of very young children. Occasional examples of such stories found their way into print in the West during the first half of the present century. But far the most impressive case-investigations in this area, indeed in any area of reincarnation research, are those conducted since 1960 by Professor Ian Stevenson of the University of Virginia. In order to carry out his investigations on the spot, Stevenson has engaged in frequent and extensive travels. The upshot has been a series of four substantial volumes (the series is still in progress), containing in all reports on fifty-two cases (153g; 153h; 153i; 153j), and various shorter accounts of individual cases. Stevenson has fifteen or twenty times as many cases on file.

The greatest strength of Stevenson's work, it seems to be, is that he has a very just appreciation of the canons of evidence against which such cases must be tried, an appreciation which he keeps at all times before his own mind, and before the minds of his readers. This is not to say that all, or even many, of his cases fully satisfy these canons, nor does he claim that they do. The point is rather that he puts before his readers, as fully and as fairly as he can, the materials which they require to form their own judgements. He has himself deliberately supplied most of the ammunition which his critics have used against him. And he has pressed for independent replications of his research.

Stevenson's methods of case-investigation, like the layout of his case reports (to which they are of course closely tied), were developed at an early stage of his research, and naturally reflect the matters upon which it is vital to have information when assessing a case of this kind. The facts or alleged facts which ostensibly link a certain young child (call him the 'present personality') to a definitely identifiable deceased person (call him the 'previous personality') may be of three sorts. There are statements made by the present personality concerning his memories of his life as the past personality; there are behaviours, skills, attitudes, abilities, and so forth, shown by the present personality, which accord with those of the previous personality; and there are recognitions by the present personality of the previous personality's relations, friends, belongings, house, etc. – when the child's parents find that the previous personality really existed, they almost always give way to curiosity and the child's demands, and arrange for him to visit the previous personality's family. Obviously the first thing we need to know is just what statements the child made, what relevant behaviours he exhibited, and at what age he began to make or exhibit them. It is especially important to know what relevant things the child said and did before he first met the previous personality's family. After the first meeting there may be 'contamination' of the present personality's memories, especially if, as not uncommonly happens, he becomes a regular visitor in the previous personality's home. In only a few cases (Stevenson – 153h, p. 144n – lists a dozen) has an investigator or independent person been able to make a list of the present personality's statements before the first meeting has taken place. Failing such a list, the investigator's best tactic is obviously to interview in detail first, of course, the child himself, and then as many persons as possible who saw him before the first meeting, heard statements from him, observed his behaviour, etc. The separate interviewing of a multiplicity of witnesses may help to offset or resolve errors of testimony, retrospective exaggerations, and tendencies to think that the child made before the first meeting statements which in fact he only produced after it.

Another crucial issue is that of how the first meeting between the present personality and the previous personality's family was conducted. Were the recognitions truly spontaneous? What cues could have been given by persons present? What mistakes may have been overlooked in the excitement of the moment? And so on. Once again we have only a few cases in which an outside investigator, alert to these possibilities, has been present as recorder on the day itself. Once again, therefore, we have generally to rely on detailed interviews with eyewitnesses, and cross-checking of their statements.

The next question to arise is clearly that of how far the child's statements and behaviour agree with what is known of the previous personality's life, death and characteristics. To ascertain this it is obviously necessary to interview members (as many as possible) of the previous personality's family, to visit their home and its surroundings, to consult public records and newspaper files, and so on. These procedures may help to throw light on the remaining crucial issue, namely whether the child could have learned relevant facts about the previous personality by normal means. With children as young as these, cryptomnesic recollection of, say, a newspaper obituary notice seems outstandingly unlikely. The possibility that the child may have picked up information through listening to adult gossip needs however to be thoroughly explored. In some cases the child is antecedently believed by the parents to be the reincarnation of another member of the family, and then of course the danger is very real. But in many cases the parents deny having known anything about the previous personality prior to the child's revelations. Their denials have, however, to be checked in the light of the geographical situations of the two homes, and of any ordinary lines of communication that can be discovered between them. The investigator's task is here very much like that of a detective. And indeed he needs, of course, to be continually watchful for signs of fraud, and of financial exploitation of the case.

Given this background of complex and interrelated problems, one can readily see why Stevenson lays out his case reports as he does. He usually begins with a short summary of the case, indicating how he first heard of it, when he first visited the families concerned, who participated in the investigation with him, and so on; he lists the people he interviewed, with or without the need for an interpreter; he sets out relevant geographical factors, and considers possible normal lines of communication; he presents his information about the life and death of the previous personality; he tabulates the relevant statements and recognitions; states whether they are correct or not, and if they are correct, gives his authority for saying so; he discusses any other relevant matters; considers the behavioural aspects of the case (the behaviour patterns, skills and attitudes which the present personality appears to share with the previous one); comments on the paranormal aspects of the case; and lastly mentions later developments, follow-up visits, etc., – it is his general and prudent practice to watch a case over a period of years to see what may come to light.

I turn now to certain general, or statistical, features of Stevenson's collection of cases. It will be convenient to mention these briefly under two headings, namely features recurring in cases from all cultures studied, and culture-bound recurrent features of the cases.

Features recurring in cases from all cultures studied

1.   Most of the subjects are between two and four years old when they start speaking about their previous lives; i.e. they start as soon as they can speak.

2.   These memories come, for the most part, in the waking state.

3.   Usually something like ninety per cent of the subject's statements about his previous life are correct.

4.   In most cases subjects stop talking about their previous lives between the ages of five and eight; memories of them usually do not survive into adulthood, though there are exceptions.

5.   In a high percentage of cases, the previous personality met a violent, and often an early death.

6.   Events connected with, or just preceding, the death of the previous personality tend to be prominent among the subject's memories.

7.   The present personality is likely to be born within a few kilometres of the previous personality's home, and to speak the same language. There are many exceptions to the former part of this rule of thumb, but the exceptions grow fewer as the distance gets greater. It has, of course, to be borne in mind that verification of the previous personality's actual existence might become more difficult with increased separation of the families concerned.

Culture-bound recurrent features of the cases

1.   Reported cases are most common in regions where reincarnation is widely believed in; e.g. in India and Sri Lanka and in Southeast Asia, or among the Druses and Alevis of Western Asia, and Tlingits of Alaska. This could obviously be explained in a variety of ways.

2.   Though in all cultures there is a high incidence of violent deaths among the previous personalities (higher than the norm of the country

concerned), the proportion varies from 38% in Sri Lanka to over 78% among the Druse cases of Syria and Lebanon.

3.   Previous lives as a member of the opposite sex are much more frequently claimed in some cultures than in others. They are unheard of among the Tlingits, Druses and Alevis, occur in 13% of Thai cases, 28% of Burmese cases, and in as much as 50% of cases among the Kutchin of northwestern Canada. Such cases occur most frequently in cultures which believe them possible, most rarely in cultures where such change is thought impossible.

4.   Instances of reincarnation within the same family are very common in Burma and among the Tlingits and the Eskimos, and rare in other cultures.

5.   The apparent interval between the death of the previous personality and the birth of the present one varies a good deal from culture to culture, the variations again being linked to culturally determined beliefs on the subject. The median interval among the Haida of Alaska and British Columbia is four months; among the Druses six months; among the Alevis 9 months; in Sri Lanka and in India 18 months; and among the Tlingits 48 months. There appears to be once again a (not very exact) link with culturally determined beliefs on the subject.

In one or two cases the previous personality has not died until *after* the birth of the present personality. The most remarkable such case is an Indian one, that of a boy named Jasbir (153g, pp. 34–52). At the age of three and a half, Jasbir became so ill with smallpox that he was thought to have died. However he gradually revived and thereafter claimed to be Sobha Ram, a recently deceased young man from a village about twenty miles away. The case has some affinities with that of Lurancy Vennum, described in the previous chapter, but unlike the Lurancy Vennum personality, the Jasbir personality never returned.

6.   'Announcing dreams', dreams in which an expectant mother receives information as to the identity of the unborn child she is carrying, are known in most cultures, but are commonest among the Burmese, the natives of northwestern North America, and the Alevis of south central Turkey.

7.   Also known in most cultures so far studied are birthmarks corresponding either to those borne by the previous personality, or else to the wounds from which he met his death. The correspondences are in some instances extremely close, and have been verified by medical records or autopsy reports concerning the previous personality. Such

cases are specially common among the Eskimos, the Tlingits, the Burmese, and the Alevis.

Having briefly described Stevenson's methods of case-investigation and case-reporting, and touched on some relevant general features of the cases in his collection, I shall now come down to a more concrete level by giving an outline of a sample case. For this purpose I have selected the case of Swarnlata (153g, pp. 67–91). This case is unusual in that the subject claimed to remember two previous incarnations. I will deal first with the earlier and more important one. Swarnlata was born on 2 March 1948, the daughter of M. L. Mishra, an assistant in the office of a district inspector of schools, and lived during the period with which we are concerned in various towns in Madhya Pradesh, India. From about the age of three and a half she exhibited ostensible memories of a previous life as Biya, daughter of a family called Pathak, in Katni, Madhya Pradesh, and (it later transpired) wife of Sri Chintamini Pandey of Maihar, a town north of Katni. It is to be noted that the Mishra family never lived closer to Katni than about a hundred miles.

Swarnlata confided fragments of her apparent memories mostly to her brothers and sisters, but also to some extent to her parents. She still retained her memories in 1958 when she met Srimati Agnihotri, a lady from Katni whom she claimed to recognize from her previous life there. This prompted M. L. Mishra, Swarnlata's father, to write down some of her statements, which he did in September 1958.

In March 1959 H. N. Banerjee, an Indian parapsychologist, spent two days with the Mishra family investigating the case. He noted down nine statements made by Swarnlata about the Pathak residence. He visited Katni, and guided by Swarnlata's statements was able to find the house of the correct Pathak family. He was the first to establish the close correspondences between Swarnlata's ostensible memories of a past life, and the life of Biya, the Pathak's daughter, who had died in 1939.

In the summer of 1959 members of the Pathak family and of Biya's husband's family travelled to Swarnlata's house. They took considerable precautions to avoid giving Swarnlata cues, and they made various attempts to mislead her. None the less she was successful in recognizing them and was not misled. Shortly afterwards Swarnlata was taken to Katni and Maihar, where Biya had lived. She recognized additional people and places, and commented on various changes that had taken place since the death of Biya. Her father, M. L. Mishra, made written notes on some of the recognitions soon after they occurred. Swarnlata seems thereafter to have been accepted as Biya by the Pathaks and Pandeys, and built up affectionate relationships with the 'brothers' and 'children' of her previous life.

Stevenson spent four days investigating the case in the summer of 1961. He interviewed fifteen persons from the three families concerned, including Swarnlata herself. Interpreters were in most instances not necessary. He also had put at his disposal documents and notes about the case prepared by H. N. Banerjee (see above) and notes made by Professor P. Pal during his study of the case in 1963. After he left he kept up a correspondence with Swarnlata and her father, and met Swarnlata again in November 1971, by which time she had obtained a BSc and an MSc with distinction in botany. She stated that she had not lost her memories of her previous life. This may have been because the Mishra family was completely tolerant of them.

I shall now present a summary list, heavily abridged from Stevenson's tabulation, of the various statements and recognitions made by Swarnlata. The first eighteen are statements made by Swarnlata before she met any members of her previous family. Most of them were written down by her father. It was items 6, 13 and 14 which enabled H. N. Banerjee to find the Pathak's house without help when he went to Katni in March 1959.

Item	Informant	Confirmed by
1. She belonged to a family named Pathak in Katni	M. L. Mishra, Swarnlata's father	Rajendra Prasad Pathak, brother of Biya
2. She had two sons, Krishna Datta and Shiva Datta	M. L. Mishra	Murli Pandey, son of Biya. (Biya had two sons; the other was named Naresh. The names given are however names of other persons in the family.)
3. Her name had been Kamlesh	M. L. Mishra	Incorrect. (This refers to the other ostensible past life recalled by Swarnlata.)
4. Her name had been Biya	Krishna Chandra, Swarnlata's brother	Rajendra Prasad Pathak
5. The head of the family was Hira Lal Pathak	M. L. Mishra	Incorrect. (A 'portmanteau' name, containing correct elements.)

6-14. The Pathak house was white; it had four stuccoed rooms, but other parts were less well furnished; the doors were black; the doors were fitted with iron bars; the front floor of the house was of stone slabs; the family had a motor car; there was a girls' school behind the house; a railway line could be seen from the house; so could lime furnaces.	M. L. Mishra	Rajendra Prasad Pathak. I. Stevenson (personal observation). All items correct.
15. Her family lived in Zhurkutia District	M. L. Mishra	M. L. Mishra; Murli Pandey, Swarnlata's son. (Name should be Zharratikuria.)
16. She had had pains in her throat and had died of throat disease	M. L. Mishra	Rajendra Prasad Pathak. Incorrect. (She had had throat trouble, but died of heart disease.)
17. She had been treated by Dr S. C. Bhabrat of Jabalpur	M. L. Mishra	Murli Pandey; (name should be S. E. Barat.)
18. She had once gone to a wedding at Tilora village with Srimati Agnihotri and they had difficulty in finding a latrine	M. L. Mishra; Krishna Chandra	M. L. Mishra; Krishna Chandra. (Srimati Agnihotri was the lady from Katni who first confirmed some of Swarnlata's past-life memories. See above.)

The next items, items 19–23, occurred when the Pathak and Pandey families first visited the Mishras in the summer of 1959 (see above).

19. Recognition of Hari Prasad, brother of Biya	M. L. Mishra; Hari Prasad Pathak	(Hari Prasad Pathak arrived unannounced and gave no name. Swarnlata at first called him Hira Lal Pathak, but recognized him as her (i.e., Biya's) younger brother, and called him 'Babu', the name by which Biya knew him.)
20 and 21. Recognition of Chintamini Pandey, husband of	M. L. Mishra; Murli Pandey	(The two anonymous visitors along with nine other men, some known to her, some

Biya, and of Murli Pandey, her son		unknown. She was asked to name them all. She told Chintamini Pandey she knew him in Katni and Maihar, and looked bashful as Hindu wives do in the presence of their husbands. She identified Murli despite his maintaining for almost 24 hours that he was not Murli but somebody else.)
22. Non-recognition of stranger unknown to Biya.	(Murli Pandey	(Murli was trying to pass off a friend he had brought with him as his brother Naresh.)
23. Chintamini Pandey took 1200 rupees from a box in which she (Biya) had kept money.	Murli Pandey	Murli Pandey. (This was told to Murli Pandey by Chintamini Pandey. No one except he and Biya had known about it.)

Items 24–49 (most of which I omit) took place on Swarnlata's visits to the Pathak and Pandey families (see above). The items I have omitted relate to recognitions of relatives and servants known to Biya, or to recognition of places, rooms, and features of houses altered since Biya's death. Swarnlata was often able to specify the relationship, and to give other appropriate details.

29. Recognition of family cowherd	Brij Kishore Pathak, fourth brother of Biya; Krishna Chandra	(Presented to Swarnlata as a specially difficult test. Brij Kishore Pathak also tried to persuade Swarnlata that the cowherd had died.)
32. Inquiring about neem tree formerly in compound of Pathak house.	Rajendra Prasad Pathak	Rajendra Prasad Pathak. (This tree had been blown down some months before Swarnlata's visit.)
33. Inquiring about a parapet at back of Pathak house.	Rajendra Prasad Pathak	Rajendra Prasad Pathak. (This had been removed since Biya's death.)
34. Non-acceptance of suggestion that Biya had lost her teeth, and statement that she had gold nails in her front teeth.	Rajendra Prasad Pathak; M. L. Mishra	Rajendra Prasad Pathak; M. L. Mishra. (Brij Kishore Pathak tried to deceive Swarnlata by saying that Biya had lost her teeth. Swarnlata denied this and insisted she had gold fillings in her front teeth. The Pathak brothers could not remember this and consulted their wives, who verified Swarnlata's statement.)

In addition to Swarnlata's correct recognitions and statements, certain aspects of her behaviour require mention. With the Mishra family she behaved like a (somewhat serious) child; but when with the Pathaks she behaved like an older sister of her 'brothers', who were in fact forty years and more older than she was. They completely accepted her, and the emotional bond between them became very strong, though it did not interfere with her affection for her natural family. When alone with the 'children' of her previous life (men much older than her) she relaxed completely and treated them as a mother would. Neither Rajendra Prasad Pathak (Biya's second brother) nor Murli Pandey (her son) had believed in reincarnation before they met Swarnlata/Biya.

The gap of nearly ten years between Biya's death, and Swarnlata's birth, is an unusually long one by the standards of such cases. Swarnlata had in fact some fragmentary ostensible memories of an intervening life at Sylhet in Bangladesh (then Assam). She gave her name as Kamlesh, and exhibited some knowledge of the geography of the district. A proper investigation was not possible. Swarnlata retained some memories of conjoined songs and dances she had supposedly learned during her Sylhet incarnation. The words of the songs were in Bengali (Swarnlata spoke only Hindi). Professor P. Pal, a native of Bengal, transcribed the songs, and translated them into English. Two out of three were clearly derived from poems of Rabindranath Tagore. The accompanying dances were of an appropriate style.

We have here an example of ostensible recitative xenoglossy (see Chapter Seven above). The question which naturally arises is whether Swarnlata could have learned the songs by ordinary means before the age of five when she first began to perform them. Stevenson considers in great detail the possibility that she might have seen them in a film (a film in a language not her own), heard them on radio, or otherwise witnessed a performance of them. He thinks it most improbable that she could have learned them normally; but I do not have space to go into the details of his arguments.

I have now, at least in a preliminary way, laid out the pieces of this puzzle, and we must now ask into what patterns the pieces can be arranged; ask, in other words, what explanation can be given of the apparently paranormal factors in the case. In tackling this question I shall try, so far as possible, to pass occasionally beyond the case of Swarnlata and offer some general comments on Stevenson's findings.

But the bulk of his work is so large that any remarks of mine are bound to be most inadequate.

The obvious starting point is with those approaches which attempt to normalize the paranormal, to demonstrate that, despite all appearances to the contrary, there is nothing in these cases which cannot be explained away in commonplace terms. The sticks with which upholders of this approach are wont to beat their opponents are, in ascending order of power to bruise, errors of memory combined with retrospective exaggeration, genetic memory, fraud and cryptomnesia.

The first two of these can be immediately dismissed, both for Stevenson's published cases in general, and for the case of Swarnlata in particular. No doubt the testimony contains a sprinkling of errors as to what the subjects did or did not say prior to their first meetings with the families of the previous personalities, and no doubt there would be a temptation to enrich the subject's supposed statements with facts gleaned after the first meeting. But I do not think that anyone who seriously studies Stevenson's case reports will conclude that this can be anything more than a very minor factor in promoting the correct statements and recognitions which these subjects are said to have made. Certainly it cannot be an important factor in the case of Swarnlata, in which a substantial number of statements were written down and passed on to an outsider before the first meeting of the two families.

Mr Ian Wilson (172, pp. 56–57) seems to think that there may be an underlying weakness in some of the evidence collected by Stevenson because two persons who assisted him in a number of case investigations in India and in Sri Lanka were ardent believers in reincarnation. I should imagine that others of Stevenson's helpers may have fallen into this category, and that Stevenson himself is not uninterested in reincarnationist philosophies. However the criticism strikes me as quite illegitimate. Neither a person's practical work, nor his arguments, can be undermined by pointing to the hopes, however strong, that may as a matter of psychological fact, have inspired them. Practical work can only be demolished by pointing to flaws in design, method, apparatus, technique, etc.; arguments can only be demolished by pointing to faulty assumptions or faulty logic. Any contrary claim must ultimately be self-defeating.

For genetic memory there is, so far as I am aware, virtually no acceptable evidence; and in the vast majority of Stevenson's cases, the present personality was certainly not, biologically speaking, directly descended from the previous one.

The possibilities of fraud are a great deal harder to assess. One has for the most part to evaluate these possibilities for each individual case. In the case of Swarnlata fraud seems exceptionally unlikely. There was no evidence that either Swarnlata or her father benefited financially. Her father received a certain amount of publicity from the affair, which to some may appear a sufficient motive for fraud. But even so the problem remains of how he could without attracting attention have obtained so much detailed and highly personal information about the private lives of the Pathaks, and have successfully coached Swarnlata in it. Nothing that Stevenson could find out about him from persons who knew him gave any grounds for suspicion that he had perpetrated a hoax, and it will be remembered that Stevenson remained in touch with both father and daughter for many years.

There seem, furthermore, to be some general reasons why fraud cannot be regarded as a likely explanation of the apparently paranormal elements in cases of this kind. One is that cases in very different parts of the world exhibit closely similar features (listed above), features for the most part lacking in those few cases in which fraud has actually been detected.

Cryptomnesia is an explanation which has likewise to be assessed case by case. In the case of Swarnlata it seems to me almost inconceivable that cryptomnesia should be the answer. The Mishra and Pathak families denied any previous acquaintance with each other and had never lived nearer each other than about a hundred miles. The chief possibility for a normal line of communication was that Swarnlata's mother came from an area where the Pathak family had business interests. Her own maiden name was in fact Pathak, though she was entirely unrelated to the Pathaks of whom Biya had been the daughter. One of Biya's brothers had some acquaintance with a cousin of Swarnlata's mother. The Mishras had also passed through Katni from time to time. However even if Swarnlata or her parents had heard something about the Pathaks of Katni, and then forgotten it (and there is nothing to suggest this) it would certainly not have included the intimate details of which Swarnlata showed knowledge, nor could it have accounted for her extremely successful recognitions of many relatives and servants of her supposed previous life.

In others of Stevenson's cases (not an overwhelming number) the likelihood of cryptomnesia seems greater – the two families concerned lived near each other or the parents of the present personality undoubtedly knew something about the life and death of the previous personality. But Stevenson very reasonably points out:

(a)   that many of his subjects were only three or even younger when they exhibited their first apparent memories of a previous existence;

(b)   unlike the subjects in many of the classic cases of demonstrated cryptomnesia, they were not hypnotized but in an ordinary waking state; and

(c)   that so far none of his cases has yielded clear evidence for cryptomnesia – there has been nothing which unmistakably linked the subject's statements to some source of information to which he undoubtedly had access.

It seems to me extremely unlikely that either fraud or cryptomnesia have been more than marginal factors in producing the correct statements and recognitions so frequently found in the pages of Stevenson's case reports. Attempts to normalize the paranormal in this area have not proved convincing. We must therefore move on to consider those explanations which invoke paranormal factors or processes. The factors or processes most commonly invoked have been ESP, obsession by the spirit of some deceased person, and actual reincarnation.

The ESP theory proposes, of course, that the 'reincarnated' subject obtains all his information about the previous personality by ESP, in most cases almost inevitably telepathy with the living. Why data concerning that particular deceased person (and usually no other) should be selected as target material remains unclear.

The telepathy theory suffers from several obvious shortcomings: In the great majority of cases the ostensibly reincarnated person shows no signs of having any special ESP abilities (Swarnlata, however, was once the percipient in a not very impressive case of apparent spontaneous ESP); some of the reincarnated personalities have exhibited skills characteristic of the previous personality, and I have already argued that skills cannot be acquired by ESP; in some cases the telepathically acquired information would have to have come from more than one source; and in a few cases the information concerned seems not just to have been acquired, but to have been *organized* in a pattern appropriate to the mind of the previous personality.

The last two points make it apparent that we are once again confronted with what can only be termed a version of the super-ESP hypothesis. It is worth quoting Stevenson's expositions of these two points in connection with the case of Swarnlata (153g, pp. 347–348):

The Pathak brothers knew the facts about the changes in the Pathak house in Katni and nearly all the other facts apparently remembered by Swarnlata about events at Katni, although they did not remember the gold fillings in the teeth of their sister, Biya. But it is extremely unlikely that they knew anything about the latrine episode which Swarnlata told Srimati Agnihotri and it is equally unlikely that they knew anything about the money taken from Biya by her husband. He had told no one about this for obvious reasons. Now it is possible that Swarnlata derived different items of information from different persons each acting as the agent for one or a few items and no others . . . But what then becomes noteworthy is the *pattern* of the information Swarnlata thus derived. Nothing not known to Biya or that happened after Biya's death was stated by Swarnlata during these declarations. We must account somehow not only for the transfer of information to Swarnlata, but for the organization of the information in her mind in a pattern quite similar to that of the mind of Biya. Extrasensory perception may account for the passage of the information, but I do not think that it alone can explain the selection and arrangement of the information in a pattern characteristic of Biya. For if Swarnlata gained her information by extrasensory perception, why did she not give the names of persons unknown to Biya when she met them for the first time? Extrasensory perception of the magnitude here proposed should not discriminate between targets unless guided by some organizing principle giving a special pattern to the persons or objects recognized. It seems to me that here we must suppose that Biya's personality somehow conferred the pattern of its mind on the contents of Swarnlata's mind.

I am quite at one with Stevenson over his doubts concerning the ESP (or super-ESP) theory, but since I have already dwelt much upon the aridity of that theory, I shall pass on to discuss the possible survivalistic interpretations of Stevenson's cases. The first of these interpretations, the theory of obsession, has been the favourite resort of Spiritualists hostile to the idea of reincarnation. Their view is that the earth-bound spirit of some disreputable deceased person becomes in some way attached to a person still in the flesh. Through a process of reciprocal telepathy (the supposed process which in previous chapters I called 'overshadowing') this psychic parasite may influence the thoughts and behaviour of his victim (usually for the worse).

It is very difficult to know what to say of this theory. We cannot list the characteristics of a number of authenticated obsession cases, and then see how far the characteristics of our reincarnation cases match up to them. Many parapsychologists would strongly deny that there are *any* authenticated cases of obsession. Perhaps the best we can do here is to argue as follows. *If* there are indeed genuine cases of obsession, the Thompson–Gifford case, which I described in the last chapter, has as good a claim to be one of them as has any other case. Let us therefore compare the experiences of the obsessed or overshadowed Gifford with those of a typical child subject in one of Stevenson's reincarnation cases. If the two are very different, then the obsession theory will have failed to get off the ground, and we may properly leave it there until such time as further discoveries succeed in re-energizing it.

It is immediately obvious that Thompson's experiences differed from those of a typical reincarnation subject in at least the following respects:

(a) He had a frequent sense of an external presence 'overshadowing' him.

(b) His paintings (exhibition of a characteristic skill characteristic of Gifford) were often done in a state of dissociation, with some degree of subsequent amnesia.

(c) Scenes for his paintings were presented to him, as if from an external source, in visions.

(d) The overshadowing presence seemed to communicate with him as if from the outside through auditory hallucinations.

(e) The scenes which came to him did not come as scenes from his own past.

(f) Mediums into whose presence Thompson was brought picked up the presence of the obsessing 'Gifford' entity (so far as I know comparable experiments have not been tried with Stevenson's subjects).

(g) Thompson did not identify with Gifford in the sense of coming to regard Gifford's family and possessions as his own, etc.

More generally one might remark that the children in Stevenson's reincarnation cases do not, on the whole, present the signs of elaborating and maintaining a subconscious romance which led Mrs Sidgwick towards the theory of overshadowing in regard to the controls and communicators of Mrs Piper.

There seem therefore to be grounds for saying that in at least one case the experiences of a supposedly obsessed person were very different from those of the subjects of Stevenson's cases of ostensible reincarnation. This appears to me a sufficient reason for consigning the obsession theory not to oblivion, but indefinitely to the shelf. For since obsession is a state in which mind and behaviour are ostensibly influenced from the outside, the fundamental evidence for it could only be psychological evidence.

It is beginning to look very much as though, having begun by expressing my very considerable distaste for the idea of reincarnation, I have now, by eliminating all the obvious alternatives, argued myself into a position where I am bound to accept it, or at any rate to begin a serious attempt to make sense of it. Can one indeed make sense of this or any other form of the survival theory? If, after my death, some recently born young person starts to exhibit memories corresponding to my memories, skills corresponding to my skills, and so on, would it therefore follow that I am come again? These are the sorts of questions we shall have to discuss in the concluding chapters.

Pending the results of this discussion, I must admit that I do not find it easy to dissent from the very moderate opinion which Stevenson expresses at the end of his most recent study (153j, pp. 369–370):

> Persons who favour the certainties of religious traditions over the uncertainties of empirical investigations may prefer to remain with the former until we have improved the latter. But other persons may welcome a growing body of evidence that permits a rational belief in reincarnation, even though this evidence falls far short of being decisive. And for the future, there is the possibility that further and improved investigations of this type may develop stronger evidence of a quality that will permit a firmer conclusion to the most important of all the questions that man can ask about himself: Whether human personality survives death.

My conclusions have so far been on balance favourable to some form of survival hypothesis. Certain mediumistic communications and certain ostensibly reincarnated personalities display so many correct and detailed apparent memories of a former existence on earth that ESP by medium or reincarnated subject scarcely seems a possible explanation, unless, indeed, we are prepared to postulate ESP of an extent and complexity for which we have no independent support. Even if we were prepared to postulate such 'super-ESP' we would still be unable to account for other aspects of the 'evidence for survival', for the manifestation of skills, personality traits, purposes, a whole point of view, characteristic of the formerly living person. The super-ESP hypothesis suffers from a large credibility gap.

To many the credibility gap of the super-ESP hypothesis, and the disputes between the supporters of that theory, and those of the survivalist theory, must seem matters of no consequence whatsoever, like arguments between rival schools of astrologers. The findings of modern biological science strongly suggest (it would be claimed) that such 'mental' phenomena as remembering, thinking, forming plans, using language, and all expressions of human 'personality', depend upon, and at the bottom simply are, aspects of the functioning of the brain. There can therefore be no question of human personality surviving the dissolution of the brain, and no rational and scientifically educated person should waste time in studying the supposed 'evidence' for survival. The evidence for ESP may be marginally more worthy of credence, but the margin is so small as to make little difference.

We come here upon issues of immense difficulty and complexity. What is in question is the nature of the relationship between mind and brain, and the widely held, almost orthodox, contemporary view that the mind is brain in action. Now these issues are too vast and too obscure to be adequately tackled here, perhaps anywhere, yet they cannot be altogether dodged for, as I have just remarked, a powerful current of opinion holds that only one sort of answer is possible, and it is an answer which puts the ostensible evidence for survival with which this book is concerned wholly out of court.

Faced with the daunting necessity to say something, however inadequate, upon this crucial topic, I have decided to adopt the following tactic. I shall discuss principally the question of whether memory is entirely a function of the brain. For, to put it somewhat over-simply, if memories are to be equated with aspects of the structure and operation of the brain, one's power to remember could not survive the destruction and dispersal of one's brain. And since evidence for the survival of memory is a central – indeed the central – part of the 'evidence for survival', all evidence for surviving memory would have to be dismissed or radically reinterpreted. Furthermore, it is likely that what holds true of memory will also hold true of the other facets of human personality with which we are principally concerned, so that by investigating the issues with respect to memory, we may be able to reach conclusions of general applicability.

The Nature of Memory

A venerable view of the nature of memory, a view going back to classical times, is this. Stimuli falling on our sense organs produce disturbances in our brains, which cause us to 'perceive' those stimuli. The disturbances in our brains leave behind 'traces', minute changes in the structure of the brain. As a result of these changes, brain activity becomes more likely to follow those same paths again, making us liable to relive the original perceptual experiences in a watered down form ('memory images'), even in the absence of the stimuli which originally produced them. Such a revival of the original experience is especially likely to be triggered off by stimuli whose own traces are intermingled, or 'associated', with those of the first stimulus.

Today this venerable theory is formulated in the terms of modern neuroscience and modern cognitive psychology. We know that the brain contains thousands of millions of specialized nerve cells (neurons), each sending out filaments which make connections (synapses) with many other cells. By means of these filaments travelling regions of electrochemical disturbance (nerve impulses) are transmitted from one nerve cell to another. In an active brain immensely complex patterns of nerve impulses are continually shifting and changing and re-establishing themselves.

Some nerve impulses and patterns of nerve impulses seem to

originate spontaneously within the brain itself. But others are set going when external stimuli strike the sense organs. Volleys of nerve impulses rush down the sensory nerves which pass from the sense organ concerned to the 'central' nervous system and the brain. Such patterns of incoming nerve impulses are usually said to *represent* or *encode* the external stimulus (object or event) which gave rise to them.

Against this background, an account of memory is commonly developed along the following lines. The incoming nerve impulses that 'encode' the external event must themselves somehow change the properties of further neurons in such a way that the changes could also be said to 'represent' or 'encode' the external stimulus, but in a different fashion. These changes – which constitute the process of *memory storage* – are usually thought to involve such alterations in the connections between nerve cells as will facilitate the revival or partial revival of the 'stored' pattern of nerve impulses. The supposed process by which the stored pattern is revived as needed, and perhaps recirculated, is known as *retrieval*. It is 'retrieval' that gives rise to the experience of remembering.

The Coding-Storage-Retrieval Model

We may call this view of memory, which is endorsed by the conventional wisdom of current psychology and brain science, the *coding-storage-retrieval* model. Curiously enough (this is perhaps a significant point) this model was widely accepted for years, indeed decades, before there was any serious evidence in its favour. In fact it was accepted despite what some regarded as weighty evidence against it. The evidence against it was as follows. If memories are stored in the brain, it is natural to ask whereabouts in the brain the store may be. It had been known for a long time that general deterioration of the brain – especially deterioration involving atrophy of nerve cells in the cerebral cortex (the layer of 'grey matter' on the outside of the brain) – leads to a general loss of intellectual faculties, including memory. But numerous attempts to show, by experiments with animals, that particular memories were 'stored in' particular parts of the cortex were largely unsuccessful. Established memories could survive the removal of considerable amounts of cortical tissue; and when deficits were produced they were more obviously related to the amount of tissue removed than to its location. There was little to suggest the existence of a memory-store, or indeed of anything resembling memory-traces as usually conceived – a fact which greatly encouraged certain believers in survival. The coding-storage-retrieval model of memory was still largely an article of faith.

However, in the last couple of decades or so, various findings have come to hand which, though they do not amount to the discovery of a memory store or of clearly localized memory traces, are at any rate consonant with the coding-storage-retrieval model of memory. For instance:

1.   Electrical stimulation of the brain (especially of the temporal lobes, the parts just in from, and in front of, the ears) by means of a small electrode sometimes produces the apparent reliving of a past experience with an hallucinatory vividness. Some workers believe that the electrodes may activate a 'retrieval' mechanism (but this interpretation of the findings is disputed).

2.   Extensive damage to the front part of the temporal lobes has been found, if it occurs on both sides of the brain, to produce a frightful memory deficit. The victim is unable to retain for more than a minute or two a memory of any new event occurring, new person met, new place visited, etc., after the date of his injury. He will not even be able to keep track of the plot of a film, play, etc! This has been interpreted variously as due to an inability to store new material, to a selective inability to retrieve material, or to an inability to encode new material.

3.   The brain may, for our purposes, be regarded as consisting of two major portions, the brain stem, which is at it were an upward and forward extension and enlargement of the spinal cord, and the large twin hemispheres, which overlie the brain stem and conceal it. The hemispheres are connected by a large bundle of nerve fibres, called the corpus callosum, and if this is severed (producing a so-called 'split brain') the two hemispheres can to some extent act independently. In experiments with animals it has been shown that each hemisphere can be taught different things, and can learn to respond differently to the same stimulus. It is as though different memory traces have been diffusely laid down and separately stored in left and right hemispheres. Analogous findings have been obtained with human patients whose brains have been 'split' for the relief of epilepsy.

4.   It has often been claimed that the injection of certain substances into the brain – for instance ones which assist or inhibit the manufacture of protein in brain cells – may have a beneficial or injurious effect on the ability to learn and retain new material. Some workers think that we must be tapping the molecular basis of memory

storage; but the proper interpretation of such findings has been much disputed.

On the face of it we seem to have here evidence for a coding-storage-retrieval model of memory, in which the coding, storage and retrieval are all activities of the brain. If this approach to memory is correct, it is clear that one's memories could not survive the dissolution of one's brain.

It is ironical that the decades which have seen the first seemingly solid pieces of physiological evidence in favour of the coding-storage-retrieval model of memory have also witnessed the beginnings of a strong and perhaps unexpected attack upon the presuppositions of that model. This attack has come mainly from what may seem an unlikely quarter, namely certain philosophers interested in the philosophy of mind (17; 20; 62a; 62b; 98a; 98b). The issues are extremely complex and difficult, and I can here give only the barest outline of them; but they are of such obvious importance to the central problems of this book that it is impossible to pass them by. Readers who prefer not to embark at all on what are to them uncharted seas will find an interim summary on pages 202–3 and a concluding summary on pages 213–4.

Before we tackle these tricky issues, it is necessary to touch upon two commonly made distinctions which will be relevant to the discussion. They are as follows:

1.   The distinction between what I shall call 'personal' memory and what I shall call 'factual' memory. By 'personal' memory I mean one's ability to recollect events, actions, persons, places, etc., which one observed oneself. By 'factual' memory I mean the ability to call to mind items of factual or propositional knowledge, such as the fact that platinum dissolves in molten lead, or the fact that King John died of a surfeit of peaches and beer. It should be noted that factual memory does not necessarily involve personal memory; one can recall a fact without recalling the occasion on which one learned it. On the other hand personal memories are always also to some extent factual memories. Thus if one remembers the dome of St Peter's one *eo ipso* remembers that St Peter's is a Cathedral with a dome.

2.   The distinction between phenomena which possess or exhibit 'intentionality' and those which do not. 'Intentionality' in this technical sense has nothing special to do with intention. It is the property which many mental states or events have of being 'about' or

'directed upon' external objects or states of affairs. Thus a hope is always a hope *for* something or *that* something will come to pass, a belief is always a belief *that* so and so is the case, a memory is always a recollection *of* something or a recollection *that* such and such is or was the case. A full specification of any such mental state requires a specification of the state of affairs which is the 'object' of that mental state; but these 'intentional objects' need not of course exist, or have existed, in the external world – I can believe ardently in things that do not exist, seem to remember something that never happened, or hope for an event which will never transpire. There is a large, and highly technical, literature about intentionality, but for present purposes we need simply note that memory (at least the kinds of memory we are here concerned with) is essentially an 'intentional' phenomenon.

We can now consider some of the more obvious objections to the coding-storage-retrieval model of memory. I shall take these under two headings:

1. Objections to the idea that one's power to remember is due to one's having in one's brain coded 'representations' or coded symbols of external events.
2. Problems that arise over the retrieval or tapping of these stored representations.

1. Objections to the Idea of Inner Representations

The central problem confronting accounts of memory which postulate stored 'representations' of external events is that of clarifying what, in this context, could be meant by 'representation'. In the ordinary sense of the term 'representation' (as when a map might be said to be a representation of a stretch of terrain, or a grouping of pipe cleaners and ping-pong balls of a complex molecule), one thing can be a representation of another only if someone creates or adopts it for that purpose, or decides, believes, claims, etc., that it is or shall be so. Creating, deciding, adopting, believing, etc., are all 'intentional' states of mind or 'intentional' mental events (i.e. they are 'about' or 'directed upon' conceived or imagined states of affairs external to themselves). It is clear that the existence of such representations requires, and cannot be used to explain, memory and other 'intentional' phenomena.

Those who explain memory ('factual' and 'personal') in terms of inner 'representations', and assume that such representations are embodied in the brain, appear to be developing their own special or technical concept of representation. The essential features of this concept are that incoming stimuli ('inputs') produce changes in the brain (one could use the old word 'traces' for these). The traces in some (unknown) manner lawfully correspond to or parallel or 'represent' some aspects of the inputs which gave rise to them.

One has, I think, only to spell out what is involved in or implied by this concept of representation to see that it cannot possibly help us to understand the phenomena of memory. The concept has commonly been developed in one of two general ways.

The simpler of these two ways has been in the past widely adhered to, and provides an account of both 'factual' and 'personal' memory. It proposes in essence that when an episode of remembering takes place a memory trace (or stored representation) is 'retrieved' or reactivated. The effect of this retrieval is rather as though the input which originally gave rise to the trace had been again received, and had been processed through the system to the point at which its nature and character were deciphered. The original perceptual experience is, as it were, partly reinstated in the form of an image; or it may be that a series of inputs have been assimilated to a single trace or representation, in which case retrieval will give rise to a general or composite image, more suited for carrying 'factual' than 'personal' memories. The supposed inner representations are usually thought of as either 'visual' or 'verbal'. They are, in short, such that when 'retrieved', they yield a visual image of some person, event, or state of affairs, or an auditory image of certain appropriate spoken words.

This version of the representational theory has of late found many critics even amongst psychologists. In the first place, it hardly seems possible, except in the limiting case of certain highly 'personal' memories, to suppose that one's memory-knowledge of any given factual or personal matter consists in or is based upon the ability or tendency to evoke or entertain a particular image, or some image or images from a delimitable set, such as inner visual or verbal representations might be supposed to generate. Take as an example my memory of the fact that King John died of a surfeit of peaches and beer. I find that I can call the facts about King John's death to mind through such images as those of a certain page of a certain elementary history textbook; of an entry in the *Dictionary of National Biography*; of the voice of a former history teacher (with whom in fact I never studied the relevant period); of a crowned figure rolling on grass; of a picnic hamper containing peaches and bottled beer; of loud intestinal rumblings; of a cartoon in *Humours of History*; of the figures 1216 superimposed on a dish of tinned peaches; and so on. Several of these images are ludicrously inappropriate, but they all appear to 'work', and any one of them might come to mind or be deliberately summoned up in some circumstances. It is obvious that my knowledge that King John died of a surfeit of peaches and beer does not derive from an ability to activate or retrieve a particular inner representation, or a representation or representations from a limited set. I can create *whatever* visual or verbal images seem at the time to constitute appropriate *expressions* of the underlying memory-knowledge. The underlying memory-knowledge transcends any such limited set of visual or verbal images as the retrieval of inner representations mirroring episodes in past history lessons, etc., might be supposed to give rise to.

There seem also to be possible episodes of 'remembering' in which retrieved representations need not figure at all. If, for instance, I decline a meal of peaches and beer with a joking reference to King John, it does not follow that I first had one of the images listed above, or indeed any image at all. My action is itself as much an expression of the memory knowledge as any visual or verbal image.

Even if we set these difficulties aside, many others still remain. The partial reinstatement or reliving of a past experience (such as *ex hypothesi* would result from the retrieval of an inner representation) could not by itself constitute an act of remembering. An image representing some past scene that I had witnessed might occur to me at regular intervals without my ever realizing that I had gone through this experience before. And similarly I might frequently find myself entertaining in my mind's eye an image of a crowned figure clutching its stomach beside a table bearing tinned peaches and bottled beer without my once linking it to the death of King John. The occurrences of the images might indeed be due to modifications in my brain caused by past inputs; but their occurrence would not constitute *remembering*. A fully-fledged act of remembering would have, in addition, to involve what can perhaps best be called an 'affirmation' that the 'intentional objects' of the images (the events or states of affairs, external to themselves, that they are 'of', 'about' or 'point to') really took place, existed, were or are the case, etc. But this element of 'affirmation', of saying to oneself, 'this is how it was (or is)', is clearly that aspect of the whole episode in which memory-knowledge is effectively deployed. And quite obviously no account of the memory-knowledge displayed in 'affirmation' can be given in terms just of revived or retrieved 'representations'; for, as I have just pointed out, a representation does not yield memory-knowledge until an affirmation has been made. The theory of visual and verbal representations misses the essence of what is involved in remembering.

A closely related point is this. If I call to mind a visual image of a crowned figure, glumly clutching its stomach, and perhaps bearing the legend 'John: 1216', or if I have a verbal image of the words, 'King John died of a surfeit of peaches and beer', I could still make nothing of these images, could 'affirm' nothing about them, if I did not already *know* that King John died in 1216, and that these images referred to that knowledge. Indeed, unless I were already furnished with a great deal of background information in the light of which the visual and verbal images concerned 'made sense', I could not interpret them at all. I would need to know, for instance, what a king is, that there was a king called John, what peaches and beer are, what eating is, that overeating or bad food may lead to stomach disorders, etc. All these essential items of background information, without which the images concerned could not be properly interpreted or understood, themselves involve or constitute memory-knowledge; so that we cannot avoid postulating that into this one act of overt remembering there covertly enters a kind of memory-knowledge that does *not* require to be embodied or presented in the form of retrieved visual or verbal images, and cannot without regress be thought to require such embodiment.

I said a few paragraphs ago that the attempt to give an account of memory in terms of inner representations has taken one of two general forms. The first was the form which we have just discussed and rejected, namely the form which supposes inner representations to be predominantly either visual or verbal. Objections such as those I have just outlined, together with the fact that people find it easier to recall the 'gist' or 'meaning' of, say, a film or a prose passage, than they do the visual details or the exact words, have led many cognitive psychologists to develop the idea of what are called 'abstract' or 'propositional' representations (useful general accounts will be found in, for instance, 3, chapter 4; 78; 84).

Propositional Representations

Abstract or propositional representations are so called because they are held to embody abstract, propositional knowledge (knowledge *that* so and so is or was the case) rather than the quasi-perceptual information derived from the sense-organs embodied in visual and verbal representations. They are supposed to embody not just individual memories or pieces of memory-knowledge, but the whole structure of our propositional knowledge in particular areas, including both conceptual knowledge ('whales are mammals') and factual knowledge ('whales swim in arctic seas'). They must thus be regarded as themselves structured, though the nature of their neural embodiment, like much else about them, remains unclear. It is supposed that the underlying propositional structure can generate a great variety of different 'surface' expressions, e.g. different sentences, different actions, different images, and that conversely it mediates our understanding of many different statements that fall, so to speak, within a given area of knowledge. The generation of the surface expressions from the underlying representations is said to be lawful. It is 'factual' memory that propositional representations are primarily designed to explain; but some authorities (with whom I tend to agree) think that even 'personal' memories are really 'factual' or propositional (i.e. are recollections *that* such and such an event of a certain kind happened to one, etc.) (See, e.g., 126).

Cognitive psychologists and psycholinguists commonly characterize propositional representations, or interconnected networks of such representations, in a somewhat technical manner by means of symbolisms derived from mathematics and formal logic. Something of the 'feel' of these characterizations may perhaps be gained in the following way. Imagine something like an encyclopaedic dictionary in which the entries are heavily cross-indexed. Thus the entries for 'whale', 'swim', 'mammal', 'arctic', and 'sea' will be cross-indexed in such a way as to indicate that (by definition) whales are mammals, and that (as a matter of fact) whales swim in arctic seas. Similarly the entries for 'blubber', 'whale', 'fat', 'skin', etc., will be cross-indexed in such a way as to indicate that blubber is an insulating layer of fat found beneath the skin of whales; and so on and so forth more or less indefinitely. Next imagine that all these cross-indexings, instead of being written into the various dictionary entries, are set out on one large sheet of paper, with key terms, or concepts, like 'whale', 'mammal', 'blubber', 'swim', etc., shown by small circles, and their meaning-relationships and factual relationships indicated by connecting lines of different colours or of different kinds and degrees of brokenness. This gives one a vague and somewhat misleading, but still,

I hope, for present purposes sufficient, idea of the sort of ways in which propositional representations have commonly been characterized.

Somewhere in the brain, it is implicitly assumed, there must be anatomical or physiological systems (propositional representations) whose structures and operations are in some sense mapped by the diagrams or symbol systems whose 'feel' I have been trying to convey. If an incoming statement or proposition so to speak harmonizes or chimes in with some part or aspect of this underlying, physiologically embodied, network, it will be understood and accepted. Conversely, the network will, so to speak, generate or permit the generation of only such propositions as are embodied in the cross-linkages of the network. Present versions of this approach deal principally with statements, and how they are produced and understood, but their proponents clearly hope to extend them to cover the generation of thoughts, judgements, images, etc., in short to all the phenomena of 'factual' memory.

I think that some of the writers who have adopted this sort of approach to the problems of memory (and of cognition in general) may look upon their delineations of the 'structure' of 'propositional representations' not as speculations about supposed inner mechanisms, but as a means of (an appropriate notation for) so to speak mapping the 'structure' of our propositional knowledge (especially our memory knowledge), of exhibiting the ways in which our concept of 'blubber' is linked to our concepts of 'mammal', 'sea', 'fat', and so on and so on. With this enterprise, though I doubt its point and long-term prospects, I have no quarrel. Others, however, seem to regard themselves as working out the groundplan of the inner mechanism through which we understand what is said to us and what goes on around us, and by means of which we know, remember, formulate propositions, etc. Broadly speaking this enterprise could take one of two forms, both of which appear to me to be quite unintelligible.

(a)   It might be supposed that propositional representations, once built up, are simply stored away and so to speak consulted when needed. This idea is quite obviously regressive, for it implies a further system which does the consulting and understands the outcome thereof, and this second system would itself need to possess concepts, intelligence and memory. (Despite the obvious regress, some neuropsychologists are prone to talk as if they thought that certain brain lesions, which interfere with the victim's grasp of semantic and conceptual relationships, were damaging a store of this kind.)

(b)   A position that seems to be commonly, if implicitly, held, is that 'propositional representations' are themselves the brain mechanisms of the understanding and production of propositional speech and thought (including thoughts and utterances which would be said to manifest or express factual and perhaps also personal memory). The diagrams and symbol systems by means of which propositional representations have been characterized are then regarded as being in effect blueprints of these underlying mechanisms, albeit blueprints of a very schematic and general kind.

It is possible, and, as I remarked a moment ago, quite legitimate to regard diagrams of propositional representations as ways of summarizing what may perhaps be called the 'intellectual competence' of a particular human being, or of human beings in particular societies. Such diagrams map the organization of a person's knowledge, his grasp of the interrelationships of the concepts embodied in the ordinary speech of his society, and so on. To regard such mappings of someone's intellectual competence not as partial specifications of what a supposed underlying mechanism would have to accomplish, but as specifications of the mechanism itself, is, on the face of it, a gross confusion. It is like taking a schematic drawing of a finished car for a blueprint of the production line which assembled that car.

Some people may, I think, have been misled into supposing otherwise, for the following reasons. When the 'finished product' which has been mapped or delineated is competence in carrying out some rule-governed activity, like playing checkers or tic-tac-toe, or constructing grammatically correct sentences, it is relatively easy to translate the map into a computer programme. The computer can furthermore be made to run through moves formally paralleling the actions of a human being who is 'competent' in the rule-governed activity concerned. The same holds true when the competence being delineated is of the kind mapped by the diagrams favoured by believers in 'propositional representations'. It is tempting to suppose that when we have programmed a computer to 'play games', emit grammatical sentences, spell out the relationships between commonly accepted propositions in a certain area, and so on, we have in effect created machines which work on the same sort of principles as we may supposed to be embodied in the brains of human beings who possess these competences. These computers must therefore in effect contain mechanical embodiments of 'propositional representations'. Surely we may assume that the human brain is likely to contain something analogous?

The mistake here consists in forgetting that what has been programmed into the computer is still, so to speak, only a 'map' or diagram of the competence concerned, and not the competence itself. The computer goes through certain changes in accordance with its 'map' and prints certain signs; these signs can be *interpreted by* an intelligent computer user as moves in a game of tic-tac-toe or checkers, or as sentences following the rules of English grammar, or whatever. But all the computer is doing here is as it were putting up bit by bit for its user's benefit a very detailed diagram of the sort of competence which a person who could really and truly play this game, understand the connections between these propositions, etc., would display. It develops many of the details as it goes along ('computes' them) from principles already built into it. None the less it can no more be said itself to 'possess' the competence concerned than a computer which can flash up road maps with distances, compute the shortest route from Land's End to John o' Groats, etc., could be said to 'know the way' from one place to another. For 'competence' in games, and in comparable rule-governed activities, does not consist in blindly going through motions into which intelligent (and 'competent') persons can 'read' the moves of the games concerned. It consists in making the proper moves (or what one conceives to be the proper moves) from the *understanding* that this is a game, that it has rules, that such and such are the *permitted* moves in this situation, and that of the permitted moves some are, in the current state of play, 'better' or more *logical* than others.

I conclude that the advocates of 'propositional representations' have so far given us only (partial) *maps* or *diagrams* of the intellectual competence displayed by persons possessing propositional or factual knowledge. They have not yet begun to approach the question of what the underlying *mechanism* of this competence might be like. That it is possible to approach the question at all remains at the moment a pious hope. Certainly it will not be possible to approach it by invoking inner 'representations' of the 'structure' of the intellectual competence concerned.

2. Problems to do with 'Retrieval'

If a stored representation, propositional or otherwise, is to give rise to an episode of remembering, it must, in terms of the coding-storage-retrieval model of memory, be 'retrieved', and as it were reactivated and partly recirculated through the system. Now if such a representation is to be retrieved from storage, it must first be located, and this in turn requires that it be labelled, tagged or coded in some way (as is the case with computer 'memories'). Otherwise the mechanism would not be able to retrieve on demand the right representation from the store. And the retrieval mechanism must possess or 'know' the various labels or tags. But (since the labels cannot be innate) this means that the mechanism must itself have a memory. And its memory cannot, without regress, be explained on the coding-storage-retrieval model. Hence this model can never give us an adequate account of memory.

It might be replied that 'content-addressable' storage systems can circumvent this difficulty. These are systems in which representations are retrieved because some element in the input (external stimulus) contains the label or 'address' of the appropriate representation. The short answer is that the external circumstances in which an intelligent person might find it appropriate to retrieve a given fact are indefinitely numerous, and are liable to an indefinitely large increase in number as time progresses. No content-addressable system could match the range of possibilities here.

These problems arise whatever kind of stored representations are in question. Special to propositional representations, however, are a further set of problems of the following kind. Propositional representations are supposed inner or 'deep' structures which generate a variety of different possible 'surface' expressions. There must, according to the theory, be rules determining which one of the possible surface expressions is generated on any particular occasion. But what can these rules be? Take as an example my memory of the interesting fact that platinum (melting point 1770°C) will dissolve in molten lead at a much lower temperature. So far as I can tell this memory does not, in my case, lead to the generation of any special or 'preferred' image or images; however, I might in some circumstances summon up various more or less appropriate images, e.g. of someone stirring a greyish, bubbling liquid, or the printed words 'melting point 1770°C', or of a voice saying, 'It will not melt, but it will dissolve'. In what actions will my memory-knowledge of this fact find expression? Probably none; or perhaps it may make me nod my head sagely when I come to read R. Austin Freeman's *Dr Thorndyke Intervenes*, a detective story in which the solubility of platinum in lead plays a part. But in what actions *might* this knowledge find expression? Well, I might pass a remark during a coffee-break conversation, or write something in an examination paper, or make a comment to my wife while looking at her wedding ring; I might write notes towards a treatise on the oddities of natural philosophy; I might in some remotely conceivable circumstances engineer a crafty escape from a platinum-built UFO. And so on and so on indefinitely.

What, then, could be the 'transformational' rules that relate the underlying propositional representation which embodies the information about the solubility of platinum in lead to the various possible surface expressions which it may generate? The trouble is that it is quite impossible to set limits on the number of possible surface expressions which the propositional representation of a fact such as we are considering might have. One can create relevant images on demand, in as much variety as the occasion requires. One will, within the limits of one's capacities, utter whatever words or carry out whatever actions an intelligent person who knows the fact in question *should* utter or carry out in the prevailing circumstances (whatever they may be). And that, I think, is the point. There is, and can be, no finite set of rules relating propositional representations to their surface expressions. Into the theory there must instead of rules surreptitiously be introduced an *intelligence* (a creative intelligence I might add) whose function is to understand and interpret the propositional representations and to direct thoughts, utterances and actions in the light of them. And this intelligence, I need hardly say, is going to require its own intentionality, and its own memory with its own retrieval system and its own intelligence to operate that retrieval system, and so on for ever.

In sum: a widely adopted approach to the explanation of memory-phenomena consists in supposing that there are laid down in our brains coded traces or 'representations' of past events or circumstances. An act of remembering occurs when one of these coded representations is 'retrieved' and so to speak put into circulation once more. I called this model of memory the 'coding-storage-retrieval' model. It is of importance in the present context because if our memories consist of 'traces' laid down in our brains, then clearly our memories cannot survive the dissolution of our brains, and a large part of the 'evidence' for survival – that involving evidence for the survival of memories – has to be abandoned or radically reinterpreted. I argued, however, that the coding-storage-retrieval model of memory, in any of the forms so far developed (and, I should like to add, in any form that could be developed), is quite incoherent.

A central part of my objections was in essence this. According to this model of memory (which is also a model of thought in general) we adjust our present thought and behaviour to the lessons of the past by retrieving and reprocessing or examining stored representations of past events (we may also use these resources to represent present events and situations to ourselves). But the stored inner representations on which we can thus supposedly draw to assist us in our dealings with the outer world would themselves constitute a kind of 'world' of their own. We would have to learn our way round this world, and learn to interpret and manipulate its contents, just as we have to learn our way round the outer world. To make use of these inner representations we would, in short, need already to have developed memory-knowledge; hence we cannot explain memory in terms of the retrieval of 'inner representations'.

I cannot of course deny that past experience may leave behind in the brain traces or representations which, when reactivated (yielding, perhaps, a 'memory-image') may cause or prompt us to remember. Such representations would, of course, simply have the status of *aides-mémoire*, and I need hardly say that an *aide-mémoire* presupposes, and does not itself constitute, a working memory. I am bound to say, however, that the idea that inner representations can have even this limited role is far from plausible. For an *aide-mémoire* is normally something that I might keep in my pocket to consult as needed. Do I then have a second *aide-mémoire* in my head which I likewise consult as needed? I am never conscious of consulting it. On what occasions do I desist from my ordinary mode of recollection (whatever that may be) and unknowingly turn to the inner *aide-mémoire*? Is it when I hesitate for a moment and *then* remember? What sort of code or language is the inner *aide-mémoire* written in? Do I as the years go by develop different codes for different purposes, corresponding to the different sorts of symbolisms (mathematical, technical, graphic, linguistic) in which knowledge in different areas is customarily set down? Or is there one universal inner language or code? If so is it innate ('built in' to the brain) or acquired? These questions, and many others equally vain, arise from the quagmires of the representational theory the moment one begins to take the *aide-mémoire* proposal seriously, like an endless series of will o' the wisps inviting pursuit.

Implications for Survival

I must emphasize that I have so far said nothing directly to challenge the supposition that memory is entirely dependent upon brain function, a supposition for which there is a great deal of empirical support. All I have done is challenge a widely received theory (or rather theoretical framework) concerning the relationship between memory and the brain. The objections to this theory, the theory of inner representations (or coding-storage-retrieval model), do, however, bear indirectly upon the problem of survival in two ways.

The first of them is as follows. The super-ESP hypothesis, the chief alternative to the survival hypothesis, seems inescapably committed to a 'representational' view of memory. For according to the super-ESP hypothesis, successful mediums must obtain much of their information about deceased persons by so to speak riffling through the memory-stores of the living and 'reading' their contents. But if there are no representations there are no memory-stores and nothing 'in' those stores which mediums can telepathically examine. The super-ESP hypothesis seems bound to collapse along with the coding-storage-retrieval theory of memory. It collapses, furthermore, whether we suppose the 'storage' to take place in the human brain, or (as some have thought) outside it – in, for example, a localized 'ether of images', a cosmic memory pool, the 'Akashic records' of the theosophists, or the mind of God. The objections to coding-storage-retrieval theories of memory would in all cases be similar.

The second way in which the collapse of the coding-storage-retrieval model of memory would indirectly affect the prospects of the survival theory is this. If memories are simply traces or representations in the brain, they cannot possibly survive the destruction of the brain. Personal survival of death is therefore absolutely ruled out (if, that is, we set aside the idea of a bodily resurrection, which would amount to the undoing or reversal of death, rather than survival of it, and is clearly not a candidate-explanation for the sorts of phenomena we are considering). If, on the other hand, the ability to remember, whatever it may consist in, is *not* based upon brain-traces or inner representations, we are, so to speak, licensed to speculate along other, less fashionable lines, some of which *may*, while others quite certainly will *not* make the survival theory once again a conceivable option for explaining certain mediumistic (and other) phenomena. In the remainder of this chapter I shall briefly explore the question of what the leading features of such an alternative approach to the problems of memory might be like.

Other Views of Memory

Any such alternative approach must, I think, to begin with emphasize a point that is not so much denied as underplayed by many proponents of representational theories, the point, namely, that human memory – at any rate the sort with which we are here concerned, – and which the representational theories are intended to explain – is essentially and before everything else a manifestation of human conceptual abilities. Very roughly one might say that concept-possession involves the capacity to group objects together in thought and to think of individual group-members *as* members of the group. In its simplest form this capacity may simply involve grouping together a miscellaneous collection of objects that one happens to find in a particular location – as when one says to oneself, 'I must tidy all that stuff away!' More commonly one groups things together not in virtue of their spatial location but because they all possess a certain characteristic or set of characteristics. One groups, say, all 'oranges' together in thought because they have similar weights, colours, textures, are edible, moist, sweet-tasting, etc.; and when one encounters an individual specimen possessing these characteristics one says of it, 'Ah, yes. One of *those*!' One may divide the class of oranges into further subgroups – Sevilles, Jaffas, mandarins, clementines, etc., – on the basis of more specific characteristics, or assimilate it to a larger grouping – 'fruit' – by restricting oneself to a small number of more general characteristics.

Now if one can say of an individual object which one encounters (an orange), 'Ah, yes! One of *those*!' (oranges as a class), one is obviously in a sense transcending the here and now; one is in thought assimilating the present specimen, on account of certain characteristics which it possesses, to a group of other objects not currently before one. One can go further and think about either the group of objects, or some individual object considered as a member of the group, in the total absence of either group or specimen. One can indeed thus 'conceive' them not just in their absence, but even if they do not exist at all, and never have existed (as when, for instance, one makes out for oneself in thought a class of diminutive human-shaped creatures possessing butterfly-like wings and magical powers).

It is at once apparent that only a being who exhibits these 'conceptual' capacities, the nature of which I have just, very crudely, tried to indicate, could truly possess memories, whether 'personal' or 'factual'. If I am to be said to remember that King John died of a surfeit of peaches and beer, I must possess such concepts as those of king, peaches, beer, illness, etc. I must be able to assign, in thought, certain objects (those which caused the king's death) to a class of things (peaches) marked out in terms of certain characteristics (size, taste, colour, growing on trees, etc.). If I could not think of these objects as belonging to that class, I could not think of them *as peaches*, and accordingly I could not recall the fact that King John died of a surfeit of peaches and beer. Even if those very words came into my mind, I should not adequately understand their meaning, and they would therefore not constitute a true recollection of the fact concerned.

It is obvious that a similar point could be made in connection with all the other terms in the proposition (king, death, beer – the proper name 'John' would require special treatment), and it is also obvious that the same problems arise in connection with 'personal' memories. I remember, for instance, the occasion on which – a hero for the first, and so far the only, time in my life – I defied the fast bowler in a house match. I could not in any real sense have this recollection at all unless I possessed such concepts as bat, ball, delivery, game, etc., etc. One's capacity to remember is part and parcel of (and is indeed inseparably linked with) one's overall conceptual capacities.

We now reach our central question, namely that of how memory-capacity and conceptual capacity in general, might be linked to brain function. It has been fashionable among physiologists and physiological psychologists to approach memory in what may be called a 'bottom up' manner. They have sought, in other words, to account for memory phenomena by postulating that experience causes changes within or between functional elements (nerve cells, protein molecules, etc.) in the brain. Since the overall pattern of relationship between these elements (the 'structure') is held to determine all levels of behaviour and mental functioning, the changes will produce corresponding alterations in these things, changes which constitute memory of facts or past events. I think that there are reasons (which I cannot spell out here) for supposing that any theory which attempts thus to derive the phenomena of memory entirely from the interactions of the elements of a system is bound to be a theory of the representational or coding-storage-retrieval sort. For if within such a system (of which a digital computer appropriately programmed would serve as a central example) past functioning (input-output relations) is systematically to influence future input-output relations, this can only be because of changes in the relations between the elements of the system, changes which systematically reflect its past input-output-input history. Such changes would almost certainly qualify by definition as inner 'representations' of past objects or events. If, therefore, the doubts which I have expressed about representational theories of memory are justified, not just representational theories, but all theories starting from supposed elements and the supposed laws of their interactions must go by the board. We must instead try out what may be called 'top down' theories, theories according to which the elements of a system sometimes act in conformity with laws which characterize the functioning of the overall system, and cannot be derived from the laws which govern the interactions of elements with their fellows. One might call the laws or principles of the working of such a system 'supervenient' laws or principles, because they supervene upon, and so to speak override or overrule, the laws of the behaviour of the elements. (A corollary of this would, I think, be that there must be a certain randomness or indeterminacy in the behaviour of the elements.)

In the case we are considering, the supervenient laws or principles are those of the 'conceptual' (or simply 'mental') level of functioning, which include of course the 'laws' of memory; the laws upon which they supervene are the commonplace and commonly accepted chemical and physiological laws which govern the behaviour of brain cells. We should have to suppose, I think, that when, during the development of the individual, or the evolution of the species, the overall spatio-temporal patterns of brain activity reach and pass a certain level of complexity, the supervenient laws appear, and begin, so to speak, partially to direct those patterns of activity, the result being, among other things, characteristic changes in the organism's behaviour. The behavioural changes will, however, not be constant from one individual organism of the species to the next, for different individuals with different histories develop different conceptual capacities and different sets of memories, and the supervenient 'laws' or 'principles' of functioning will differ correspondingly from one individual to the next. Thus, from a standpoint, so to speak, at the level of brain cells and their summed individual activities and relationships, memory (along with other manifestations of conceptual capacities) will involve supervenient principles of functioning, principles differing somewhat in detail from one individual to the next, and not derivable from any amount of information concerning structural changes within and between brain cells.

The supervenient principles which, according to the hypothesis we are considering, emerge and develop when the overall spatio-temporal pattern of brain activity reaches a certain kind and degree of complexity, might be supposed either:

1. to inhere in the stuff of the universe in ways which contemporary physical science has as yet scarcely begun to glimpse, and to be 'released' when patterns of the right kind and complexity are generated; or

2. to be created, brought into being, by complex patterns of brain activity; or

3. to result from the interaction between some influence outside the brain, and brain activity of a sufficiently complex kind (one might say that when an active brain is blown upon by the cosmic wind, or swims in the holomovement or the sea of hidden variables, strange and unforeseen phenomena come into being); or

4. to come from outside the brain and be *permitted expression* when a brain exhibits a certain kind of highly complex activity-pattern.

I do not think that, for present purposes, it greatly matters which of the above positions we adopt, for, without specifically adhering to any one of them, we can make some plausible further suggestions as to how the supervenient level of function might be supposed to be related to the patterns of activity of brain cells. These suggestions are six in number:

1. It seems fairly clear that, within certain modest limits, there is no intrinsic or necessary link between specific instances of supervenient functioning (particular thoughts, particular memories, etc.) and the firing of particular sets of brain-cells. Once the critical level of complexity of brain-activity has been passed, the thinking of a particular thought is likely to be compatible with the firing of any one of a very large number of possible subsets of brain cells; and vice versa. There are various kinds of reason for saying this. One kind of reason is empirical: there are many examples in which the power of conceptual thought has been gravely impaired following considerable loss of brain tissue, and has subsequently to a greater or lesser extent been re-established. There have also been many cases of early loss of brain tissue (sometimes as much as a whole cerebral hemisphere) or of congenital abnormalities leading to a similar result, in which conceptual functioning has developed to lie within normal limits. In both these sorts of case it seems inevitable that we should have to say that this, that, or the other thought (supervenient level of functioning)

now occurs in connection with, or is mediated by, the activity of a set of brain cells other than the set with whose actitivity it was once associated, or would have been associated had earlier circumstances been different.

Another kind of reason is logical. According to the hypothesis we are considering (the hypothesis, indeed, to which we have been driven by the breakdown of the coding-storage-retrieval model of memory) the supervenient level of functioning reflects back upon, and directs, the neural events which accompany it. The supervenient level of functioning could not have this kind of autonomy, and could not thus act as a factor or principle ordering neural events, if each actual or possible supervenient (mental, conceptual) event or state were uniquely related to the activation of one and only one set of brain cells. For if the supervenient level of function is to be thought of as bringing about changes in the pattern of neural events rather than as merely accompanying such changes, it must, so to speak, change first, and bring the neural events into line afterwards.

I do not, of course, wish to go to the opposite extreme and suggest that the firing of any sufficiently complex subset of brain cells is compatible with the appearance of any kind of supervenient functioning whatsoever. The particular kind of higher functioning that appears or emerges will be constrained though not determined in detail by aspects or features of the overall complex spatio-temporal pattern of brain activity, and it is not impossible that such constraints will become stricter as the organism grows older. Thus dreams occur when the brain exhibits certain patterns of electrical activity (perhaps linked to regenerative processes in brain cells); the brain activity may constrain mental activity into a certain mode (dreaming) without determining the content of the dream in any detail. Other (perhaps partly overlapping) patterns of brain activity may be particularly conducive to (say) rational, or verbal, or musical, or depressive, or action-oriented modes of thought. The way in which mental states follow one another (their sequence) may be determined through the 'higher' level of function constraining the 'lower', or vice versa; or some admixture of both.

2.   It seems likely that more complex patterns of brain activity will permit the appearance of more complex kinds of supervenient functioning (it would, however, be no light task to give an adequate definition of complexity here). This is, I think, basically a matter of observed fact (though one might find reasons for regarding it as

antecedently likely). As a human being grows towards mental maturity, so the interconnections between his brain cells grow immeasurably more complicated. This in turn makes for an immense increase in the possible complexity and variety of spatio-temporal patterns of nervous activity. The multiplication of links between brain-cells is generally regarded as due to, or rather as constituting, learning. I should, however, be inclined to suppose that much of this multiplication represents the basis for a general increase in the number and complexity of possible patterns of nerve cell activity, and hence of possible modes of supervenient (mental) functioning, and not the basis for the canalization of mental activity into determinate channels.

3.   If, as I suggested a moment ago, there may be, or may develop, some, though not a strict, association between certain general features of the overall pattern of brain activity, and the emergence of certain modes of supervenient functioning (dreaming, rational thought, musical thought, etc.), the following further issue arises. What happens when circumstances require the simultaneous production of more than one of these supervenient modes of functioning, for instance the musical and the verbal? Suppose that the particular mode of supervenient function to emerge is related (as seems inescapable) to the pattern of activity, of *all* or *much* of the brain. Now the *whole brain* cannot simultaneously exhibit two different patterns of activity. But perhaps in so large and intricate a brain as that possessed by humans two different complex patterns of activity might develop in two different parts, say the left and right hemispheres, thus permitting the simultaneous emergence of verbal and musical functioning. Could one then sing the National Anthem as distinct from having to choose between humming the tune and reciting the words? Not necessarily; but probably one could do so provided that the patterns of activity in the two brain regions involved stood in whatever (presently unknown) spatio-temporal relationships to each other and to patterns of activity in the rest of the brain are necessary to make them sub-patterns within an overall pattern of a kind upon which this new and 'higher' kind of functioning might supervene.

Of course this example is immensely oversimplified; but there is, as is well known, a good deal of evidence for the 'localization' of specific psychological functions 'in' specific parts of the brain. Damage to the parts of the brain concerned leads to impairment of the psychological function. 'Disconnection' of two such parts (i.e. destruction of the nervous pathways connecting them) will impair performance in any task that required the integration of both the psychological functions concerned. (Conventional thinking on this last matter supposes that coded 'representations' can no longer be shunted around as required.) The approach we are exploring would lead us to take a somewhat different view of the effects of brain damage on psychological functioning. If (to return to my over-simplified example) that region of the brain in which the 'music' pattern had become established were destroyed, the 'musical' function would no longer supervene, at least until that pattern had re-established itself elsewhere, or the function become linked to a somewhat different pattern. If the 'verbal' region became 'disconnected' from the 'musical' region, the two patterns might be thrown out of gear in such a way that the supervenient function would be rendered at least temporarily incoherent, and attempts to sing the National Anthem would be dismal failures.

The suggestions I have so far explored concerning the possible relationship between the postulated 'supervenient' level of functioning and patterns of brain activity have mostly concerned conceptual functioning in general. My final suggestions have more specifically to do with memory.

4. I am not, of course, suggesting that once the 'higher' level of functioning has supervened, memory (as an aspect of this higher level of functioning) is independent of, or unaffected by, activities and changes at cellular level. We might make some plausible guesses at the relations between the two levels of functioning. For instance, suppose that when I first grasped that interesting point about the solubility of platinum in molten lead, my brain was exhibiting such and such a spatio-temporal pattern of activity – a pattern from a limited but still extensive range of possible patterns, any one of which might have permitted or underpinned my moment of understanding. Thereafter two tendencies come into play:

(a) When I next think about, remember, exercise my understanding of, platinum and lead (a higher level or supervenient activity), that pattern of brain activity will be more likely to come into being than others from the same range (this might underlie the fact that an action which, when first executed, is carefully thought out, may with repetition become automatic).

(b) The recurrence of that pattern of brain activity will tend to bring me once again to think about platinum and its solubility in lead (the combination of this tendency with the preceding one might facilitate reinstatement of my knowledge of the solubility of platinum in lead as soon as my thought began to turn in the right direction).

These two changes may well involve changes at synapses (the junctions between nerve cells), giving some possible patterns advantages over others.

5. I think we shall also have to suppose some kind of law of inertia with regard to the formation of memories. Not every new piece of information that comes one's way results in a change in one's conceptual equipment, in the supervenient principles of functioning of which I have spoken. Indeed one would not wish to have it otherwise, for the disadvantages of having a perfect memory would be considerable. There must be a tendency for the 'supervenient' principles to remain as they were, or to subside again into their previous state, unless there is some positive feature of the situation which permits or promotes change. One must remember that the relationship between 'lower' and 'higher' levels of functioning is a two-way one. Lower level events constrain higher level events as well as vice versa. If lower level conditions (the pattern of electrochemical happenings in the brain cells) are not right, changes in the supervenient principles will not come about, or the system will quickly subside again into the *status quo*. The effect of an epileptic fit, an electric shock to the brain or a blow to the head may well be to precipitate just such a return to the *status quo*, leading to complete amnesia (loss of memory) for events immediately preceding the traumatic happening. Perhaps a less devastating influence of the same kind – say a continued diffuse bombardment of the hemispheres by nerve impulses originating from the brain stem – is always at work and needs to be inhibited or modulated in some unknown fashion before any permanent change in the supervenient principles can get under way. Removal of the modulating influence would lead to a grave impairment in the ability to learn new material, an effect which is of course produced by certain brain lesions.

6. Memory will of course also be impaired (along with all other manifestations of conceptual capacities) by any factor which interferes with the complex patterns of brain activity upon which the 'higher' level of functioning supervenes. For instance the senile and pre-senile dementias, which involve a general deterioration of all intellectual faculties, are marked by an extensive degeneration of cortical nerve-cells, a degeneration which would without doubt disrupt and ultimately abolish the intricate spatio-temporal patterns of brain activity necessary for the emergence of the 'higher' level of functioning.

Summary

This brief excursus on memory and the brain is, of course, to be taken with a grain of salt. Its purpose is illustrative rather than expository. I argued in the first part of the chapter that the coding-storage-retrieval model of memory, with its assumption that memories are traces or representations in the brain, and its consequent incompatibility with survivalist theories of the sorts of phenomena we have been discussing in this book, is quite incoherent and must be abandoned. What I have been trying to illustrate in later parts of the chapter is that it is by no means difficult to dream up other, and quite different, accounts of how memory may be related to brain function, accounts which can accommodate basic facts about localization of function in the brain, the effect of brain damage on memory, and so forth, with at any rate no greater implausibility than attends the (far from convincing) explanations of the same facts given by proponents of the coding-storage-retrieval model.

My own account is, as I said, intended to be merely illustrative. But it does have at least one feature which (it seems to me) any longer and more serious account would have to have. It places the phenomena of memory among a class of psychological phenomena which cannot be explained in terms of, but rather supervene upon, the complex patterns of electrochemical activity manifested by the brain – at least as these are conceived by contemporary science. From the standpoint of the activities of one's brain-cells, one's memories represent supervenient principles of ordering which in part direct and constrain those activities. And since my personal and many of my factual memories are different from your memories, it could be said that in a sense each brain has *its own* set of supervenient principles of ordering.

Now if memories are not 'written in' to the brain, but involve an emergent or supervenient level of function which constitutes, relative to the activities of nerve cells in the brain, a principle or principles of ordering not derivable within the framework of conventional neurophysiology, then possibilities remain open which bear upon the tenability of the survival hypothesis. The principles of ordering which supervene upon the 'lower level' functioning of each person's brain have *ex hypothesi* some degree of autonomy from the neural events which they 'constrain'; and certainly memories 'lost' after shock or actual damage to the brain may sometimes reinstate themselves in ways that suggest that they are now sustained or underpinned by the activity of neural elements other than those which originally sustained them. Could this autonomy extend so far as reinstatement in some other setting altogether? I have tried to show that this possibility cannot at the moment be effectively ruled out on neuropsychological or neurophysiological grounds. One might well demand very strong evidence indeed before conceding that the possibility may in fact be realized. Yet I think it might fairly be said that some of the evidence presented in this book – and it is only a small part of the total evidence – is at least exceedingly curious.

14 Out-of-the-Body Experiences and Apparitions

I suggested in the previous chapter that memory, and phenomena involving concept-possession, must be regarded as manifestations of a level of function which supervenes upon, and cannot be explained in terms of, electrochemical events within and between brain cells, at any rate as these events are currently understood. I suggested further that from the standpoint of the activities of the cells in a given individual's brain, his particular memories, memory-knowledge, and conceptual abilities in general, must constitute supervenient principles of functioning special to him. His surviving the death of his brain would involve, amongst other things, the continued operation of these principles in some other setting than that of the brain with which they were originally associated. And evidence for survival, such as we have been discussing in this book, could reasonably be said to constitute evidence for such continued operation – for the 'supervenient level of functioning' approach to memory does not rule out this possibility in the way that the 'inner representation' approach does.

Now if we are to take the survival theory seriously, two further questions immediately suggest themselves. The first is this. Would the survival of the supervenient principles of functioning once associated with a particular person's brain involve or amount to or require the survival of that person as a conscious individual? This is an extraordinarily difficult problem, to which I have no ready answer. In the case of mediumistic communicators one might try to develop an argument along the following lines. If we encounter and communicate with a skilled and purposive intelligence which exhibits an apparently coherent stream of memories, then we *must* accept that we are dealing with a conscious individual. For we have no other criteria, and no other possible criteria, for the presence of such an individual. The presence, e.g., of a moving and breathing body would not be a sufficient criterion (some would, however, wish to argue – mistakenly in my view – that it is a necessary one). The issue, therefore, that we have to decide when confronted with the apparently surviving memories, purposes, etc., of some person now deceased is not whether they indicate the presence of a conscious individual, but whether or not the conscious individual whose presence they indicate is some living and embodied human being, e.g. a medium in a state of dissociation exercising her powers of super-ESP. If we are prepared to rule out the super-ESP hypothesis, is there any remaining hypothesis other than that of survival that even begins to make sense?

The only alternatives I can think of are of the most nebulous kind. The most frequently canvassed has been the 'psychic factor' theory developed, though not necessarily endorsed, by the late Professor C. D. Broad (18a, pp. 536–551; 18c, pp. 419–430). According to this theory, when a person dies something survives, but it is a something much less than a whole person. In and of itself it is not sentient or purposive, but it is none the less a vehicle for memory traces and perhaps for other kinds of dispositions. It is capable under certain circumstances of entering into such a relationship with the nervous system of a living person as will enable that person (medium, percipient) to develop a transient and perhaps dissociated stream of consciousness which will exhibit some of the memories, purposes, etc., once characteristic of the deceased person concerned. Broad seems to think of 'psychic factors' as being spatially localized entities, but no doubt it would be possible to develop versions of the theory which made 'psychic factors' something like holograms, i.e. not localised in themselves, but capable of localized manifestations.

The psychic factor theory would, I think, run into considerable difficulties if the criticisms of trace theories of memory, which I presented in the last chapter, are correct. For the insentient psychic factor would have to be the bearer not of a store of inert memory 'traces', which a medium might in some way 'read', but rather of a whole complex and interrelated set of conceptual capacities, capacities which (I have argued) cannot possibly be based upon inner traces or representations in any substance whatsoever, but instead constitute principles in accordance with which the whole system behaves. However I cannot form a sufficiently clear idea of what a 'psychic factor' might consist in to criticize the notion further.

Cases of ostensible reincarnation raise somewhat similar issues, though in one way at least the issues are simpler. Whereas in cases of mental mediumship two questions are at stake, namely:

(a)　whether or not there is at work in the communications a stream of consciousness other than that (or those) of the medium who now confronts us, and

(b)   whether it is continuous with that of a formerly incarnated person, in reincarnation cases we have only to ask whether the consciousness of the incarnated person who now confronts us is (in the same sense) continuous with that formerly associated with another body at an earlier period of time.

Some people would argue that (as a matter of logic rather than of fact) we can only reidentify something as the same thing we previously encountered if it can be shown or agreed to have had a continous spatio-temporal history in the interim. Hence in reincarnation cases we cannot identify the present personality with the previous one however accurate are the former's apparent memories of events in the life of the latter. (Analogous arguments are held to show that 'disembodied' survival is a meaningless notion; we could not lay down criteria by means of which to decide whether or not a disembodied entity had a continuous spatio-temporal history, or, indeed, a spatio-temporal history distinct from that of other such entities; hence a disembodied entity could not be reidentified as the erstwhile occupant of a formerly living body.) I do not agree with these arguments, but the relevant literature is considerable (see e.g. 31; 40; 46; 91; 119), and I cannot delve into it here.

The 'psychic factor' theory could also be tried out on cases of apparent reincarnation. It would involve saying that some part or element or aspect of the previous personality survives, and, coming somehow to influence the nervous system of the present personality, causes the present personality to have experiences as of remembering events which in fact belonged to the life of the previous personality. However the same obscurities beset the psychic factor theory here as beset it in connection with mediumistic controls and communicators. In addition various further *ad hoc* assumptions would have to be built into it to account, for instance, for the fact that the present personality is prepared to affirm that the 'past life' experiences he recalls were *his* experiences, and for the fact that (in contrast to mediums) the subjects of reincarnation cases are only influenced by one psychic factor, or at any rate by no more than one psychic factor from a given period in the past.

There is, besides, a certain scarcely rational arbitrariness about attempts to apply the psychic factor hypothesis to at any rate the better reincarnation cases. For it is being proposed that something (a formerly incarnated entity of a peculiar kind) was once conscious and possessed certain conceptual capacities, memories, etc., and that something (a presently incarnated entity) is conscious and possesses very similar conceptual capacities, memories, etc., (and furthermore claims continuity of consciousness with the formerly incarnated entity), and yet that there is in fact no continuity of consciousness between the two, the apparent continuity being effected by the aimless intervention of an insentient psychic factor whose nature is unknown.

The second of the two further questions which suggest themselves if we take the survival hypothesis seriously is equally difficult. It is as follows. I have spoken of each person's memories, and his conceptual capacities in general, as sets of principles of functioning which supervene upon and constrain, and are not reducible to, the patterns of electrochemical activities exhibited by assemblages of cells in his brain. If human personality does, in any meaningful sense, survive death, it is these principles of functioning (different sets for different people) which must survive and manifest again. But 'principles of functioning' cannot just exist in a void. They must be principles of *something's* functioning. And if they can survive the destruction of the brain with which they were originally associated, then they cannot have been primarily, but only derivatively, principles of the operation of *that brain*, and must instead have been the principles of operation of something that so to speak *worked through* that brain. What could this something be? A mind or soul as conceived in the tradition of Western theological and philosophical thought? One of Broad's 'psychic factors'? A portion of the Divine mind or World-soul? Some kind of physical emanation or field of whose inner nature we have at the moment no inkling? An aspect of the 'holomovement'? Where did this something come from? Was it created by the activities of the brain when these pass a certain level of complexity? Did it result from the interaction of brain activity with some influence external to the brain? Did it exist in its own right and merely manifest through the brain when the activities of the latter reached a level of complexity that permitted it to do so? To all these questions, and many others, I must confess myself stumped for answers. Many, indeed, would find the questions themselves ridiculous or unintelligible. Perhaps they are. I can only reply that so far as I can tell it is because of facts and arguments rather than of pre-existing bias that I find myself led to ask them.

I have discussed these two interesting questions in the abstract, but there are of course phenomena which many would assume bear immediately upon the answers to them. Some would say that the 'controls' of mediums have many times told us all that we can or need to know upon these matters. All such controls (so far as I know) claim that they, and other deceased persons, are fully conscious individuals just as they were before death; indeed more so. And many controls have favoured us with a great deal of purported information, often of a scientific or pseudo-scientific character, about what it is that is supposed to survive the death of the body. A suggestion commonly made is that we have a second body (sometimes more than one) of a subtle and tenuous kind, made, it is sometimes said, of matter at a higher rate of 'vibration' than the matter of our present bodies. This second body (or 'soul') is the true housing or vehicle of that indwelling spark of the divine (the 'spirit') which constitutes our animating intelligence both here and hereafter.

Now if a mediumistic control first gives us convincing 'evidence of identity', and then proceeds to favour us with copious teachings about the next world and its inhabitants, we might well feel that what he had to say, containing as it does inside information, must be well worth listening to. The snag, alas, lies in the considerations which I advanced in Chapter Eight above. There is every reason to suppose that, whatever the ultimate source of the 'evidential' statements made by the controls of trance mediums, those controls themselves are dramatizations by some level of the medium's own mind. Hence it is entirely possible that any teachings the controls may deliver or purportedly scientific statements they may make, emanate from the medium in this world rather than from the control in the next. One would not, of course, wish to reject these statements out of hand because of this possibility; one would merely wish to test them in the same way as one would test any other purported statements of scientific fact – by observation and experiment. Unfortunately I have not as yet heard of any such statement which has been sufficiently explicit and sufficiently in tune with the tendencies of modern science to render it testable.

There are however certain phenomena – common enough, and adequately recorded – which seem on the face of it to shed some direct light upon the two questions we have been discussing. The phenomena concerned are those of 'out-of-the-body' experiences (OBEs) and of apparitions. Cases falling under both these headings have from time to time been collected and published on a considerable scale by members of the SPR and the ASPR. A comprehensive review of this large literature does not fall within the scope of the present volume. Readers who wish to embark upon a more extensive study of it may consult two books in the present series, *Hauntings and Apparitions* by Andrew MacKenzie, and *Beyond the Body* by Susan Blackmore, or some of the quite numerous other works on the same subjects (e.g. 8; 51; 52; 115; 162c). I shall say just enough about these cases to indicate their possible bearing upon the questions with which we are here concerned, and upon the problem of survival in general.

OBEs

Out-of-the-body experiences (OBEs) are those curious, and usually brief, experiences in which a person seems to himself to leave his body and to observe the world from a point of view other than that which he would have were he still 'in' his body. In some cases the experients claim that they 'saw' and 'heard' things (objects which were really there, events and conversations which really took place) which they could not have seen or heard from the actual positions of their bodies. OBEs are surprisingly common; different surveys have yielded somewhat differing results, but all in all I think that one would not be too far wrong if one said that somewhere between one person in ten and one person in twenty is likely to have had such an experience at least once (for a survey of the surveys see 13, pp. 82–93).

OBEs are most frequent during sleep, during unconsciousness following anaesthesia or a bang on the head, and during stress. But they can occur during almost any kind of activity. Green (53, pp. 63–64) cites a couple of cases in which motor-cyclists, riding at speed, suddenly found themselves floating above their machines looking down on their own bodies still driving along. Accidents did not ensue. I have been informed, by an authority on aviation medicine, that pilots of high-flying aeroplanes (perhaps affected by absence of vibration, and uniformity of sensory stimulation) have similarly found themselves apparently outside their aircraft struggling to get in. One might well struggle frantically under such circumstances.

Not all OBEs occur spontaneously. Some people have, by various techniques, cultivated the faculty of inducing them more or less as desired, and a number have written detailed accounts of their experiences. These accounts do not always in all respects square with accounts given by persons who have undergone spontaneous OBEs. For instance the great majority of voluntary 'astral travellers' state that they find themselves still embodied, but in a body whose shape, external characteristics, and spatial location are easily altered at will, and an appreciable number refer to an elastic 'silver cord' joining their new body to their old one. A much smaller percentage of those who undergo spontaneous OBEs mention being embodied, and some specifically state that they found themselves disembodied. The 'silver cord' is quite rarely mentioned. It is hard to avoid suspecting that many features of self-induced OBEs are determined by the subject's reading and his antecedent expectations.

OBEs, especially spontaneous ones, are often very vivid, and resemble everyday, waking experiences rather than dreams, and they may make a considerable impression on those who undergo them. Such persons may find it hard to believe that they did not in fact leave their bodies, and may draw the conclusion that we possess a separable soul, perhaps linked to a second body, which will survive in a state of full consciousness, perhaps even of enhanced consciousness, after death. Death would be, as it were, an OBE in which one did not succeed in getting back into one's body.

Such conclusions present themselves even more forcefully to the minds of those who have undergone the variety of OBE known as a 'near death experience' or NDE. It is not uncommon for persons who have been to the brink of death and returned – following, say, a heart stoppage or serious injuries from an accident – to report an experience (commonly of a great vividness and impressiveness) as of leaving their bodies, and travelling (often in a duplicate body) to the border of a new and wonderful realm. At the border they are stopped by a 'presence', or by a deceased friend or relation, and sent back again, because, so they are informed, their time is not yet. They awake to find themselves back in their bodies.

NDEs, even more than OBEs, have lately caught the public imagination, especially in the United States (see e.g. 13, pp. 142-152; 102a; 102b; 132), and recent surveys of patients who have had close encounters with death, suggest that NDEs are much commoner than had previously been thought. Undergoing an NDE may change a patient's whole religious and philosophical outlook. He has, it seems to him, learned by experience what it is like to die.

A school of thought has grown up within parapsychology, and around its fringes, which takes such ideas very seriously indeed. We may refer to this school of thought as the 'animistic' school, 'animism' being the view that every human mind, whether in its before death or after death state, 'is essentially and inseparably bound up with some kind of extended *quasi*-physical vehicle, which is not normally perceptible to the senses of human beings in their present life' (18c, p. 339). An argument which one commonly hears from members of the animistic school is this. OBEs and NDEs are, so far as we can tell, universal. They have been reported from many different parts of the world and many different historical eras. The experiences of the persons concerned therefore *must* reflect genuine features of the human constitution; for we cannot possibly suppose that they derive from a common stream of religious tradition or folk-belief – the societies from which they have been reported are too widely separated in space and time for that to be a possibility.

The most powerful shot in the animist's locker remains, however, still to be mentioned. There are some cases – by no means a negligible number – in which a person who is undergoing an OBE, and finds himself at or 'projects' himself to a particular spot distant from his physical body, has been seen at that very spot by some person present there. Such cases are generally known as 'reciprocal' cases, and I proceed next to give an example. The following is an extract (26, p. 29) from a statement sent to the ASPR in May 1957 by Miss 'Martha Johnson', a woman of 26 from Plains, Illinois. She describes a dream which she had early in the morning of 27 January 1957. She dreamed that she had travelled, by walking or floating, to the home of her mother in northern Minnesota, 926 miles away.

> After a little while I seemed to be alone going through a great blackness. Then all at once way down below me, as though I were at a great height, I could see a small bright oasis of light in the vast sea of darkness. I started on an incline towards it as I knew it was the teacherage (a small house by the school) where my mother lives . . . After I entered, I leaned up against the dish cupboard with folded arms, a pose I often assume. I looked at my Mother who was bending over something white and doing something with her hands. She did not appear to see me at first, but she finally looked up. I had a sort of pleased feeling and then after standing a second more, I turned and walked about four steps.

She awoke from her dream at 2.10 A. M. (1.10 A. M. Minnesota time). The mother gives her account of her own experiences in two letters to her daughter, dated 29 January 1957 and 7 February 1957, from which I extract the following:

> I believe it was Saturday night, 1.10, 26 January, or maybe the 27th. It

would have been 10 after two, your time. I was pressing a blouse here in the kitchen . . . I looked up and there you were by the cupboard just standing smiling at me. I started to speak and you were gone. I forgot for a minute where I was. I think the dogs saw you too. They got so excited and wanted out – just like they thought you were by the door – sniffed and were so tickled.

Your hair was combed nice – just back in a pony tail with the pretty roll in front. Your blouse was neat and light – seemed almost white. [Miss Johnson confirmed in correspondence that she had 'travelled' got up in this way.]

In this case, the 'traveller' perceived correct details of the scene which she visited, so her experience can hardly have been just an hallucination; and the body in which she believed herself to be corresponded in hair style and clothing with details of the form which her mother saw standing by the cupboard. Surely we cannot avoid supposing that something (a duplicate body?) went forth from Miss Johnson which acted as a vehicle for her consciousness, or was perhaps in part a product of it, and at the end of its voyage was actually seen by her mother and would also have been seen by any other person with the right kind of sensitivity who happened to be on the spot. And is it not equally obvious that had Miss Johnson's ordinary physical body been destroyed during her 'absence' from it she would have been left, so to speak, stranded, but still conscious, still a whole person, and still the occupant of some kind of subtle or rarefied body?

Thus the animist, starting from his study of OBEs and NDEs, comes up with answers to the two questions which I posed at the beginning of this chapter. He claims to have direct evidence that after death:

(a) we remain the conscious individuals that we always have been; and

(b) that the 'vehicle' of our surviving memories and other psychological dispositions is a surrogate body whose properties (other perhaps than that of being malleable by thought) are, he would admit, largely unknown.

In addition to taking OBEs and NDEs as themselves evidence for survival, the animist might well feel able to offer the following argument for regarding a further class of phenomena as evidence for survival. There is in the literature on apparitions (the topic which I shall next come to) a substantial sprinkling of cases of apparitions of deceased persons, some of which have been seen by witnesses who did not know the deceased in life. An extensive statistical investigation by the late Professor Hornell Hart (60a) strongly suggests that apparitions of the dead and the phantasms of living 'projectors' in reciprocal cases are, as classes, indistinguishable from each other in what may be called their 'external characteristics' – such as whether the figure was solid, dressed in ordinary clothes, seen by more than one person, whether it spoke, adjusted itself to its physical surroundings, etc. Now we know that in reciprocal cases the phantasm of the projector is in some sense a centre of or a vehicle for consciousness, namely the consciousness of the projector. Since apparitions of the dead and of living projectors manifestly belong to the same class of objects or events, we may properly infer that since the apparitions of living projectors are vehicles for the consciousness of the person in question, this must be true of apparitions of the dead also. Hence the consciousness of deceased persons survives and may either have, or make use of, a kind of body.

Apparitions

I wish now to approach the same ground again from a somewhat different starting point, a starting point, to wit, in the phenomena of apparitions, some aspects of which I have just briefly mentioned. Stories of apparitions ('ghosts') have been reported from all societies of which we have adequate records. Modern surveys suggest that in western society perhaps one person in ten will (while sane, sober and awake) have seen a human figure or heard a human voice to which no person present corresponded. (Sometimes the figure that is seen is also heard to speak; only rather rarely is it additionally perceived by the sense of touch.) The most commonly proferred explanation of apparitions has, historically, been some version or another of the animistic hypothesis which I have just discussed. This theory is, however, rejected by the great majority of modern parapsychologists, most of whom regard apparitions as hallucinations, as figments of the mind having no external reality. Their principal reasons (162c, pp. 53–60) for holding this view are as follows. Although apparitions, with a few exceptions, tend to look and behave much like ordinary people, they have a habit of suddenly vanishing into thin air, leaving not a trace behind; they may perform feats which physical objects could not perform, such as passing through doors and walls; they are apt to move instantaneously from one place to another. Sometimes they are accompanied by phantasmal and clearly symbolical appurtenances, such as hearses or coffins. If they are seen to open a door or move an object, the object will afterwards be found not to have moved and the door to be still locked and bolted. Door-openings and object-movements were part not so much of an hallucination as of a whole hallucinatory scene.

The hallucination theory of apparitions has clearly a good deal in its favour. But it also confronts certain difficulties. The most obvious of these arise over the fact that in a not inconsiderable number of apparition cases the hallucinations concerned may be described as 'veridical'. By this is meant that they correspond in ways for which we can offer no ordinary explanation, either with some event external to themselves or with the experiences of another percipient or percipients. The principal classes of veridical hallucinations are these.

1. *Crisis Apparitions.* These constitute by far the largest class of veridical hallucinations. The percipient sees (or hears the voice of – but for simplicity I shall for the most part confine myself to visual cases) a person known to him, who then suddenly vanishes in an inexplicable manner. Subsequently it turns out that the person who was seen died, or underwent some other unpleasant crisis, at or about the time of the apparition. (By convention, a 'crisis' apparition must occur within twelve hours either way of the crisis involved.)

2. *Collectively Perceived Apparitions.* Two or more persons simultaneously see the same phantasmal figure in the same place (hallucinations of all the other classes may in addition be collectively perceived).

3. *Apparitions of Deceased Persons ('Post-Mortem Apparitions').* (By convention, an apparition is classified as post-mortem only if the person it represents has been dead for at least twelve hours.) Such hallucinations may be classed as 'veridical' if either:

(a) the percipient did not know that the person he saw had died;

(b) the apparition, though not known to the percipient, was subsequently identified by him (e.g. from a photograph) as that of a deceased person formerly connected with the spot in question;

(c) the figure conveyed some information once known to the deceased person concerned, but previously unknown to the percipient; or

(d) the figure manifested some purpose characteristic of or appropriate to the deceased person, but unknown to, and not characteristic of, the percipient.

4. *Haunting Apparitions.* The same figure is seen in the same locality on a series of different occasions by the same (or better still) different percipients. Such apparitions are usually assumed to be those of deceased persons, but evidence of identity is often lacking.

5. *Apparitions of Living Persons.* Such apparitions may be termed veridical if, for instance, the figure seen is that of a living person who formerly frequented that spot, or that of a living person who is about to arrive there (for preference unexpectedly).

Of each of these classes we have well-authenticated instances; instances, at least, which seem to me to be well-authenticated. I shall later on give examples from some, but not all, of these classes. Readers may care to follow up the references given above, and study some of the testimony for themselves. Now if we accept that cases of these five categories do occur, how is the hallucination theory to accommodate them? The answer is fairly obvious. The hallucination theory must be supplemented by the introduction of the factor of ESP. The percipient builds into his hallucination, and as it were fleshes it out with, information obtained by ESP. That is where the 'veridicality' comes from. The form of ESP that has to be involved is, in all categories other than the first, usually that of telepathy. In some cases (apparitions of the dead, haunting apparitions) we could invoke either telepathy with the living or telepathy with the departed. For the moment I shall stick to the version that postulates only telepathy with the living.

When the hallucination theory is supplemented by introducing ESP, we come up with a variety of possible explanations of the various categories of veridical hallucination. In crisis apparitions, the percipient learns by ESP of the death or impending death of the person involved. The information is received by some unconscious or subliminal level of the personality, and has some difficulty in finding its way into ordinary consciousness. It manages to crash the barrier in the form of a 'sensory automatism' (see Chapter Two above). In collectively perceived apparitions, one percipient becomes telepathically aware of the other's hallucination, and constructs a corresponding hallucination himself; or perhaps both telepathically contact an outside source. In cases of haunting apparitions and of apparitions of the dead, the present witness makes telepathic contact with some living person who remembers the deceased person who died at that spot, or perhaps he clairvoyantly scrutinizes a photograph album in which that person's picture is to be found; and so on. It can all (if one does not analyse it too carefully) be made to sound most plausible.

When proponents of the hallucination theory of apparitions have, to their own satisfaction, chased members of the animistic school off this territory, they are apt to pursue them back into their own ground. In other words they try to develop an hallucination theory of OBEs, NDEs and reciprocal cases. They tend to argue along the following lines. It may be true that OBEs and NDEs are of world-wide distribution, and that we cannot attribute the universal propensity to undergo such experiences to the shaping influence of a common cultural tradition. But it does not follow from this that these experiences therefore reflect some basic fact about the human constitution (e.g. that we are a compound of body, soul and spirit). Rather do they reflect the fact that, in fundamentals, peoples' minds work the same way even in very different cultures. The soul-theory of the human constitution is a very obvious one, given certain striking, but not uncommon, sorts of events (dreams, hallucinations, ESP, loss of loved ones). That the soul-theory emerges and shapes peoples' experiences in all quarters of the globe is a fact no more surprising than the fact that certain recurrent themes crop up in folktales from widely separated cultures. And the experiences (like the mythological themes) tend to emerge in certain situations (dreams, drug-states, hallucination) and in response to certain external stresses (worry, anaesthesia, shortage of oxygen in the brain following a heart attack), usually stresses which the experient can do nothing to relieve. OBEs and NDEs and certain sorts of related hallucinations are, according to this view, generated as a means of coping with otherwise unendurable psychological pressures.

Indeed if one examines numerous reports of OBEs and NDEs one can see quite plainly that the underlying themes are heavily influenced by cultural factors, which would hardly be the case if the experiences were insights into the nature of the soul and of the world to come. The self-induced OBEs of 'astral travellers' in our society differ, as I have already pointed out, in important respects from the spontaneous ones. The self-induced OBEs of shamans and witch-doctors are wildly different from those of our own tame astral travellers (see 37, *passim*). Those undergoing NDEs in our society tend to find themselves moving towards a peaceful and harmonious realm of indescribable beauty; mediaeval NDEs contain horrific visions of hell, as well as visions of a heaven which not everyone would enjoy (21, II, pp. 197–202, 225–233); an eighteenth century Quaker finds himself approaching a realm resounding with 'songs of praise unto the Lord God and the Lamb' (166); and so on and so on.

What of those cases in which a person who has been 'out of the body' has apparently brought back information which he could not have obtained had he been at the location of his physical body? Since we have already argued that facts acquired by ESP can be incorporated in various kinds of hallucinations, the proposal that such insights may also be incorporated in yet another bizarre kind of hallucination should create no additional difficulty. As for reciprocal cases: things are, of course, a little more complicated here; still, we can without too much difficulty develop an account along the following lines. The 'projectionist' acquires by ESP information about objects and events at some distant spot, and constructs therefrom an hallucination representing that scene as observed from a certain point of view. The 'percipient' at that scene telepathically learns that the projectionist is having an hallucination as of being at that spot. He embodies this information in an hallucinatory representation of him.

Thus we have disposed of reciprocal cases too. And indeed the animist's theory that in such cases the projectionist goes forth clad in a second and subtle body is obvious nonsense. Consider the following reciprocal case, collected by Nils Jacobson, a Swedish psychiatrist much interested in unusual experiences. The two persons concerned had agreed to experiment. I extract from their statements (73, p. 112):

JAKOB: . . . The day after our decision I drove my daughter to her job, the time was 6 P.M. I was suddenly reminded of this agreement with Eva. Then I transported myself astrally to her home and found her sitting on the sofa, reading something. I made her notice my presence by calling her name and showing her that I was driving my car. She looked up and saw me. After that I left her and was back in the car which I had been driving all the while without any special awareness of the driving . . .

EVA: I was sitting alone in the room in an easy chair . . . Suddenly I saw Jakob sitting in front of me in the car, saw about half the car as if I were in it with him. He sat at the wheel: I only saw the upper part of his body. I also saw the clock in the car, I think it was a couple of minutes before six. The car was not headed towards our house but in another direction . . .

Even if (which I doubt) one could tinker with the animistic theory in such a way as to give a plausible account of how 'duplicate' bodies form their outer parts into the semblance of clothes, one could hardly extend the supposition to cover their transforming themselves into the semblance of half a car, complete with clock showing the correct time.

At this point a supporter of the hallucination theory would no doubt feel that he had swept the supporters of the animistic theory completely off the field of play, even off their favourite corner of it – the one devoted to OBEs, NDEs and reciprocal cases. And for my part I find it hard to dissent. At least – I can at the moment find among the phenomena of OBEs and NDEs no strong grounds for disagreement with the hallucination theory, though I would not be altogether surprised if some grounds for disagreement were eventually to be unearthed. For instance some quite intensive studies have recently been carried out in the United States (most notably by Osis, Morris and Roll – see 13, pp. 220–224) of persons claiming to be able to travel out of the body at will. Attempts have been made to ascertain:

(a)   whether such persons can 'home in on' and correctly identify target objects placed in special screened localities;

(b)   whether, when they do so home in, they can in any way influence 'detectors' – human, animal or instrumental – placed around those targets; and

(c)   whether success in (a) correlates significantly with success in (b).

The results to date have been equivocal and somewhat frustrating. I think it would be fair to say that while occasional apparent successes have been reported under all three headings, successes have not been consistent or striking enough for us to be able either to accept or to reject them with confidence. Unless future experiments produce unmistakably positive results we must, I think, continue to refuse credence to the animistic hypothesis.

Summary

I began this chapter by discussing two questions:

(a)   would survival of a person's memories, and other conceptual capacities, involve or amount to the survival of that person as a conscious individual; and

(b)   what could be the nature of that which survives, the presumed 'vehicle' of the surviving memories, etc?

After briefly discussing these questions, I turned to the answers to them given by a school of thought whose members I called 'animists', and who have interested themselves especially in OBEs, NDEs and reciprocal cases. These answers I have been unable to accept. So we are back again to the beginning of the chapter. Has the whole excursus then been a waste of time? I hope not; for in the first place the phenomena I have briefly and inadequately touched upon (OBEs, NDEs, reciprocal cases, apparitions) are ones frequently introduced into discussion of the problem of survival, so that it is desirable that they should have been at least mentioned; and in the second place I propose to use what I have said in this chapter as a jumping-off ground for a further exposition of the hallucination theory of apparitions and its possible bearing upon the problem of survival.

15   Apparitions of the Dead

In the previous chapter I explained why it is that most parapsychologists regard apparitions as having no objective reality, as being hallucinations constructed by the mind of the beholder. So compelling are the reasons for this view that when presented with cases in which the figure has for instance conveyed to the percipient information which he did not previously know, parapsychologists, reluctant to admit that some being external to the percipient might have been objectively there, have tended to suggest that the percipient obtained the information by his own ESP, and, for obscure psychological reasons, dressed it up before his own mind in the form of an hallucination. I adopted the standpoint of the hallucination theory in order to cast doubt upon its main rival, the animistic theory. With deplorable perverseness. I am now going to raise doubts about the hallucination theory.

The doubts I shall raise concern principally the applications of the theory to certain sorts of post-mortem apparitions. (It may or may not be the case that analogous doubts could be raised concerning its application to other sort of cases.) The post-mortem apparitions in question belong to kinds which have often been thought to constitute evidence for survival – the apparition has been of some recognized or subsequently identified deceased person, has in one way or another conveyed information which the deceased person might be expected to have possessed, but of which the percipient was unaware, has manifested purposes characteristic of the deceased person, but not necessarily of the living percipient, and so on. So, while not letting the questions raised in the last chapter drop altogether out of sight, I shall in exploring the hallucination theory be presenting some further kinds of ostensible evidence for survival.

The hallucination theory of apparitions has, as I pointed out in the previous chapter, to be supplemented with proposals to the effect that in a substantial number of cases the occurrence of the hallucination, or its contents, or both, are supplied by the percipient's own ESP. Without this assumption the theory can give no account of the various kinds of 'veridical hallucinations' which I listed in the previous chapter; unless, indeed, it were simply to find grounds for denying that they ever occur, a stance which, for the reasons I sketched in Chapter One, seems to me indefensible. The upshot, as I hope shortly to illustrate, is that the hallucination theory is forced to postulate the occurrence of ESP of extraordinary complexity. In fact the hallucination theory becomes just one of the many guises of our old friend (or enemy) the super-ESP hypothesis. I shall, in what follows use the terms 'hallucination theory' and 'super-ESP hypothesis' more or less interchangeably.

What one may call the 'strong' form of the super-ESP hypothesis – the form against which I have directed a good many arguments in earlier parts of this book – invokes either clairvoyance or telepathy with living persons. This would involve one's saying, in the current context, that the percipients of veridical apparitions get all their information either through clairvoyance or through telepathy with living persons. It is also possible to frame what one may call a 'weak' form of the super-ESP hypothesis, a form which admits the possibility of telepathy with the departed. The theory of 'overshadowing' which I discussed in Chapters Nine and Ten was in effect a theory of this kind. Applied to veridical hallucinations, the weak form of the super-ESP hypothesis would allow us to say that the information which percipients embody in their hallucinations may sometimes come through telepathy with the dead.

I shall argue, with special reference to three classes of apparition, that both the strong and the weak forms of the super-ESP hypothesis are alike untenable. The three classes of apparition concerned are as follows:

1.   Certain cases of seemingly purposive post-mortem apparitions.
2.   Collectively perceived apparitions (with special reference to a post-mortem example).
3.   Haunting apparitions (again with special reference to a post-mortem example).

1. Post-Mortem Apparitions Exhibiting Purpose

The first class of case which I shall discuss consists of post-mortem apparitions which convey information previously unknown to the percipient, and convey it, perhaps in a characteristic manner, in pursuit of a goal presumably favoured by the deceased, but not consciously entertained by the percipient. Such cases on the face of it are bound to strain the 'strong' form of the super-ESP-cum-hallucination hypothesis, for they suggest rather forcefully that the contents of the experience were somehow imposed on the percipient by an outside agency. Let us try out the strong form of the super-ESP hypothesis upon the following series of abridged case-reports.

a.   A young man owns a tow boat which he runs to help support his family. The engine keeps breaking down. One night the young man is lying awake worrying about it. His lately deceased father comes through the closed bedroom door. They have a conversation about the engine, and the father correctly advises him how to set it right (129, pp 155–156).

One might simply suppose here that 'deep down' the young man already knew the answer; for obscure psychological reasons it found its way into consciousness in the form of an hallucination.

(b)   A man (who had had other visions) sees an exalted or angelic spirit (identity unknown) who tells him that his sister is in need, and that he is to send her a certain sum of money. He complies, and afterwards finds that at that time she had been in great difficulties, and had been praying for help (100).

Here one might propose that the percipient learned by ESP of his sister's distress, which he would naturally wish to relieve. His psychological quirks were such that the ESP, instead of taking a direct route (an intuition, a 'call' in his sister's voice), was dressed up in the form of a visit from a spiritual being.

(c)   Mr J. P. Chaffin, whose father had died nearly four years previously, dreams on a number of occasions that his father appears at his bedside. On the last occasion his father is wearing his old black overcoat, and shows him the pocket, saying, 'You will find my will in my overcoat pocket.' (The percipient was not clear whether this experience was a dream or a waking apparition – there are in fact a number of cases in which the former has passed into the latter.) Mr Chaffin searches the pocket of this coat, and finds therein a roll of paper which reveals the location of a hitherto unsuspected second will (139a).

With this case the ESP hypothesis must move towards the super-ESP hypothesis. We have to say that Mr J. P. Chaffin learned by ESP not just where a clue to the will was, but that there was a will at all. This involves his 'reading' what was written on the rolled up paper in the overcoat pocket, a task requiring ESP of a degree hardly paralleled in any experimental investigation. For obscure psychological reasons, his unconscious mind dressed up the information as though it were coming from his late father.

(d) A naval officer, Lieutenant H., and his wife are assigned new quarters in a house which they share with another family, the Gs. On four occasions he clearly sees, for up to fifteen minutes, the figure of a man (previously unknown to him), which seems as though about to speak, but vanishes into thin air when approached. On one occasion the figure blocks light from electric light bulbs; on another, two dogs are alarmed prior to its appearance. It transpires that the ghost closely resembles Mrs G.'s late father, who had never been to the house. Lieutenant H. picks out his photograph from among about twenty others (56).

The ESP hypothesis has now to become the super-ESP hypothesis. One might suppose that Mrs G.'s thoughts were dwelling much upon her late father. Lieutenant H. telepathically 'read' those thoughts, and externalized the information in the form of an hallucinatory figure of the old gentleman. But there are numerous problems. Can we make sense of the idea that one might telepathically 'read' or 'perceive' events in someone else's mind, when it makes no sense to talk of reading or perceiving them by any form of sense perception? Furthermore the ESP that is here being postulated is of a very remarkable degree, and was exercised by a person who had had no other such experience to weaken his scepticism. What, next, of the behaviour of the dogs? They become excited immediately *before* Lieutenant H. first saw the figure, and could not therefore have picked up his astonishment. Can we really suppose that they too both happened to read Mrs G.'s mind at that moment? Lastly, there is the question of motive. In most, though not all, cases of spontaneous ESP, the experient might be supposed to desire to have the information that is conveyed to him; and sometimes the presumed telepathic agent might be supposed to wish to convey it. In this case, however, Lieutenant H. had no motive to wish for information about Mrs G.'s father, nor had Mrs G. any motive for wishing him to receive it.

(e) Mrs P., a lady who has once before had an hallucination – a non-veridical one however – is lying in bed waiting to feed her baby. A lamp is burning. Suddenly she sees a tall man, dressed in naval officer's uniform, come to the end of the bed. She rouses her husband, who also sees the figure. It speaks reproachfully to her husband. He then leaps out of bed. The figure moves away, transiently blocking the light from the lamp, and vanishes into the wall. Mr P. tells her the apparition was that of his father, who had been dead fourteen years. Later she learned that her husband was prevented by this vision from taking financial advice which would have proved ruinous (110a, II, pp. 326–329).

On the super-ESP hypothesis we would have to tackle this case as follows. Mr P. was or had been brooding or dreaming about his long-dead father, wondering what he would have thought about his great financial difficulties, etc. There is no evidence of this, but we might suppose that he was brooding unconsciously. Mrs P. read her husband's mind, and constructed therefrom an hallucination of his father standing in a certain spot. When she roused Mr P., he telepathically picked up her vision and externalized a corresponding one himself. The purpose apparently manifested by the phantom – to reprove Mr P. – was really Mr P.'s own. In his heart of hearts he wanted to stop himself from the course of action he was about to embark on, but his psychological quirks were such that he could best do so by manufacturing the monitory hallucination of his deceased father. That Mr and Mrs P. should on this one occasion alone have exhibited reciprocal ESP of so extraordinary an extent may be explained on the grounds that worry facilitates ESP – or upon any other grounds one can dream up.

It cannot, I think, be denied that the super-ESP theory's account of these cases, especially (c), (d) and (e), is *ad hoc* and convoluted to the last degree. In fact a flat-earther in full cry could hardly support his hypothesis with more tortuous argumentation, or with proposals less open to direct test. It is, of course, correspondingly difficult to prove the super-ESP theory wrong. We don't know the limits (if any) of ESP, or of the dramatic inventiveness of the unconscious mind. But still, isn't it obviously simpler to suppose that in each of these cases there was at work some further agency, to be identified with a still surviving portion of a formerly incarnate human being, which somehow shaped the experience of the percipient or percipients in accordance with its own persisting knowledge and persisting purposes? That way we can avoid such bizarre notions as that persons hitherto not known to be psychically gifted can suddenly develop powers of ESP comparable to, if not exceeding, the most remarkable that have ever been experimentally demonstrated; that two people without any conscious thought of doing any such thing can at an unconscious level telepathically link up with each other and hammer out the details of an hallucinatory figure which both shall see; that animals may to some extent share in this process; that the information thus acquired will be dressed up by processes unknown and presumably unconscious and presented to the conscious mind quite indirectly in the form of dramatic but really irrelevant interventions by deceased persons; and that the purposes promoted by the hallucinatory episodes, even when ostensibly more appropriate to the supposed deceased person, are really those of the living percipient or of some other living person whose mind telepathically influences his. All these proposals, and many others that seem likely to emerge from the super-ESP theory, appear in the present state of our knowledge to be quite untestable against any actual or conceivable findings; and we ought therefore in accordance with the pragmatic principle laid down in Chapter One that one should, when one can, avoid a likely dead end, refrain if possible from adopting them.

The problem, of course, is whether or not any form of survival theory really is going to prove itself more straightforward and more open to empirical test than the super-ESP hypothesis. Whilst a survivalist theory might be thought to simplify questions of motive, and of the tortuous paths taken by alleged ESP, it does not free us from the necessity of postulating ESP, sometimes quite complex ESP. For how, other than through a process that would fall under the catch-all heading of ESP, could a discarnate entity communicate with living persons (sometimes with two or more of them at once)? We have here, of course, what I called the 'weak' form of the super-ESP hypothesis – the one that permits telepathy with deceased persons. Suppose we attempt to apply this version of the theory to case (e) above. Then we should have to suppose something like the following web of telepathic relationships. Mr P.'s father, the late Mr P. senior, learns through telepathic contact with his son that the latter is in danger of accepting unsound financial advice. He wishes to avert the impending catastrophe and perhaps tries in some way to influence his son. However he manages at first only to influence his son's wife, who never knew him. He telepathically conveys to her not a warning about her husband's financial rashness, but information as to his own appearance, information which she externalizes into an hallucination of him. Frightened, she awakens her husband, Mr P. junior. He too picks up the telepathic influence from Mr P. senior, and likewise externalizes it in the shape of an hallucination. Either because Mr and Mrs P. are in telepathic rapport with each other, or because Mr P.

senior is a telepathic 'sender' of great skill and power, the two hallucinations ('his' and 'hers') are made to coincide with each other in location, dress, speech, movements and disappearance; they do not (so far as we can tell) get 'out of synchrony' with each other.

It would, of course, be possible, from the point of view of the 'weak' super-ESP theory, to analyse the supposed network of telepathic relations in this case in various other ways. But I do not think any of them would be appreciably simpler than the one I have adopted. And the one I have adopted involves postulating telepathy of a detail and complexity for which no experimental investigation provides the remotest parallel. The weak form of the super-ESP hypothesis is here scarcely simpler than the strong.

2. Collectively Perceived Apparitions

Collective percipience is not too uncommon, and may take place with apparitions of all classes – crisis, post-mortem, visual, auditory, etc. I have already cited one case of a collectively perceived post-mortem apparition. Here are extracts from the witnesses' statements in another (8, pp. 139–141). Two girls are staying one night in a Lincolnshire farmhouse about twenty years prior to the time of writing (1891):

> We retired to rest about the usual farmhouse hours. We slept in an old-fashioned four-post bedstead, at about four feet from the wall. In the centre of the wall, at the side of the bed, was a cupboard.
>
> We had been in bed about half a hour when I looked towards the door of the cupboard. I saw a little, ruddy-faced old lady, with a frilled white cap on her head, a white handkerchief folded round her neck, and a white apron, as if she was sitting with her hands folded in her lap. It seemed almost as if it were a painting on the door; it looked exactly as if it were living. I gave a sudden start, and said to Miss Quilty, 'Did you see anything?' and her answer was the same, 'Did you see anything?' I related to her what I had seen, and Miss Quilty had seen exactly the same as myself; our rest was disturbed for the night. On relating our story, the next morning, it proved the exact likeness of the farmer's mother, who had lived there before him, and died in that bedroom.

S. MOORE

The other witness, Miss Ellen Quilty, gives fuller details of the room and of the surrounding circumstances. Her account of what she saw is as follows:

> Standing back in the wall I had seen a little old woman, with a white muslin handkerchief neatly arranged on her shoulders; a white bordered cap fitting close to a sweet, calm face, her arms folded, and an apron of the same material as the kerchief.

It is very tempting to say of this case, and others like it, that if two or more persons (and cases with more than two percipients are by no means unknown) simultaneously see the same thing in the same place, then we have evidence that that thing is objectively there. In fact 'evidence' may be the wrong word. Perhaps it would be more appropriate to say that part of what we *mean* by calling a thing or event 'objective' is that more than one person can observe it. We must also mean that different percipients' views of the object are mutually interrelated in such a way that the rules of perspective are not violated. And this condition also seems to hold in most instances of collective apparitions. There are examples in which a figure has been seen full-face by a person confronting it, in right profile by a person to its right side and in left profile by a person to its left side (12). There are even a few cases of a ghost being apparently reflected in a mirror (e.g. 8, cases 56 and 60). I do not know of any case in which a phantasm perceived by several persons in a slightly scattered group has simultaneously appeared full face to each of them.

How, then, could we set about undermining the proposition that when an apparition is collectively perceived there really must be something objectively present at the spot in question? First of all one might soften up this thesis by pointing out that even if some sort of entity is objectively present, it is a very odd sort of entity, one that could be called 'objective' only in an attenuated or Pickwickian sense. If six people are in a position to perceive it, three may do so and three not. It leaves no physical traces. One might next point out that collectively perceived apparitions as a class do not differ in external characteristics from other sorts of apparitions, many of which must, for the reasons already given, be looked upon as purely hallucinatory.

So far, so good. The crunch for the non-objective (or pure hallucination) approach to crisis apparitions comes when it has to give an account of the fact that the hallucinations suffered simultaneously by the various percipients of a collective apparition are so remarkably alike. Some writers (52, pp. 41–48) have tried to lessen the impact by suggesting that the witnesses' statements often lack enough details for us properly to judge the extent of the similarity, and that, when details are given, these may not in fact agree. Perhaps the hallucinations of the different percipients have merely a common theme, elaborated by each person in his own way.

I cannot say that I find this argument convincing. The differences between the statements of the separate witnesses of a collective apparition seem to me generally not to exceed what one might expect had a real object or event been involved, and the similarities are sometimes numerous and detailed. (Examples of both agreement in detail, and occasional disagreement, may be seen in the sample statements which I quoted a moment ago). Hart and Hart, in an extensive review of relevant material, reach the same conclusion. They cite eleven of the cases in their sample and conclude (61, p. 245): 'Here then are eleven cases, in each of which two or more percipients (in so far as their accounts relate the facts) saw the same figure in the same [spatial] location, wearing the same clothes, with the same facial expressions and doing the same things. Although these are perhaps the most striking cases, much the same thing might be said of the other collective perceptions of apparitions.'

If this way of avoiding the problem be rejected, those who deny the objective reality of collectively perceived apparitions – and in particular of collectively perceived post-mortem apparitions, which are those of especial concern to us at the moment – seem stuck with one or other of two possible theories, viz. the theory of super-ESP involving only the living (the 'strong' form), and the theory of super-ESP including telepathy from the dead (the 'weak' form).

The first of these theories may be briefly expounded, with special reference to veridical post-mortem apparitions, as follows. One of the two (or more) percipients picks up by means of ESP the information that is to be externalized in the form of the hallucination. Let us say (using the specimen case given above) that she telepathically obtains from the farmer's mind a picture of his late mother, or that she clairvoyantly perceives a photograph of her, shut within the massive covers of the family album. Then the second percipient picks up all this information telepathically from the first percipient; or else she too, marvellous to relate, happens to scan by ESP the mind of the farmer of the photograph of the farmer's mother at just the moment when the first percipient did the same thing. Finally the (unconscious) minds of the two percipients have somehow to make contact with each other to ensure that when, as a result of all this ESP, they each construct an hallucination, the two hallucinations are reciprocally adjusted to allow for differences of perspective, etc., whilst the main details of both are kept constant.

To say that this is a tall order is a great understatement. I do not think that there are any examples of experimental ESP of anything like this detail and complexity, and precious few such examples of spontaneous ESP other than apparitions. It is possible that some instances of ostensible spontaneous ESP in dreams fill the bill. But even so, the following difficulty remains. In a sample of cases studied by Hart (60a, p. 204), there were 46 in which there was a second person in a position to have seen the apparition if the apparition were like a real object. In 26 of these 46 cases the second person did see it. These figures are supported by the findings of the well-known Census of Hallucinations (it polled 17,000 persons) conducted in the early days of the SPR (146). The census obtained 283 cases of visual hallucinations in which the percipient had a waking companion, and 90 cases of auditory hallucinations (voices); 95 of the former hallucinations and 34 of the latter were shared. The census committee issued certain warnings about the possibility that real objects and real sounds might have been thought hallucinatory – the percentage of collectivity was higher in outdoor cases – but even so we must recognize that if a person has an hallucination of the kinds we are considering (i.e. ones not due to insanity, drugs, fever, hypnosis, etc.), there is an appreciable probability that any companion he has will share it. This remains true whether or not the hallucination is otherwise veridical (i.e. is a crisis case, etc.). It follows that if we regard the sharing of an hallucination as due to ESP exercised by both percipients, we are in effect proposing that ESP abilities of an extraordinarily high order are very widely distributed among the population at large, and could presumably be tapped experimentally if only the right circumstances could be hit upon. Of this, alas, there is, so far as I know, no evidence at all. Nor is there much evidence that when spontaneous ESP takes forms other than the hallucinatory (the intuitions, realistic dreams and unrealistic dreams of Louisa Rhine's classification), there is any great likelihood that it will be shared. There are some convincing cases of shared or reciprocal dreams, but they only constitute a minute fraction of the total dreams dreamed. If one of two people sharing a bed sees an apparition, it is quite likely that the other person, if awake, will see it also. It is immensely unlikely that they will share a dream, even though it be precognitive.

This must surely count as evidence against the theory of super-ESP involving only the living. Furthermore it is far from clear what, at least in the present state of parapsychology, could count as evidence for it. The unconscious minds of the percipients are supposed to get together to arrange the details, perspective, etc., of their reciprocally related hallucinations. This is a process unobservable in principle. In the example I quoted, we had to suppose that one or another or both of the girls clairvoyantly observed a picture of the farmer's mother, or telepathically found one in the farmer's mind. There was no actual evidence that such a picture existed, or that the farmer had been especially thinking about his late mother. Perhaps the girls dug the image out of the farmer's unconscious mind (or out of the memory-stores in his brain). No further evidence which might throw a light on such proposals seems at the moment within the realms of possibility. Surely (following the 'avoid dead ends' principle which I proposed in Chapter One) we must dismiss the theory of super-ESP involving only the living as one with which, in the prsent state of our knowledge, we can get no further.

Suppose, then, we admit discarnate agency into our theorizing, and instead try out that approach to collectively perceived apparitions which I called the 'theory of super-ESP including telepathy from the dead'. This theory would enable us to say that the girls got the information about the farmer's late mother through telepathic contact with the lady herself, and not through some more circuitous channel. But does this supposition really help? It lands our theory with extra deadweight in the form of the idea of a discarnate human being, a notion that is at best far from easy to elucidate. And we are still left not just with telepathy of a degree that might well be called 'super-ESP' between the two girls, and between the girls and the deceased lady, but with a problem over how the girls could have gleaned from the old lady's mind the sort of detailed image of her that they actually saw. If the old lady had been brooding about her former home, her mind would presumably have been filled with memories of walking around the rooms, looking out of the windows, etc., not with third-person pictures of what she herself would have looked like walking or sitting or standing there. Suppose, as in a number of cases, that the collectively perceived apparition had been that of an animal, such as a cat (8, cases 97 to 101). Could we seriously suppose that the various witnesses built up their similar hallucinations of it by externalizing the information gleaned from telepathic contact with its surviving spirit, as the latter relived in recollection the pleasures of prowling around the house or garden concerned? This theory has all the difficulties of the previous one, plus some extra problems of its own.

The ESP which proponents of the hallucination theory are forced to invoke in order to account for cases of collective percipience is so complex, so devious, so detailed, and so unsubstantiated by any independent empirical evidence, that one might well be tempted to revert to the supposition that some entity of a kind not as yet understood is objectively present at the spot where the apparition is seen. But no amount of evidence for the objective presence of such an entity could possibly resuscitate the crude animistic theory which I discussed in the previous chapter.

3. Haunting Apparitions

Yet another class of veridical apparition story which might be thought to provide evidence for 'objectivity' is that of haunting apparitions; cases, that is, in which the same, or apparently the same, figure is seen, or the same voice, etc., heard, in the same locality on a series of occasions by the same, or different (and preferably independent) percipients. The archives of the SPR contain a number of such cases in which the statements of the various witnesses have been obtained. I shall now summarize and quote from the statements in one sample case (122a, pp. 270–276). It is not, evidentially speaking, one of the very strongest, but it has the advantage of being relatively short. It also has the advantage that although the four percipients saw the same, or a very similar, figure, none had previously heard of the experiences of the others. The witnesses concerned were Dr H., the proprietor of the haunted house, his daughters Miss G.H. and Miss A.H., and a cousin, Miss J.A.A. The first three accounts date from the latter part of 1883.

1.   Some time between 1863 and 1865, Dr H. (we have this from his *wife's* statement, apparently confirmed by him) was going upstairs about 9.00 P.M. He was 'rather startled to see on the landing (a few steps higher) a little child, who ran before him into my [Mrs H.'s] room. My little boy B., about two or three years of age, was at that time sleeping in a small child's bed at my bedside. Dr H. followed and spoke, calling the boy by name, but he gave no answer. The gas was burning on the landing outside my room, but there was no light inside . . . He lighted a candle, searched my room, and also saw the boy was unmistakably asleep. He expected to find one of the other children, as the figure appeared to be taller than that of the boy.'
2.   Early one morning in January 1877, Miss G.H. passed the door of the room in which the youngest sister slept. The door was open. 'Taking hold of the handle, I was about to shut it (the door opened inwards), when I was startled by the figure of a child, standing in a corner formed by a wardrobe which was placed against the wall about a foot and a half from the doorway. Thinking it was my sister, I exclaimed, 'Oh, M., you shouldn't startle me so!' and shut the door; but in the same instant, before I had time to quit my hold of the handle, I opened it again, feeling sure that it could not be my sister; and, sure enough, she was in fact asleep in bed so far from

the door that it would not have been possible for her to have crossed from the door to her bedside in the short space of time when I was closing the door. In the corner where the child had been there was nothing, and I felt that I must have seen a ghost, for I was suddenly seized with a feeling of horror which could not have been caused by anything imaginary. The child had a dark complexion, hair and eyes, and a thin oval face; it was not white, as when seen by Miss A., but it gave me a mournful look as if full of trouble. Had it been a living child, I should have imagined it to be one who enjoyed none of the thoughtlessness and carelessness of childhood, but whose young life, on the contrary, was filled with premature cares. Its age might be about nine or 10; its dress I could not distinguish, as I only seemed to see its head and face; the expression struck me most; so vividly did I see it that if I were able to draw I could, I believe, give an accurate representation of it, even now after about five years.'

3. Miss A.H. (later Mrs A.), Miss G.H.'s eldest sister, had a similar experience only a few minutes later. Looking into Miss G.H.'s empty room she saw 'a little figure in white standing near a table'. It made her so nervous that she ran from the room.

4. Miss J.A.A.'s statement concerned an experience in July 1879. It first appeared in *Notes and Queries* for 20 March 1880. She was woken one night about daybreak by her bedroom door being opened and shut and then opened again. 'Almost at the same time that the door opened for the second time, I was a little startled by the rustling of some curtains belonging to a hanging wardrobe, which stood by the side of the bed; the rustling continued, and I was seized with a most uncomfortable feeling, not exactly of fright, but a strange unearthly sensation *that I was not alone*. I had had that feeling for some minutes, when I saw at the foot of the bed a child about seven or nine years old. The child seemed as if it were on the bed, and came gliding towards me as I lay. It was the figure of a little girl in her night-dress – a little girl with dark hair and a very white face. I tried to speak to her, but could not. She came slowly up to the top of the bed, and then I saw her face clearly. She seemed in great trouble; her hands were clasped and her eyes were turned up with a look of entreaty, an almost agonized look. Then, slowly unclasping her hands, she touched me on the shoulder. The hand felt icy cold, and while I strove to speak she was gone. I felt more frightened after the child was gone than before, and began to be very anxious for the time when the servant could make her appearance.'

5. In the early part of 1885 Dr H. reported hearing a number of series of knocks in the house, for which he could offer no normal explanations. It does not appear that anyone else heard them.

Mrs H. believed the apparition to be that of a little girl, J.M., who had died in the house in 1854. She remembered her as having 'fine dark eyes, black hair, oval face, and a pale olive complexion'. This child had died in the room in which Miss A.H. saw the figure. At the time of her death this room was in the next-door house. The houses were subsequently joined together, and the other three appearances were not in the part of the house in which the child had lived.

It is unusual to find a case in which there are even these rather limited grounds for identifying the apparition with a particular deceased person (for a somewhat comparable case see 85). There are in the literature, however, a number of cases in which the apparition has been seen more frequently, and in which the witnesses' testimony is fuller and more recent. The obvious interpretation of such cases (obvious, at any rate, to persons uncontaminated by the sophistries of parapsychologists) is certainly the animistic one, the suggestion that in the house in question there is actually to be found, at least from time to time, a persisting and peculiar quasi-physical entity, to be identified or linked with some now deceased human being who formerly dwelt there. But the objections to be offered to the animistic theory in this context are in essence the same as, and just as insuperable as, the ones I have run through in other contexts, and I shall not pursue them further.

Frank Podmore, who first published the case I have just outlined, was strongly averse to any form of the survivalist and subtle body theories, and instead developed various forms of the super-ESP hypothesis. He applies it to this case as follows (122a, p. 276).

> It is not difficult to trace the probable genesis of the first appearance. A hardworking country doctor, who has on various occasions in his life experienced hallucinations, visual and auditory, coming home late one evening, after a long day's work, sees a figure bearing a vague resemblance to one of his children – a purely subjective hallucination. The later appearances, if in fact there was no communication of Dr H.'s experience, are more difficult of explanation. The two earlier may have been the result of hereditary predisposition to hallucination. But it seems at least possible that all three were due to thought-transference, with Dr H., or perhaps Mrs H., on whom the first appearance seems to have made some impression, as the agent. In this way also the general resemblance which appears to have existed between the various appearances may be most readily accounted for. This explanation may seem far-fetched and improbable: the critic should be reminded that we have much evidence for the operation of telepathy betwen living minds, but we have very little for the existence or the agency of disembodied spirits.

This sort of hypothesis would become even more involved if it were applied to cases in which, as sometimes happens, a haunting apparition continues to manifest in a particular house through several changes of occupancy; or, indeed, manifests not in a house at all, but in, say, a particular stretch of road (95, pp. 114–123). One would have to suppose that someone, not present at the spot, is continually brooding over and inwardly revolving events which once happened there; somehow persons now occupying or passing through that place become telepathically linked to this distant person, and externalize the information thus gained in the form of hallucinatory figures. The figure seen is usually not that of the distant telepathic agent; but, depending upon the direction which his broodings take, may represent a person or persons, or even (as Podmore postulates) a frightening hallucination from his past. This accounts for the occasional cases in which various different figures are seen. What one says of cases in which the apparition wears clothes from a past era is not made clear.

Podmore's description of his hypothesis as 'far-fetched and improbable' seems entirely justified. It is also cumbersome and utterly *ad hoc*. In no case that I know of is there any actual evidence to relate the recurrent manifestation of a post-mortem apparition in a particular spot to the distant broodings of some living person formerly associated with that spot. The telepathic links between the distant agent and the various percipients must be supposed to be established simply by the fact that the various percipients are in a locality once well-known to the agent. Yet if links of such strength really can be established in this way, why do not, for example, the successive long-term occupants of a particular prison cell enjoy lives regularly enriched by telepathic contact with previous inmates now free? Furthermore in some cases haunting apparitions have been collectively perceived, so that we have to add to the above difficulties, those difficulties, already discussed, raised for the super-ESP hypothesis by examples of collective percipiency. Finally there is the question of motive. In very many, though by no means all, cases of spontaneous ESP, the experient has some reason for being concerned with the welfare of the person to whom his experience relates. In the great majority of examples of haunting apparitions, the ghost, if identifiable with any plausibility, has been that of a person with whom the percipients had no kind of special connection.

The various difficulties which confront the super-ESP hypothesis as applied to haunting apparitions are, it seems to me, in no wise diminished if we substitute for the telepathic agency of some unknown living person, that of a deceased person who once flourished at the place in question. Perhaps, indeed, this proposal would help us over cases in which the ghost wears the clothes of a past age. But to counterbalance this, we are again confronted with the problem of what sort of information telepathic contact with the mind of a brooding or dreaming deceased person might be supposed to yield. Primarily, one would suppose, the information would concern what it felt like to walk through a certain house, examine the furniture, etc., etc. Only secondarily would it have to do with what the telepathic agent looked like as he or she moved from room to room. If, indeed, the supposed telepathic agent were a deceased cat (and cats are certainly place-loving animals), I have no idea what sort of information one might glean. I suspect a lot of it would have to do with the smell of food in the kitchen.

I find it hard – indeed impossible – to resist the conclusion that no account of haunting apparitions can be given in terms of telepathic or clairvoyant links between the various persons successively associated with the haunted spot, not even if one extends the range of permissible links to include persons now deceased. Something in, or about, or to do with *the place itself* plays a crucial role in generating the phenomena.

This conclusion perhaps receives support from the following additional circumstances (into which I do not have the space to enter fully). A house which is troubled by a haunting apparition is not unlikely to be troubled also by other kinds of disturbances. These include the appearance of luminous patches, balls of light, etc.; the turning of doorhandles and opening of doors; tugging at bedclothes; loud bangs on doors or sequences of inexplicable raps; movement or displacement of small objects; and above all imitative noises – sounds as of the dragging of furniture, the dropping of weights, the breaking of crockery, the opening of drawers, etc., also footsteps, voices, groans, etc., all without any determinable cause. In some cases – generally called 'hauntings' (45, Chapters 10–12, 15) – phenomena of these kinds may take place without any recurrent apparition, or with only occasional tantalizing glimpses of shadows, misty figures, etc. It is worth noting that, unlike apparitions and person-centred poltergeists, hauntings tend to be primarily nocturnal. Tennyson captured the essence of hauntings in some memorable lines:

> A footstep, a low throbbing in the walls,
> A noise of falling weights that never fell,
> Weird whispers, bells that rang without a hand,
> Door-handles turn'd when none was at the door,
> And bolted doors that open'd of themselves:
> And one betwixt the dark and light had seen
> *Her*, bending by the cradle of her babe.

The issue which such cases raise for our immediate purposes is this.

Cases of hauntings shade without perceptible break into cases of haunting apparitions. We clearly have here not two classes of case but only one. But the phenomena of hauntings include some that are ostensibly objective and physical. It is as though 'haunted' houses, in addition to being visited by elusive phantoms, are the playgrounds of unseen but physically localized agencies of limited intelligence and mischievous proclivities. How does this fact, if fact it be, bear upon the theory that apparitions are purely hallucinatory, that when one is seen nothing is 'objectively there'?

The answer of many parapsychologists has been to deny that the ostensibly physical phenomena of hauntings are really physical at all. If they are not susceptible of ordinary explanations, then they must be hallucinatory, just as the figures seen are hallucinatory. This proposal greatly increases the pressure inside that over-stretched balloon, the super-ESP theory. For we have now to say not just that the apparitions are hallucinations generated by complex processes of ESP involving past and present occupants of the house, but that the footsteps, noises, door openings, raps, etc., all of which, one might add, may be collectively perceived, have a similar origin. I have argued at length elsewhere against this position (45, Chapter 10), and will not recapitulate my arguments here. I shall simply point out that cases of hauntings, which shade at one end into cases of 'pure' haunting apparitions, shade at the other into cases so marked by physical phenomena that they have often been classified as poltergeists, despite the fact that they have not centred around any obvious poltergeist 'agent'.

Now if there is indeed a tendency for the places frequented by a haunting apparition to be also the scenes of peculiar physical happenings of the kinds indicated, this must surely strengthen the view that haunting apparitions either are, or are in some way produced by, localized and objective entities or factors. For neither haunting apparitions nor 'disturbed' houses are so common that we can regard the relatively frequent associations or overlaps between the two sorts of phenomena as due to chance. Whatever produces the one set of phenomena must also be instrumental in producing the other. And in 'hauntings' the apparently physical effects show every sign of being objective and localized, and of having a localized source.

Let me now summarize the general conclusion to be drawn from the preceding discussion of the three classes of case which I singled out for special scrutiny in this chapter.

The hallucination theory, when combined with what I called the 'strong' form of the super-ESP hypothesis – the one which does not admit telepathy with the dead – seems to me quite untenable. It is forced not just to postulate ESP of an extent and complexity for which there is no other warrant, but also to make utterly *ad hoc* assumptions about psychological processes and peculiarities in both percipients and presumed agents ('senders').

The breakdown of the 'strong' form of the super-ESP hypothesis would seem on the face of it to open the door to the survival hypothesis. For in certain cases (including some more remarkable than those in which, for reasons of space, I have had to confine my illustrations) information unknown to the percipient, but known to the deceased person has been conveyed, and purposes more appropriate to the deceased person than to anyone living have been manifested. If we are not able to explain these facts in terms of the strong form of the super-ESP hypothesis, we must surely turn to some form of survival theory.

The obvious snag here is this. If the information and the purposes concerned are communicated from the dead to the living, or obtained from the deceased person by the living one, the process of communication must be one which we can only call ESP. We have turned, in fact, to what I called the 'weak' form of the super-ESP hypothesis. But earlier in the chapter I explored this version of the theory in several different contexts, and each time reached the conclusion that it is scarcely, if at all, more tenable than the 'strong' form.

One further theory I will unhesitatingly reject. It is what may be called the retrocognitive or 'playback' theory of haunting apparitions and of post-mortem apparitions in general. The idea is that the percipients of such apparitions are simply witnessing a playback of a past scene or scenes. Perhaps that scene is somehow imprinted or recorded on the physical locality in which it happened; perhaps there is a recurring kink or loop in space-time at that point. But either way the upshot is much the same. The percipients 'tune-in', or slip out of present time for a moment, and witness a past event, scene, or sequence of happenings.

Now there are certain cases which, if accepted, might be interpreted in this way – I refer to such phenomena as apparent visions of past battles, etc. But I don't think post-mortem apparitions can, in general, be so interpreted. For although some such apparitions act in a somewhat zombie-like and automatic manner, rather as though they were in a trance, they are none the less not always wholly repetitive in their behaviour, and sometimes seem responsive to persons in their vicinity, on rare occasions even speaking. So I will set the playback theory aside.

Must we then once more try out the animistic theory that we earlier on rejected? There are certainly some features of these cases that seem quite strongly to suggest the presence of some sort of localized entity: the fact that when an apparition (post-mortem or otherwise) is collectively perceived, each percipient will see it in the appropriate perspective; the fact that if one person in a particular spot sees an apparition (post-mortem or otherwise) any other person present stands a far greater chance of seeing it also than he does of telepathically participating in another person's experience under any other circumstances whatsoever; the fact that haunting apparitions are, as a class, not distinct from 'hauntings', in which phenomena of an objective kind do seem to occur. But the difficulties which confront the animistic hypothesis remain as intractable as ever. We seem to have reached a complete impasse.

16 A Theory of Apparitions

I have now discussed the chief categories of 'veridical' post-mortem apparitions, and I have considered each of them in relation to the two major sorts of theory of such apparitions, namely the hallucination plus super-ESP hypothesis and the animistic theory. The super-ESP theory has usually been given an anti-survivalistic turn, but many, perhaps most, forms of survival theory have also had to postulate what is in effect super-ESP. In either case we are in what seems to me a total dead end. The animistic theory has, so far as I know, always been linked to the survivalist position. Taken at face value, it is not just a dead end but a road to a realm of fantasy; and if that sounds like a contradiction, it nicely reflects the theory. All in all this is a baffling and dispiriting state of affairs. Yet I, for one, can find no excuse for dismissing the phenomena, nor any way of lulling myself into the belief that they do not occur.

In this unhappy situation it appears worth briefly considering one further theory, a theory which may well seem to some even more fantastic than those I have just rejected. It is the theory developed by F. W. H. Myers (55, II, pp. 277–316; 110a, Chapters 6 and 7), who found himself, even so early as 1886, in very much the dilemma that I have just mapped out.

The starting point of his attempt to resolve the dilemma is reciprocal cases like those discussed in Chapter Fourteen. He proposes that when a voluntary or involuntary 'projector' views a distant scene as if from a point within or confronting that scene, and obtains correct information about it, there may be an actual modification of space at the spot where he conceives himself to be. This portion of space may be modified 'not materially nor optically, but in such a manner that persons perceptive in a certain fashion would discern in that part of space an image approximately corresponding to the conception' of his own aspect latent in the projector's mind (110a, I, p. 268). Myers is most insistent that he is not postulating the going forth of an etheric body or 'metaorganism'; he clearly held, however, and later unequivocally stated, that there is in such cases 'a real transference of something from the agent, involving an alteration of some kind in a particular part of space'. This 'something' would not itself be that which is directly perceived when the projector's phantasm is seen; rather it would be, as it were, the seed which by some unknown means causes non-optical perceptions of the phantasm to burgeon in appropriate perspective around it as if they emanated from a 'radiant point'. If the agent's latent conception of himself at that moment included such accessories as a hat, a horse, or half a motor car, these too could emerge as features of the phantasm. Cases in which a voice is heard can be treated analogously.

Those other kinds of veridical apparitions of the living in which the projector brings back no recollection of his supposed excursus (for instance 'arrival' cases, in which the figure arrives on the scene just before its original) Myers treats more or less as imperfect examples of the foregoing. He supposes that there is some kind of excursus, but that the projector fails to remember it, because the excursus is of a dissociated or dream stratum of the personality (according to Myers such dissociated or 'subliminal' mental activity is going on in us all the time). In some cases the phantasm of a particular living person has been repeatedly seen. Myers describes such persons as having a 'psychorrhagic diathesis', literally a capacity to let the soul break loose. It is hardly surprising that this term has not caught on, but the fact is fairly well supported (I once myself knew quite well a person – a member of the SPR! – whose double had formerly been often seen and heard).

Myers does not apply his theory extensively to crisis apparitions, many of which, he seems to think, may be 'ordinary' hallucinations, but he proposes that it can be of help in those crisis (and other) cases in which either:

(a)   there is collective percipience; or

(b)   the figure is seen by a bystander and not by the 'intended' or appropriate person.

With regard to cases of the former kind Myers says (110a, I, p. 263): 'When two or three persons see what seems to be the same phantasm in the same place and at the same time, does that mean that that special part of space is somehow modified? Or does it mean that a mental impression, conveyed by the distant agent . . . to one of the percipients is reflected telepathically from that percipient's mind to the minds of the other . . . percipients? . . . I observe as telling against that other view, of psychical contagion – that in certain collective cases we discern no probable link between any of the percipient minds and the distant agent.' With regard to cases of the latter sort Myers says (110a, I, p. 266): 'If in such a case a bystander perceives the invading figure, I must think that he perceives it merely as a bystander – not as a person telepathically influenced by the intended percipient, who does not in fact perceive anything whatsoever.'

It will by now be obvious how Myers can apply his theory to post-mortem apparitions. A post-mortem apparition in which the phantasm appears intelligent and purposeful, conveys information, etc., is different in only one important respect from the conscious projection of a purposeful living agent (as in 'experimental' cases) – that respect is, of course, that the agent, having died, is now permanently detached from his body. As for haunting apparitions, 'I am inclined,' says Myers (110a, II, p. 75), 'to lay stress on the parallel between these narratives of haunting and those phantasms of the living which I have already classed as *psychorrhagic*. In each case, as it seems to me, there is an involuntary detachment of some element of the spirit, probably with no knowledge thereof at the main centre of consciousness. Those "haunts by the living", as they may be called – where, for instance, a man is seen phantasmally standing by his own fireplace – seem to me to be repeated, perhaps more readily, after the spirit is freed from the flesh.' Haunting apparitions may be due to the dreams of the departed.

Myers says of his theory, not without justice, that it 'suffers from the complexity and apparent absurdity inevitable in dealing with phenomena which greatly transcend known laws' (110a, I, p. 264). He also says of it that it does in its way colligate a good many cases of odd and varying types. This claim, too, is hard to deny. But before attempting to assess the theory I shall propose certain revisions of it (whether major or minor will depend on one's point of view). They have the effect of whittling down its basic assumptions. Thus the theory I shall actually assess will not be Myers' theory, but another and related hypothesis. The revisions which I propose are as follows:

1.   Let us take as a basic assumption, or rather perhaps as a basic fact, that some people, under certain obscure circumstances, can produce an effect at a spatial location more or less distant from their bodies, such that persons appropriately positioned, and endowed with

a certain form of peculiar sensitivity, will see at that location a phantasm corresponding in appearance, position and orientation to some conception latent in the agent's mind. That conception may be, but *need not necessarily be*, the agent's conception of himself. After all, if an agent can generate a phantasm of himself seated on a horse, or driving a car, why should he not, under some circumstances, generate a phantasm just of the horse, or just of the car, or indeed of some person other than himself? Thus a collectively perceived crisis apparition *might* be generated by the dying person who is its original; but it *might*, on the other hand, be generated by a living person (probably one of the percipients) in response to extrasensorially acquired information about his death. We could even, perhaps, devise along the latter lines some explanation of the occasional stories of animal apparitions, or of bizarre or grotesque non-human or super-human apparitions, which most parapsychologists would not dare to compromise their scientific respectability by investigating.

It would, of course, similarly be *possible* to try to explain away *all* cases of veridical apparitions of the dead in this way, i.e. as generated by a conception latent in the mind of some still living person who is merely brooding about the deceased person concerned. Thus the theory could explain such apparitions in *either* survivalist *or* non-survivalist terms. Its general tendency is, however, as Myers holds, survivalistic, for the following reasons. In cases of veridical post-mortem apparitions, the generator of the phantasm cannot (or usually cannot) on Myers' theory be among the percipients of it. For to the extent that the apparition is 'veridical' – to the extent, in other words, that it contains details and conveys information unknown to the witnesses, represents a person with whom they were not acquainted, ostensibly pursues a goal which they do not consciously entertain, etc. – it *cannot* (assuming, that is, that we refuse to credit them with powers of super-ESP such as we have just rejected) represent a conception in the mind of any of the percipients. If anyone other than the deceased original of the phantasm generates that phantasm it must be some person not present at the time and place of its appearance. But this view does not seem easy to defend:

(a) Often no plausible candidate for the role clearly emerges. There is no person who is known to be still brooding over, dwelling upon, or grieving over the deceased, with peculiar intensity, or who has some powerful motive for attempting to generate a phantasm of some person other than himself.

(b)   Cases in which a person has apparently generated a phantasm, visible to others, of some one other than himself, are fairly rare, and I do not know a single one in which the supposed generator has not been himself among the percipients.

2.   If we allow the possibility that someone might generate a phantasm of a peson other than himself, we must also abandon the idea, at first sight so natural, that some aspect of the personality necessarily makes an excursion to the spot at which the apparition is seen and there plays a causal role in its genesis. If the figure need not be that of the person who produces it, this idea loses its intuitive plausibility, and moreover it did not in the first place accord very well with cases in which the presumed projector retained no memory of his excursion. I should be inclined to regard the generation of the phantasm as usually the product, or more probably the unsought by-product, of psychological processes in a distant agent. Among these psychological processes is certainly the state of what used to be called 'travelling clairvoyance', or seeming to see a distant scene as if from a point within that scene. Of course it *might* be the case that during successful travelling clairvoyance, some conscious entity of unknown kind does sometimes leave the projector's organism, and that it is round this spatially localized entity that the phantasm is seen. But even were this so, I should still be inclined to suggest that the phantasm is generated at the projected entity's own location because the projector's latent conception of himself is of a clothed and embodied person at the spot where he now is. To see the phantasm is *not* to see the projected entity, nor is the phantasm in any sense the *vehicle* of consciousness.

It is possible (I do not put it more strongly) that the distinction just propounded between the local modification of space (the 'phantasmogenetic focus') which causes certain persons to see an apparition, and the temporarily or permanently disembodied projector who produces the local modification of space, but sometimes *is* and sometimes *is not* himself at the site of that modification, might be usefully applied to some of the more bizarre cases of haunting. One might suppose that when in a certain house the occasional appearance of a phantasm is part of a complex of odd and probably nocturnal happenings, some of which are almost certainly physical, there is present, or occasionally present, on the site a localized entity, perhaps identical in some way with an element in the personality of some formerly living human being, which *both* induces a 'phantasmogenetic' modification of a portion of space, perhaps of that portion surrounding itself, *and,* by accreting energy to itself and deploying it in some way not yet understood, is able to cause the paranormal physical effects. The phantasm, the figure seen, would of course not be itself directly instrumental in producing the physical phenomena, not even if it were seen apparently effecting them. If it were photographed, nothing would appear on the film, or at any rate (since one would not wish to rule out the physical detection of a putative energy source) nothing much resembling what the percipients reported. All this is the wildest speculation; but it is at any rate consistent with the range of alleged phenomena which we have to explain.

3.   Although Myers emphasizes that apparitions are not material objects, nor yet quasi-physical meta-objects like etheric bodies, he none the less undoubtedly believed that the 'local modifications of space' which constitute or underlie his postulated 'phantasmogenetic centres' are modifications in a realm of being (the 'metetherial') other than the physical world with which ordinary sense perception acquaints us. Other distinguished writers in the field (for instance H. H. Price, 123) have developed similar ideas. None the less I think we shall, at least in the foreseeable state of our knowledge, be well advised to steer clear of such notions. They raise at the moment no issues that can be scientifically investigated, and will lead only to dead ends of the kind which, I proposed in the first chapter, we should try to avoid. For present purposes it is enough if we accept as a fact, or postulate for the sake of argument, that certain persons in certain circumstances are able so to modify a certain region of space that other persons, visiting that region, may see there a figure corresponding to some latent conception in the agent's mind.

But, it might be asked, are the percipients systematically hallucinated, or is there really some peculiar, but publicly accessible, object which they all perceive? Isn't the tendency of the theory, with its talk of local modifications of space, to suggest that there is indeed some peculiar kind of object (call it a 'thought-form') where an apparition, at any rate a collectively perceived apparition, is seen? Can we prove or disprove this suggestion, and with it therefore the theory?

I think – although I have not space to elaborate the point here – that this argument misconceives the logic of the situation. It is quite likely that we know as much about the characteristics of apparitions as we ever shall. We know that in some ways they resemble physical objects, and in other ways they do not. They generally look and sound and behave much like ordinary physical objects, and may be seen in appropriate perspective by several persons simultaneously; on the other hand they do not last very long, they do not affect physical objects around them, and they may not be perceived by everyone in a position to perceive them. Under these conditions, the question whether they are hallucinations or 'real' objects is surely no longer a factual one; it is a matter of which way of speaking, which linguistic convention, it is simpler to adopt, and which coheres best with our fashions of discourse upon related matters. The issue is philosophical rather than factual. Shall we talk of an agent's capacity to create a sort of radiant point around which persons are liable to suffer systematically related hallucinations? Or shall we talk of an agent's capacity to create a kind of object that does not affect physical instruments and is perceptible only to people with a certain kind of non-optical sensitivity? The former way of talking leaves the systematic relatedness of the hallucinations without a rational basis; the latter leaves the presence or absence, or the perceptibility, of the object, more than a little arbitrary. My guess (and presumably Myers' too) would be that on the whole the shortcomings of the second way of talking would be easier to live with than those of the first. But perhaps we can simply dodge making a choice.

4.   Whichever way of talking we adopt, we are confronted with the following further problem. The process of 'non-optical' perception by which Myers thinks we become aware of apparitions would seem, at least when the apparition is veridical, to fall under the general heading of ESP – it involves the acquisition of information without the use of the known sense-organs. But it does not fall readily under the heading of 'telepathy' nor yet under that of 'clairvoyance'. The 'local modifications of space' which bring about apparitions may be *caused by* 'conceptions latent in the mind' of the agent; but by no stretch *are* they those conceptions or literally part of the agent's mind. Apparitions are only the *effects* of the agent's mental activities, just as are, say, his paintings or his poems. Hence the 'perception' of them cannot be classed as telepathic, for it does not amount to direct and non-inferential knowledge of what is in the agent's mind. Since clairvoyance is defined as extra-sensory knowledge of *physical* events or states of affairs, we cannot say that the 'non-optical perception' concerned is a form of clairvoyance. We seem to have here a form of ESP that can be labelled neither as telepathy nor as clairvoyance. At least this proposal consorts well with the fact (mentioned in the

previous chapter) that apparitions are not infrequently shared by those in a position to share them, whereas ESP manifesting in other forms is rarely shared. We need a new word for this further form of ESP; but I will not tax my ingenuity, nor add to parapsychology's extensive verbal lumber, by trying to invent one.

That completes my account of Myers's theory of apparitions (in a slightly doctored version), and it is now time to attempt an assessment. Its strong point is clearly that it can account for the 'veridicality' of veridical cases without resort to the complexities of super-ESP, and can explain the apparent objectivity of the phantasms seen in cases of collective percipience and haunting ghosts without pitching us into the absurdities of the animistic theory. It confronts, however, numerous difficulties. Let us begin with a minor one. It is often suggested that most people have a relatively imperfect idea of how they look to others, especially from behind, or in profile. That being so, how can we possibly propose that an agent's 'latent conception' of himself can so modify a certain region of space that suitably gifted persons see a realistic phantasm of him there? This argument has, I think, some weight, but not a great deal. Is the average person's idea of how he looks likely to differ so much from how he actually looks that a percipient would be likely to notice the difference? Perhaps peoples' ideas of how they look are not so much conditioned by their images in their mirrors as one might suppose. Schatzman (141) has recently conducted some brief but immensely intriguing experiments with a subject, 'Ruth', who possesses in a remarkable degree the ability to create for herself totally realistic hallucinations (ones which from all accounts, though unlike the hallucinations of epileptics, alcoholics, drug-takers, the insane, etc., closely resemble the figures seen in classic apparition cases). So 'real' are her hallucinations that when she summoned one up to interpose between her eyes and a source of flickering light, her brain's normal electrical response to the light ceased. Ruth can with equal facility create hallucinations of herself or of other people, and the hallucinations are not just visual, but auditory, tactile and olfactory (the figures talk, and she can feel and smell them). When Ruth creates an hallucination of herself the hallucination is apparently quite realistic and is not a mirror image.

The most important criticism is so obvious that it may be stated briefly. The theory gives credit to numerous unknowns, and a shortfall in any one of them would bankrupt it. It postulates 'phantasmogenetic' modifications, nature unknown, of particular spatial localities; an unknown process whereby certain persons can cause such modifications; an unknown form of sensitivity by means of which certain persons can perceive the phantasms thus generated; discarnate intelligences of which we know nothing except that they were formerly incarnated as particular human beings; and (presumably) some totally unknown faculty of ESP by means of which these discarnate intelligences obtain their information about this world and the next. No sensible theorist would entrust his intellectual capital to such unknowns, for unknowns are not credit-worthy.

The trouble is, it seems to me, that we have little choice but to allow Myers' theory, unknowns and all, just a little credit. The theory, as he remarks, ties together a good many phenomena of 'odd and varying types', and even if his account of them is highly implausible, it does not, and this is the important point, appear quite such a dead end as are the super-ESP and the animistic theories. There do seem to be, even in the present state of our knowledge, certain further empirical inquiries to which it might lead. We might, for example, investigate the 'phantasmogenetic' capacities of such gifted subjects as 'Ruth'. Schatzman experimented with Ruth to see whether her hallucinations could be shared by others. They were not. However on two occasions, when no experiment was in progress, other persons apparently observed phantasms which she had created (a similar incident is described by David-Neel, 28). One person actually held a conversation with the figure, which he believed to be that of a real person, viz. Ruth herself. Once a dog became greatly disturbed when Ruth generated a phantasm in its vicinity – a phenomenon for which the literature of apparitions holds numerous parallels. The findings so far yield no certainties, but raise many intriguing possibilities.

At the beginning of Chapter Fourteen I posed two questions which arose from the fact that we seemed forced by the facts and the considerations advanced earlier in the book to take the survival theory seriously. The two questions were:

1. Would the survival of a person's memories, and his conceptual capacities in general, involve or amount to his survival as a conscious individual?

2. If such memories and capacities survive, what could underpin their survival, be, so to speak, their vehicle?

It was, partly, in pursuit of answers to these questions that I embarked on the discussion of OBEs and of apparitions. At the end of this discussion I have found myself, despite its numerous obscurities, taking seriously Myers's 'phantasmogenetic centre' theory of apparitions. Does this theory, if true, or rather if in some (probably minor) degree an approximation to the truth, have any bearing upon the above two questions?

With regard to the first question, one would, I suppose, naturally assume that if the evidence suggests that certain sorts of phantasms (veridical post-mortem ones) are generated by surviving portions of formerly living human beings, whatever survives and generates them must possess very much the same memories and conceptual abilities as are possessed by the living persons who sometimes similarly seem to generate phatasms of themselves. For *ex hypothesi* the phantasms are in some sense externalizations of 'conceptions latent in the minds of' the projectors. One could, at any rate, without doubt put up a defence of this view. But there are many difficulties. There seem, as Myers remarks, to be cases of projection by living projectors in which the projector has no awareness of what he is about, in which the projection is, as it were, automatic and a function of some unconscious level of the personality. Could something survive which was not conscious, was less than a personality, a mere vestige or trace, which could none the less still give rise to 'automatic' projections? A reply to this difficulty might make a distinction between those phatasms which seem, as it were, intelligent and responsive to living persons, and those which are mere zombies or automata. The former could only be generated by conscious and intelligent projectors. But debate on these topics could go on more or less indefinitely, for we know at the moment absolutely nothing of the process by which 'phantasmogenetic centres' are created by living projectors, of the relationships between this process and the physical world, and the dependence or otherwise of the process upon particular kinds of brain functioning. We are even more in the dark when we begin to speculate as to what may be involved in the creation of such centres by deceased projectors.

As for the second question, that concerning the supposed 'vehicle' of surviving memories and capacities, Myers' theory carries, so far as I can see, no specific implications, but adopting it might well set one off on some such train of thought as this. If, as seems to be the case, some people can, even during their lifetimes, sometimes create phantasmogenetic centres at considerable distances from their own bodies and nervous systems, can themselves perceive phantasms emanating from such centres when the latter are created by themselves or by other people, can exercise other forms of ESP directed upon distant events or persons, can perhaps even influence physical events around them other than by ordinary bodily actions, then the relationship between perceiving and indeed creative mind, and the physical world, must be utterly different from, and far more complicated than, anything which we now envisage. I would emphasize the word 'creative', for it would appear that we may in a sense be able in our insignificant ways to meddle with the universe, or rather with our local corners of it, by means as yet totally beyond our comprehension. (It may be that a control's ability to 'overshadow' a medium is another facet of this power to meddle.) How much further beyond our present comprehension, then, must be the relationship between any portion of the personality which survives death and the known and unknown physical world.

These professions of present and probable future ignorance in the face of immensely difficult problems will please no one. Many religious believers of one kind and another already have, and may centre their lives and thought around, simple or seeming-simple answers to these problems. Such persons are apt to think those who remain unconvinced by their simple answers, or who do not find them simple, merely obstinate and perverse. On the other hand those *esprits forts* who make almost a religion out of science, or rather out of the scientific knowledge we currently possess, and who pride themselves on their educated scepticism, will be even less happy with my professions of ignorance; for while it is proper and even laudable for a scientist sometimes to admit ignorance or temporary bafflement, the ignorance I am professing is of the wrong kind. I am professing the sort of ignorance which implicitly disparages the present state of our scentific knowledge, and does so on the basis of what many would assume to be a few marginal phenomena. And indeed it certainly seems to me that at the moment we know about as much of these matters as the Greeks did of electricity when they discovered that if you rub pieces of amber on your sleeve they will pick up straws.

17 Concluding Remarks

With regard to the evidence for survival, I have now said, probably several times over, nearly everything that I have to say. I cannot dismiss this evidence *en bloc* as bad evidence, as entirely the product of fraud, misrecording, malobservation, wishful thinking, or plain chance coincidence. I can find no other decisive reasons for rejecting it. I have separately argued in connection with the phenomena of mediumship, with apparitions, and with certain cases of ostensible reincarnation, that the super-ESP hypothesis will not suffice to explain the quantity of correct and appropriate information sometimes furnished. I have further pointed out that some cases present features suggestive not just of surviving memories (the sphere in which the alternative super-ESP explanation might seem to be at its strongest) but of more positive personality characteristics – distinctive purposes, skills, capacities, habits, turns of phrase, struggles to communicate, wishes, point of view. Readers must assess these aspects of the puzzle for themselves. For myself I can only say that it seems to me that there is in each of the main areas I have considered a sprinkling of cases which rather forcefully suggest some form of survival. At least – the supposition that a recognizable fragment of the personality of a deceased person may manifest again after his death without there being some underlying causal factor common to the original manifestations and the later, aberrant ones, seems impossibly magical. And it is hard to see in what terms we could conceive this underlying causal factor except those of an individual consciousness of some degree of coherence and complexity. The hypothesis of an insentient 'psychic factor' seems, as I pointed out at the beginning of Chapter Fourteen, to present numerous difficulties. But in this area, and in important related areas, what we know stands in proportion to what we do not know as a bucketful does to the ocean. Certainty is not to be had, nor even a strong conviction that the area of one's uncertainty has been narrowed to a manageable compass.

Even if one accepts that in the present state of our knowledge some sort of survival theory gives the readiest account of the observed phenomena, many issues remain undecided. In the vast majority even of favourable cases the 'surviving' personality which claims continuity with a formerly living, or previously incarnated, personality, is only able to demonstrate such apparent continuity on a very limited number of fronts, and may, indeed, markedly fail to demonstrate it on others. This does not, of course, mean that behind the observed manifestations there does not lie the fullest possible continuity; but equally it means that the hypothesis of complete continuity is unproven, and all sorts of possibilities remain open. Is there partial or complete survival? Sentient survival, or (far worse than mere extinction) survival with just a lingering, dim consciousness? Is there long-term survival or survival during a brief period of progressive disintegration? Is there enjoyable survival, or survival such as one would wish to avoid? Survival with a physical substrate, or disembodied survival? Survival as individual, or survival with one's individuality for the most part dissolved in something larger? Is survival the rule, or is it just a freak? To these and many other questions I can at the moment see no very clear answers.

Many people, indeed, do not require, or perhaps wish for, clear answers. They will take the mere rejection of the super-ESP hypothesis as justifying the view that God's in His heaven and all's right with the world.

> Oh, easy creed
> That our beloved ones are not lost indeed
> But, somewhere far and fainter, live secure,
> While yet they plead
> With voices heard in visions live and pure,
> With touch upon the hand, that they endure,
> Only withdrawn!

For my part I think that any further decisive progress will have to wait upon the results of a great deal of further difficult and time-consuming work on a number of different fronts. By the time this work has been even partly carried out, most of us will be dead, and will thus know the answers anyway, or not know them as the case may be. And the results of the work may be to point away from the survivalist theory once again. As to this, one can at best express a tentative view as to the likely future trend of the evidence. I have given my own view. Others will estimate the situation differently.

To those hot for certainty – whether it be certainty of survival or of extinction – this answer may seem dusty enough. However it will not seem dusty to everyone. For, as I have tried to show, it is possible from a properly informed consideration of the evidence to build up a rational case for belief in some form of survival, and also a rational case against it. And a rational case, of either tendency, built on evidence, however difficult to interpret, is to be preferred to any amount of blind belief or blind disbelief. Furthermore, to persons such as myself, with an overdeveloped bump of curiosity and a liking for mysteries, what may be called a Chinese box universe – a universe made up, so to speak, of a puzzle containing another puzzle deep within it, and so on indefinitely – has much appeal. And maybe at the heart of all truth and justice lie hidden, and brought to light, will prevail. Or maybe not. But in either case the puzzles are there, and their fascination is irresistible.

What, then, of the future? How might these puzzles be further studied? I do not think that there are any short cuts to a solution, or to a dismissal of the problem. The idea of a decisive 'test of survival' has commended itself to many, and some public-spirited individuals have left behind them sealed packages, the contents of which they hoped to communicate after death. In only a few instances has any degree of success been reported (e.g. 110a, II, pp. 182–185; 139c); and even had successes been more frequent they might have been attributed to clairvoyance by the medium.

Recently, more sophisticated forms of test have been suggested. Thouless (159b) has proposed that persons who wish to leave a 'test' behind them should encipher and deposit with a reputable organization some prose passage of appropriate content. All they would need to communicate would be the keyword. A control against the possibility that mediums could crack the code by super-ESP would be obtained by having them attempt to obtain the keyword while the subject is still alive. If they fail to obtain it we must assume that it is beyond the reach of ESP. Perhaps such a project will work – a supposed Richard Hodgson communicated through Mrs Piper a 'password' which turned out to be the name of her own daughter enciphered in a complex manner almost certainly known to Hodgson in life (109, pp. 204n–205n). Stevenson (153a) has initiated a similar project using combination locks instead of ciphers. A positive result in such a test would obviously be of great interest and importance; but to constitute strong evidence for survival it would, I think, still need to be combined with evidence for the survival of purposes, personality characteristics, other sorts of memories, etc.

Such 'tests of survival' apart, it seems to me that work on the question of survival will have to proceed, piece by piece, on two broad fronts. The first would involve the slow and patient sifting and accumulation of ostensible 'evidence for survival' such as I have presented and discussed in this book. The second (much harder to define) would involve the sort of inquiries, factual and conceptual, which might result in our being able to build up a general framework of thought within which survival and the various categories of evidence for survival will cohere and made sense, and will cohere also with the findings of other branches of science. (On the other hand we might decisively fail to achieve such a framework of thought, and that too would be a matter of great significance.) We have (as I have tried to show) already acquired a good deal of material on the former front; but we have acquired very little on the latter. If the evidence for survival were a great deal more copious and more startling than it actually is (and it is fairly copious and sometimes quite startling) we could perhaps get by with little accumulation of material on the latter front. I can certainly *imagine* a state of affairs in which, as a matter of fact, no one, or no one except philosophers when actually philosophizing, would express doubts about survival. Suppose, for example, that persons 'out of the body' were regularly able to act as living communicators, conveyed fluent and appropriate information, etc., and could give on their 'return' full accounts of what had transpired, and after their own deaths continued to communicate in much the same way right up to the moment of their reincarnation as one of Stevenson's child subjects. But such a state of affairs does not obtain. Hence, it seems to me, it has become as important to attempt to progress on the second front as on the first. We already have quite a lot of ostensible evidence for survival; we do not have a conceptual framework into which we can satisfactorily fit it.

I shall accordingly not pursue the question of what further ostensible 'evidence for survival' we might obtain, but shall instead move immediately to the second of the two 'broad fronts' on which (I argued) work on the problem of survival needs to proceed. What steps might be taken to enlarge our relevant 'background' knowledge in such a way that the evidence for survival comes to 'make sense' in an overall context which includes the findings of other sciences as well as those of parapsychology? I should expect progress on this front, if progress there is, to be slow and painful, a gradual fitting together of laboriously acquired pieces, rather than a sudden insight into their true relations. And one can set no limit beforehand upon the number of 'pieces' which might in the end prove relevant. In previous chapters I have suggested various kinds of parapsychological work which, it seems to me, might have relevance to this endeavour. For example:

1. Experiments directed towards obtaining mediumistic communications from living persons. Living communicators might turn out to face much the same difficulties and to get into much the same muddles, as discarnate ones; and then we might perhaps obtain some clues as to the mechanism of communication, and the tenability of what I called the theory of 'overshadowing', and so forth. The work might or might not cohere or combine with work on OBEs. Equally, the upshot might be to suggest that the Gordon Davis and John Ferguson cases were not freaks or frauds, and hence to strengthen the background to the super-ESP hypothesis.

2. Likewise capable of supporting the super-ESP hypothesis would be experiments with sensitives (if such could be found) resembling those studied by Osty (see Chapter Ten above). I do not think that the status of the super-ESP hypothesis can be adequately established until such experiments have been carried out utilizing modern methods of experimental design and statistical assessment, features conspicuously absent from Osty's pioneering work.

3. Full and extensive studies of the abilities of such gifted subjects as 'Ruth' (see previous chapter) to generate hallucinations in themselves and sometimes, apparently in other people, might, as I pointed out, throw light on the tenability or otherwise of the theory of veridicial apparitions which I discussed in Chapter Sixteen.

4. The most urgently needed investigation in the area of spontaneous cases is, it seems to me, a detailed investigation by competent and properly equipped persons into the physical aspects of a really marked 'haunting'. For in such cases we have, very often, localized physical disturbances that are *prima facie* not susceptible of an ordinary explanation; and we have also (at least sometimes) apparitions; and the problem of the relation between these two is absolutely central to all questions concerning the nature and genesis of apparitions, and ramifies into other questions. Furthermore, in some hauntings, there are certain signs of an intelligence (whose origins and nature remain to be elucidated). One might try bringing different mediums and sensitives to the spot independently of each other to see if there was any agreement in their 'diagnoses', and thus obtain both

'mental' and 'physical' avenues of approach to the same case (cf. 97; 106; 143). From a number of such investigations, one might (with an immense and unlikely amount of luck) begin to glimpse an overall pattern within which several different kinds of ostensible survival evidence might fall into place.

However, as I remarked a moment ago, relevant discoveries are likely to come – I think will have to come – from outside parapsychology altogether. From what I said in Chapter Thirteen, it should be clear that the physiology of memory processes will constitute an area of central concern. Wider aspects of biology may come to have relevance (144). There are also many signs – which I cannot detail here – that progress in the frontier regions of physics and mathematical physics may open up new ideas for parapsychology. Recently published work on the 'metal-bending' phenomenon constitutes an empiral focus for these speculative ideas, but the ramification of these ideas could extend much more widely than that.

The problem that confronts survival research is not shortage of things to do, but shortage of funds, with which necessarily goes shortage of personnel. When the SPR was first founded, it had a number of very able members with private means and ample leisure. It was these persons who were primarily responsible for the immense amount of work and the significant progress that marked the first three or four decades of the Society's existence. The situation today has radically changed. There are fewer wealthy and leisured persons, and some of the investigations that are now desirable would require sophisticated and expensive scientific equipment. Governments and grant-giving agencies have not enough funds for tackling problems in this world, and will certainly not subsidize the study of problems relating to the next. It is only if a sufficient number of interested individuals band together and contribute their money and their time that we may hope for any concerted rather than piece-meal progress to be made. There continues to be a vital role for the SPR, the ASPR, and kindred societies. The recent work of Stevenson and Osis, as well as the original labours of the SPR's founders, have shown how much can be accomplished even by a small number of dedicated persons with moderate funds and facilities at their disposal.

Substantial parts of this book have been taken up with an attempt to reconcile the apparently irreconcilable; to reconcile, in other words, the data of modern psychology and modern neuroscience, with certain odd empirical facts that apparently suggest that human personality may at least sometimes survive bodily death. I do not for a moment pretend that I have satisfactorily harmonized these bodies of data. Each time I tie up, with fumbling fingers, a couple of loose ends, a third one slips free again. Most of the protagonists will continue to reject the opposite camp's data without any adequate scrutiny and purely on faith – faith, that is, that because their own findings and interpretations are unshakable, or at least shakable only in inessentials, the other fellow's findings and interpretations cannot merit serious study. It is not just, say, neuroscientists who have this attitude to the ostensible evidence for survival. Some parapsychologists (from the experimental camp) tend to take this view of the data gathered by other parapsychologists (those interested in the topics of this book). Some Spiritualists would accord a like negligent dismissal to the findings of neuroscience. I do not like this rejection of data on faith – it is at best a not very honest way of protecting oneself from the labour of having to adjust one's opinions. A far bigger act of faith – one to which I must confess I cannot at all times rise – is to accept both sets of data, and to assume that since the universe is not in the last resort disorderly, some way of reconciling them will in the end be found.

Bibliography

1. Alexander, P. P. *Spiritualism: a Narrative with a Discussion* (Edinburgh: W. P. Nimmo, 1871).

2. Allison, L. W. *Leonard and Soule Experiments* (Boston: Boston Society for Psychic Research, 1929).

3. Anderson, J. R. *Cognitive Psychology and its Implications* (San Fransisco: W. H. Freeman, 1980).

4. Angoff, A. and Barth, D., eds. *Parapsychology and Anthropology* (New York; Parapsychology Foundation, 1974).

5a. Balfour, G. W. 'Some Recent Scripts Affording Evidence of Personal Survival' (*Proceedings of the Society for Psychical Research*, 1914-5, 27, pp. 221-243).

5b. Balfour, G W. 'The Ear of Dionysius: Further Scripts Affording Evidence of Personal Survival' (*Proceedings of the Society for Psychical Research*, 1918, 29, pp. 197-243).

5c. Balfour, G. W. 'The Ear of Dionysius: a Reply' (*Proceedings of the Society for Psychical Research*, 1918, 29, pp. 270-286).

5d. Balfour, G. W. 'A Study of the Psychological Aspects of Mrs Willett's Mediumship' (*Proceedings of the Society for Psychical Research*, 1935, 43, pp. 43-318).

6. Balfour, J. 'The "Palm Sunday" Case: New Light on an Old Love Story' (*Proceedings of the Society for Psychical Research*, 1958-60, 52, pp. 79-267).

7. Beattie, J., and Middleton, J. *Spirit Mediumship and Society in Africa* (London: Routledge and Kegan Paul, 1969).

8. Bennett, E. *Apparitions and Haunted Houses* (London: Faber and Faber, 1939).

9. Bernstein, M. *The Search for Bridey Murphy* (Garden City, NY: Doubleday, 1956).

10. Besterman, T. 'Further Inquiries into the Element of Chance in Booktests' (*Proceedings of the Society for Psychical Research*, 1931-2, 40. pp. 59-98).

11. Besterman, T., and Heard, G. 'Note on an Attempt to locate in Space the Alleged Direct Voice Observed in Sittings with Mrs Leonard' (*Journal of the Society for Psychical Research*, 1933, 28, pp. 84–85).

12. [Bird, J. M.] 'Two Striking Cases of Collective Apparitions' (*Journal of the American Society for Psychical Research*, 1928, 22, pp. 429–432).

13. Blackmore, S. J. *Beyond the Body: an Investigation of Out-of-the-Body Experiences* (London: Heinemann, 1982).

14. Bozzano, E. *Discarnate Influence in Human Life* (London: J. M. Watkins, n.d.).

15a. Bradley, H. D. *Towards the Stars* (London: T. Werner Laurie, 1924).

15b. Bradley, H. D. *The Wisdom of the Gods* (London: T. Werner Laurie, 1925).

15c. Bradley, H. D. *And After . . .* (London, T. Werner Laurie, 1931).

16. Braud, W. G. 'Liability and Inertia in Conformance Behavior' (*Journal of the American Society for Psychical Research*, 1980, 74, pp. 297–318).

17. Braude, S. *ESP and Psychokinesis: a Philosophical Examination* (Philadelphia: Temple University Press, 1980).

18a. Broad, C. D. *The Mind and its Place in Nature* (London: Routledge and Kegan Paul, 1925).

18b. Broad, C. D. *Religion, Philosophy and Psychical Research* (London: Routledge and Kegan Paul, 1953).

18c. Broad, C. D. *Lectures on Psychical Research* (London: Routledge and Kegan Paul, 1962).

18d. Broad, C. D. 'Autobiography' (in Schilpp, P. A., ed., *The Philosophy of C. D. Broad*. New York: Tudor Publishing Co., 1959, pp. 3–68).

19. Brown, S. *The Hey-Day of Spiritualism* (New York: Hawthorn Books, 1970).

20. Bursen, H. A. *Dismantling the Memory Machine* (Dordrecht, Holland: Reidel, 1978).

21. Calmet, A. *The Phantom World: or, the philosophy of Spirits, Apparitions, etc.* (2 vols. London: R. Bentley, 1850).

22a. Carington, W. W. 'The Quantitative Study of Trance Personalities. Part I.' (*Proceedings of the Society for Psychical Research*, 1934, 42, pp. 173–240).

22b.   Carington, W. W. 'The Quantitative Study of Trance
Personalities. Part II.' (*Proceedings of the Society for Psychical
Research*, 1935, 43, pp. 319–361).

22c.   Carington, W. W. 'The Quantitative Study of Trance
Personalities. Part III.' (*Proceedings of the Society for Psychical
Research*, 1936–7, 44, pp. 189–222).

23.   Carrington, H. *An Instrumental Test of the Independence of a
Spirit Control* (New York: American Psychical Institute, [1933]).

24.   Christie-Murray, D. *Reincarnation: Ancient Beliefs and Modern
Evidence* (Newton Abbot: David and Charles, 1981).

25.   Crapanzano, V., and Garrison, V. *Case Studies in Spirit Possession*
(New York: Wiley, 1977).

26.   Dale, L. A., White, R. and Murphy, G. 'A Selection of Cases
from a Recent Survey of Spontaneous ESP Phenomena' (*Journal of
the American Society for Psychical Research*, 1962, 56, pp. 3–47).

27.   Dallas, H. A. 'Communications from the Still Incarnate at a
Distance from the Body' (*Occult Review*, 1924, 40, pp. 26–32).

28.   David-Neel, A. *Magic and Mystery in Tibet* (London: Souvenir
Press, 1961).

29.   Delanne, G. *Documents pour servir à l'étude de la réincarnation*
(Paris: Editions de la B.P.S., 1924).

30.   Dickinson, G. L. 'A Case of Emergence of a Latent Memory
under Hypnosis' (*Proceedings of the Society for Psychical Research*, 1911,
25, pp. 455–467).

31.   Dilley, F. B. 'What is Wrong with Disembodied Spirits?'
(*Research Letter of the Parapsychology Laboratory, University of Utrecht*,
No. 11, Aug. 1981, pp. 31–41).

32.   Dingwall, E. J. ed. *Abnormal Hypnotic Phenomena: a Survey of
Nineteenth-Century Cases* (4 vols. London: J. and A. Churchill,
1967–8).

33.   Dodds, E. R. 'Why I do not Believe in Survival' (*Proceedings of the
Society for Psychical Research*, 1934, 42, pp. 147–172).

34a.   Ducasse, C. J. *A Critical Examination of the Belief in a Life
after Death* (Springfield, Illinois: C. C. Thomas, 1961).

34b.   Ducasse, C. J. 'What Would Constitute Evidence of Life after
Death?' (*Journal of the Society for Psychical Research*, 1962, 41, pp. 401–
406).

35.   Edge, H. L. 'A Philosophical Justification for the Conformance
Behavior Model' (*Journal of the American Society for Psychical
Research*, 1978, 72, pp. 215–231).

36.   Eeden, F. van. 'Account of Sittings with Mrs Thompson'

(*Proceedings of the Society for Psychical Research*, 102, 17, pp. 75–115).

37. Eliade, M. *Shamanism: Archaic Techniques of Ecstasy* (2nd ed. London: Routledge and Kegan Paul, 1970).

38. Elliott, A. J. A. *Chinese Spirit-Medium Cults in Singapore* (London: London School of Economics, 1955).

39. Ellis, D. J. *The Mediumship of the Tape Recorder* (Harlow, Essex: D. J. Ellis, 1978).

40. Flew, A. G. N. 'Is there a Case for Disembodied Survival?' (*Journal of the American Society for Psychical Research*, 1972, 66, pp. 129–144).

41. Flournoy, T. *From India to the Planet Mars* (New York: University Books, 1963).

42. Frazer, J. G. *The Belief in Immortality* (Vol. I. London: Macmillan, 1913).

43. Freeborn, H. 'Temporary Reminiscence of a Long-forgotten Language during Delirium' (*Journal of the Society for Psychical Research*, 1902, 10, pp. 279–283).

44a. Gauld, A. 'Mr Hall and the SPR' (*Journal of the Society for Psychical Research*, 1965, 43, pp. 53–62).

44b. Gauld, A. *The Founders of Psychical Research* (London: Routledge and Kegan Paul, 1968).

44c. Gauld, A. 'A Series of "Drop-in" Communicators' (*Proceedings of the Society for Psychical Research*, 1966–72, 55, pp. 273–340).

44d. Gauld, A. 'ESP and Attempts to Explain it' (in Thakur, S. C., ed. *Philosophy and Psychical Research*. London: G. Allen and Unwin, 1976, pp. 17–45).

44e. Gauld, A. 'Discarnate Survival' (in Wolman, B. B., ed., *Handbook of Parapsychology*. New York: Van Nostrand Reinhold, 1977, pp. 577–630).

45. Gauld, A., and Cornell, A. D. *Poltergeists* (London: Routledge and Kegan Paul, 1979).

46. Geach, P. *God and the Soul* (London: Routledge and Kegan Paul, 1969).

47. Gelfand, M. *Witch Doctor* (London: Harvill Press, 1964).

48. Gibbes, E. B. 'Have we Indisputable Evidence of Survival?' (*Journal of the American Society for Psychical Research*, 1937, 31, pp. 65–79).

49. Gibson, E. P. 'An Examination of Motivation as Found in Selected Cases from *Phantasms of the Living*' (*Journal of the American Society for Psychical Research*, 1944, 36, pp. 83–105).

50. Glenconner, P. *The Earthen Vessel* (London: John Lane, 1921).

51. Green, C. E. *Out-of-the-Body Experiences* (Oxford: Institute of Psychophysical Research, 1968).

52. Green, C. E., and McCreery, C. *Apparitions* (London: Hamish Hamilton, 1975).

53a. Guirdham, A. *The Cathars and Reincarnation* (London: Neville Spearman, 1970).

53b. Guirdham, A. *We Are One Another* (London: Neville Spearman, 1974).

54. Gurney, E. 'The Nature of Evidence in Matters Extraordinary' (in Gurney, E., *Tertium Quid*. London: Kegan Paul, Trench and Co., 1887, vol, I, pp. 227–273).

55. Gurney, E., Myers, F. W. H., and Podmore, F. *Phantasms of the Living* (2 vols. London: Trübner, 1886).

56. H., A.M. 'An Apparition Identified from a Photograph' (*Journal of the American Society for Psychical Research*, 1931, 20, pp. 53–57).

57. Haraldsson, E. 'Apparitions of the Dead: a Representative Survey in Iceland' (in Roll, W. G., Beloff, J., and McAllister, J., eds. *Research in Parapsychology 1980*. Metuchen, N. J.: The Scarecrow Press, 1981, pp. 3–5).

58. Haraldsson, E., Gudmundsdottir, A., Ragnarsson, A., Loftsson, J., and Jonsson, S. 'National Survey of Psychical Experiences and Attitudes towards the Paranormal in Iceland' (in Morris, J. D., Roll, W. G., and Morris, R. L., eds. *Research in Parapsychology 1976*. Metuchen, N. J.: The Scarecrow Press, 1977, pp. 182–186).

59a. Haraldsson, E., and Stevenson, I. 'A Communicator of the "Drop in" Type in Iceland: the Case of Runolfur Runolfsson' (*Journal of the American Society for Psychical Research*, 1975, 69, pp. 33–59).

59b. Haraldsson, E., and Stevenson, I. 'A Communicator of the "Drop in" Type in Iceland: the Case of Gudni Magnusson' (*Journal of the American Society for Psychical Research*, 1975, 69, pp. 245–261).

60a. Hart., H. 'Six Theories about Apparitions' (*Proceedings of the Society for Psychical Research*, 1953–6, 50, pp. 153–239).

60b. Hart, H., *The Enigma of Survival* (London: Rider, 1959).

61. Hart, H., and Hart, E. B. 'Visions and Apparitions Collectively and Reciprocally Perceived' (*Proceedings of the Society for Psychical Research*, 1932–3, 41, pp. 205–249).

62a. Heil, J. 'Cognition and Representation' (*Australasian Journal of Philosophy*, 1980, 58, pp. 158–168).

62b. Heil, J. 'Does Cognitive Psychology Rest on a Mistake?' (*Mind*, 1981, 90, pp. 321–342).

63. Hilgard, E. R. *Divided Consciousness: Multiple Controls in Human Thought and Action* (New York: Wiley, 1977).

64a. Hill, J. A. *Spiritualism: its History, Phenomena and Doctrine* (London: Cassell, 1918).

64b. Hill, J. A. *Experiences with Mediums* (London: Rider, [1934]).

65. Hitchcock, J. N., and Jones, R. L. *Spirit Possession in the Nepal Himalayas* (Warminster: Avis and Phillips, 1977).

66a. Hodgson, R. 'A record of Observations of Certain Phenomena of Trance' (*Proceedings of the Society for Psychical Research*, 1892, 8, pp. 1–167).

66b. Hodgson, R. 'A Further Record of Observations of Certain Phenomena of Trance' (*Proceedings of the Society for Psychical Research*, 1897–8, 13, pp. 284–582).

67. Holt, H. *On the Cosmic Relations* (2 vols. London: Williams and Norgate, 1915).

68. Hope, C. 'Report on Some Sittings with Valiantine and Phoenix in 1927' (*Proceedings of the Society for Psychical Research*, 1931–2, 40, pp. 411–417).

69. Hughes, I. M. 'A Paranormal Dream' (*Journal of the Society for Psychical Research*, 1958, 39, pp. 186–188).

70. Hulme, A. J. H., and Wood, F. H. *Ancient Egypt Speaks* (London: Rider, 1937).

71a. Hyslop, J. H. 'A Case of Veridical Hallucinations' (*Proceedings of the American Society for Psychical Research*, 1909, 3, pp. 1–469).

71b. Hyslop, J. H. 'The Doris Case of Multiple Personality' (*Proceedings of the American Society for Psychical Research*, 1917, 11, pp. 5–866).

71c. Hyslop, J. H. *Contact with the Other World*. (New York: the Century Company, 1919).

72. Iverson, J. *More Lives than One?* (London: Souvenir Press, 1976).

73. Jacobson, N. *Life without Death?* (London: Turnstone, 1974).

74. James, W. 'Report on Mrs Piper's Hodgson Control' (*Proceedings of the Society for Psychical Research*', 1910, 23, pp. 2–121).

75a. Johnson, A. 'On the Automatic Writing of Mrs Holland' (*Proceedings of the Society for Psychical Research*, 1908–9, 21, pp. 166–391).

75b. Johnson, A. 'Second Report on Mrs Holland's Script' (*Proceedings of the Society for Psychical Research, 1910, 24, pp. 201–263).

75c. Johnson, A. 'Third Report on Mrs Holland's Script' (*Proceedings of the Society for Psychical Research*, 1911, 25, pp. 218–303).

75d. Johnson, A. 'A Reconstruction of Some "Concordant Automatisms"' (*Proceedings of the Society for Psychical Research*, 1914–5, 27, pp. 1–156).

76. Jones, L. A. 'Presidential Address' (*Proceedings of the Society for Psychical Research*, 1928–9, 38, pp. 17–48).

77. Jung, C. G. *Synchronicity* (London: Routledge and Kegan Paul, 1972).

78. Jusczyk, P. W. and Earhard, B. 'The *Lingua Mentis* and its Role in Thought' (in Jusczyk, P. W., and Klein, R. M., eds., *The Nature of Thought: Essays in Honor of D. O. Hebb*. Hillsdale, N. J.: L. Erlbaum, 1980, pp. 155–186).

79. Kampman, R. 'Hypnotically induced Multiple Personality: an Experimental Study' (*Acta Universitatis Oulensis Series D Medica, No 6, Psychiatrica No 3* Oulu: University of Oulu, 1973).

80. Kampman, R., and Hirvenoja, R. 'Dynamic Relation of the Secondary Personality Induced by Hypnosis to the Present Personality' (in Frankel, F. H., and Zamansky, H. S., eds., *Hypnosis at its Bicentennial*. New York: Plenum, 1978).

81. Kenny, M. G. 'Multiple Personality and Spirit Possession' (*Psychiatry*, 1981, 44, pp. 337–358).

82. Koestler, A. *The Roots of Coincidence* (London: Hutchinson, 1972).

83. Kohr, R. L. 'A Survey of Psi Experiences among Members of a Special Population' (*Journal of the American Society for Psychical Research*, 1980, 74, pp. 395–411).

84. Kosslyn, S. M., and Pomerantz, J. R. 'Imagery, Propositions and the Form of Internal Representations' (in Block, N., ed., *Readings in the Philosophy of Psychology I*. London: Methuen, 1981, pp. 150–169).

85. Lambert, G. W. 'An Apparition of a Child: the Case of Johnnie M.' (*Journal of the Society for Psychical Research*, 1966, 43, pp. 428–431).

86a. Lambert, H. C. 'Experiments in Psychic Healing by Titus Bull, M. D.' (*Psychic Science*, 1927, 6, pp. 83–89).

86b. Lambert, H. C. 'The Case of Mr C. E., an Obsession Case Treated by Titus, Bull, M.D.' (*Psychic Science*, 1928, 7, pp. 197–214).

87a. Lang, A. *Cock Lane and Common-Sense* (London: Longmans, Green & Co., 1894).

87b. Lang, A. 'Reflections on Mrs Piper and Telepathy' (*Proceedings of the Society for Psychical Research*, 1900-1, 15, pp. 39-52).

88. Larusdottir, E. *Midillinn Hafsteinn Bjornsson* (Iceland: Nordri, 1946).

89. Leonard, G. O. *My Life in Two Worlds* (London: Cassell, 1931).

90. [Lewis, E. E.] *A Report of the Mysterious Noises Heard in the House of Mr John D. Fox* . . . (Canandaigua: E. E. Lewis, 1848).

91. Lewis, H. D. *Persons and Life after Death* (London: Macmillan, 1978).

92. Lewis, I. M. *Ecstatic Religion: an Anthropological Study of Spirit Possession and Shamanism* (Harmondsworth: Penguin, 1978).

93. Lodge, O. *Raymond, or Life and Death* (London: Methuen, 1916).

94. Long, J. K., ed. *Extrasensory Ecology: Parapsychology and Anthropology*) (Metuchen, N. J.: Scarecrow Press, 1977).

95. MacKenzie, A. *Hauntings and Apparitions* (London: Heinemann, 1982).

96. Magnin, E. 'Quelques guérisons en médecine psychiatrique dues à l'emploi des procédés métapsychiques' (in Vett, C., ed., *Le compte-rendu officiel du Premier Congrès International des Recherches Psychiques à Copenhagen 26 Août - 2 Septembre 1921*. Copenhagen: Internationale des comités pour les recherches psychiques, 1922, pp. 314-333).

97. Maher, M., and Schmeidler, G. R. 'Quantitative Investigation of a Recurrent Apparition' (*Journal of the American Society for Psychical Research*, 1975, 69, pp. 341-352).

98a. Malcolm, N. 'Memory and Representation' (*Nous*, 1970, 4, pp. 59-70).

98b. Malcolm, N. *Memory and Mind* (Ithaca: Cornell University Press, 1977).

99. Markwick, B. 'The Soal-Goldney Experiments with Basil Shackleton: New Evidence of Data Manipulation' (*Proceedings of the Society for Psychical Research*, 1978, 56, pp. 250-277).

100. Mattiesen, E. 'A Case of Telepathic Hallucination' (*Journal of the Society for Psychical Research*, 1913, 16, pp. 118-126).

101. Millar, B. 'The Observational Theories: a Primer' (*European Journal of Parapsychology*, 1978, 2, pp. 304-332).

102a. Moody, R. A. *Life after Life* (New York: Bantam, 1976).

102b. Moody, R. A. *Reflections on Life after Life* (London: Corgi Books, 1977).

103. Moore, W. U. *The Voices* (London: Watts, 1913).

104. Moreil, A. *La vie et l'oeuvre d'Allan Kardec* (Paris: Éditions Sperar, 1961).

105. Moss, P. and Keeton, J. *Encounters with the Past* (Harmonsworth: Penguin, 1981).

106. Moss, T., and Schmeidler, G. R. 'Quantitative Investigation of a "Haunted House" with Sensitives and a Control Group' (*Journal of the American Society for Psychical Research*, 1968, 62, pp. 399–410).

107. Mühl, A. M. *Automatic Writing: an Approach to the Unconscious* New York: Helix Press, 1963).

108. Murphy, G. *Three Papers on the Survival Problem* (New York: American Society for Psychical Research, [1955]).

109. Murphy, G., and Ballou, R. O. *William James on Psychical Research* (London: Chatto and Windus, 1961).

110a. Myers, F. W. H. *Human Personality and its Survival of Bodily Death* (2 vols. London: Longmans, Green and Co., 1903).

110b. Myers, F. W. H. *Fragments of Inner Life* (London: Society for Psychical Research, 1961).

111. Myers, F. W. H., Lodge, O., Leaf, W., and James, W. 'A Record of Observations of Certain Phenomena of Trance' (*Proceedings of the Society for Psychical Research*, 1889–90, 6, pp. 436–659).

112. Newbold, W. R. 'A Further Record of Observations of Certain Phenomena of Trance' (*Proceedings of the Society for Psychical Research*, 1898–9, 14, pp. 6–49).

113. Oesterreich, T. K. *Possession, Demoniacal and Other* (New York: R. R. Smith, 1930).

114. Osborn, A. W. *The Superphysical* (London: I. Nicholson and Watson, 1937).

115. Osis, K., and Haraldsson, E. *At the Hour of Death* (New York: Avon Books, 1977).

116. Osty, E. *Supernormal Faculties in Man* (London: Methuen, 1923).

117. Pagenstecher, G. 'Past Events Seership: a Study in Psychometry' (*Proceedings of the American Society for Psychical Research*, 1922, 16, pp. 1–136).

118a. Palmer, J. 'Extrasensory Perception: Research Findings' (in Krippner, S., ed., *Advances in Parapsychological Research 2: Extrasensory Perception*. New York: Plenum Press, 1978, pp. 59–243).

118b. Palmer, J. 'A Community Mail Survey of Psychic Experiences' (*Journal of the American Society for Psychical Research*, 1979, 73, pp. 221–251).

118c. Palmer, J. 'Parapsychology as a Probabilistic Science: Facing the

Implications' (in Roll, W. G., ed., *Research in Parapsychology 1979*. Metuchen, N. J.: The Scarecrow Press, 1980, pp. 189–215).

119. Penelhum, T. *Survival and Disembodied Existence* (London: Routledge and Kegan Paul, 1970).

120a. Piddington, J. G. 'On the Types of Phenomena Displayed in Mrs Thompson's Trance' (*Proceedings of the Society for Psychical Research*, 1903-4, 18, pp. 104-307).

120b. Piddington, J. G. 'A Series of Concordant Automatisms' (*Proceedings of the Society for Psychical Research*, 1908, 22, pp. 19-416).

120c. Piddington, J. G. 'Three Incidents from the Sittings: Lethe, the Sibyl; the Horace Ode Question' (*Proceedings of the Society for Psychical Research*, 1910. 24, pp. 86–169).

120d. Piddington, J. G. 'Postscript to the Lethe Incident: Note on 'Olympus' (*Proceedings of the Society for Psychical Research*, 1910, 24, pp. 327–328).

121. Piper, A. L. *The Life and Work of Mrs Piper* (London: Kegan Paul, 1929).

122a. Podmore, F. 'Phantasms of the Dead from Another Point of View' (*Proceedings of the Society for Psychical Research*, 1898-9, 14, pp. 50–70).

122b. Podmore, F. 'Discussion of the Trance Phenomena of Mrs Piper' (*Proceedings of the Society for Psychical Research*, 1898-9, 14, pp. 50-70).

122c. Podmore, F. *Modern Spiritualism: a History and a Criticism* (2 vols. London: Methuen, 1902).

122d. Podmore, F. *Mesmerism and Christian Science* (London: Methuen, 1909).

122e. Podmore, F. *The Newer Spiritualism* (London: Fisher Unwin, 1910).

123. Price, H. H. 'Survival and the Idea of Another World' (*Proceedings of the Society for Psychical Research*, 1953-6, 50, pp. 1-25).

124. Prince, R., ed. *Trance and Possession States* (Montreal: R. M. Bucke Memorial Society, 1968).

125a. Prince, W. F. 'The Doris Case of Multiple Personality' (*Proceedings of the American Society for Psychical Research*, 1915, 9, pp. 1-700, and 1916, 10, pp. 701-1419).

125b. Prince, W. F. 'The Doris Case of Quintuple Personality' (*Journal of Abnormal Psychology*, 1916, 11, pp, 73-122).

125c. Prince, W. F., 'Psychometric Experiments with Señora Maria

Reyes de Z.' (*Proceedings of the American Society for Psychical Research*, 1921, 15, pp. 189–314).

125d. Prince, W. F. 'Certain Characteristics of Veridical Mediumistic Phenomena Compared with those of Phenomena Generally Conceded to be Telepathic ' (in Vett, C., ed., *Le compte-rendu officiel du Premier Congrès International des Recherches Psychiques à Copenhague 26 Aout – 2 Septembre 1921*. Copenhagen: Internationale des Comités pour les Recherches Psychiques, 1922, pp. 101–122).

125e. Prince, W. F. 'Studies in Psychometry' (*Proceedings of the American Society for Psychical Research*, 1924, 18, pp. 178–352).

125f. Prince, W. F. *The Psychic in the House* (Boston: Boston Society for Psychic Research, 1926).

126. Pylyshyn, Z. 'What the Mind's Eye Tells the Mind's Brain: a Critique of Mental Imagery' (*Psychological Bulletin*, 1973, 80, pp.

127. Radclyffe-Hall, M., and Troubridge, U. 'On a Series of Sittings with Mrs Osborne Leonard' (*Proceedings of the Society for Psychical Research*, 1920, 30, pp. 339–554).

128a. Rao, K. R. 'Studies in the Preferential Effect. II. A Language ESP Test Involving Precognition and 'Intervention' (*Journal of Parapsychology*, 1963, pp. 147–160).

128b. Rao, K. R. 'Theories of Psi' (in Krippner, S., ed., *Advances in Parapsychologal Research 2: Extrasensory Perception*. New York: Plenum Press, 1978, pp. 245–295).

129. Rhine, L. *The Invisible Picture: a Study of Psychic Experiences* (Jefferson, N. C.: McFarland and Co., 1981).

130. Richet, C. 'Xénoglossie, l'écriture automatique en langues étrangères' (*Proceedings of the Society for Psychical Research*, 1905–7, 19, pp. 162–194).

131. Richmond, Z. *Evidence of Purpose* (London: Bell, 1938).

132. Ring, K. *Life at Death* (New York: Coward, McCann and Geoghegan, 1980).

133. Rochas, A. de *Les vies successives* (Paris: Chacornac, 1911).

134. Rogo, D. S. 'Titus Bull, American Exorcist' (in Ebon, M., ed., *Exorcism: Fact not Fiction*. New York: Signet Books, 1974, pp. 167–176).

135. Ryall, E. W. *Second Time Round* (Jersey: Neville Spearman, 1974).

136. Sage, M. *Mrs Piper and the Society for Psychical Research* (London: Brimley Johnson, 1903).

137. Sahay, K. K. N. *Reincarnation: Verified Cases of Rebirth after Death* (Bareilly: N. L. Gupta, [1927]).

138a. Salter. H. de G. 'On the Element of Chance in Book Tests' (*Proceedings of the Society for Psychical Research*, 1923, 33, pp. 606–620).

138b. Salter, H. de G. 'Some Incidents Occurring at Sittings with Mrs Leonard which may Throw some Light on their *Modus Operandi*' (*Proceedings of the Society for Psychical Research*, 1930–1, pp. 306–332).

138c. Salter, H. de G. 'The History of George Valiantine' (*Proceedings of the Society for Psychical Research*, 1932, 40, pp. 363–410).

139a. [Salter, W. H.] 'Case of the Will of Mr James L. Chaffin' (*Proceedings of the Society for Psychical Research*, 1928, 36, pp. 517–524).

139b. Salter, W. H. 'An Experiment in Pseudo-Scripts' (*Proceedings of the Society for Psychical Research*, 36, 1928, pp. 525–554).

139c. Salter, W. H. 'F. W. H. Myers's Posthumous Message' (*Proceedings of the Society for Psychical Research*, 1958–60, 52, pp. 1–32).

140. Saltmarsh, H. F. *Evidence of Personal Survival from Cross Correspondences* (London: Bell, 1938).

141. Schatzman, M. *The Story of Ruth* (London: Duckworth, 1981).

142. Schiller, F. C. S. 'A Case of Apparent Communication through a Person Living, but Suffering from Senile Dementia' (*Journal of the Society for Psychical Research*, 1923, 21, pp. 87–92).

143. Schmeidler, G. R. 'Quantitative Investigation into a 'Haunted House' (*Journal of the American Society for Psychical Research*, 1966, pp. 138–149).

144. Sheldrake, R. *A New Science of Life* (London: Blond and Briggs, 1981).

145a. Sidgwick, E. M. 'Discussion of the Trance Phenomena of Mrs Piper' (*Proceedings of the Society for Psychical Research*, 1900–1, 15, pp. 16–38).

145b. Sidgwick, E. M. 'A Contribution to the Study of the Psychology of Mrs Piper's Trance Phenomena' (*Proceedings of the Society for Psychical Research*, 1915, 28, pp. 1–657).

145c. Sidgwick, E. M. 'An Examination of Book-tests Obtained in Sittings with Mrs Leonard' (*Proceedings of the Society for Psychical Research*, 1921, 31, pp. 241–400).

145d. Sidgwick, E. M. 'Phantasms of the Living' (*Proceedings of the Society for Psychical Research*, 1923, 33, pp. 23–429).

146. [Sidgwick, H., Sidgwick, E. M., and Johnson, A.] 'Report on the Census of Hallucinations' (*Proceedings of the Society for Psychical Research*, 1894, 10, pp. 25–422).

147. Soal, S. G. 'A Report on Some Communications Received through Mrs Blanche Cooper' (*Proceedings of the Society for Psychical Research*, 1925, 35, pp. 471–594).

148. 'Society for Psychical Research, etc., the: Objects of the Society' (*Proceedings of the Society for Psychical Research*, 1882–3, 1, pp. 3–6).

149a. Stanford, R. G. 'Towards Reinterpreting Psi Events' (*Journal of the American Society for Psychical Research*, 1978, 72, pp. 197–214).

149b. Stanford, R. G. 'The Influence of Auditory Ganzfeld Characteristics upon Free-response ESP Performance' (*Journal of the American Society for Psychical Research*, 1979, 73, pp. 253–272).

150. Stawell, F. M. 'The Ear of Dionysius: a Discussion of the Evidence' (*Proceedings of the Society for Psychical Research*, 1918, 29, pp. 260–269).

151. Stearn, J. *The Second Life of Susan Ganier* (London: Leslie Frewin, 1968).

152. Stevens, E. W. *The Watseka Wonder* (Chicago: Religio-Philosophical Publishing House, 1887).

153a. Stevenson, I. 'The Combination Lock Test for Survival' (*Journal of the American Society for Psychical Research*, 1968, 62, pp. 246–254).

153b. Stevenson, I. 'The Substantiality of Spontaneous Cases' (*Proceedings of the Parapsychological Association*, 1968, 5, pp. 91–128).

153c. Stevenson, I. 'Telepathic Impressions: a Review and Report of Thirty-five New Cases' (*Proceedings of the Society for Psychical Research*, 1970, 29, pp. 1–198).

153d. Stevenson, I. 'A Communicator Unknown to Medium and Sitters' (*Journal of the American Society for Psychical Research*, 1970, 64, pp. 53–65).

153e. Stevenson, I. 'A Communicator of the 'Drop-in' Type in France: the Case of Robert Marie' (*Journal of the American Society for Psychical Research*, 1973, 67, pp. 47–76).

153f. Stevenson, I. *Xenoglossy: a Review and Report of a Case* (Bristol: Wright, 1974).

153g. Stevenson, I. *Twenty Cases Suggestive of Reincarnation* (Charlotteville: University Press of Virginia, 1974).

153h. Stevenson, I. *Cases of the Reincarnation Type. Vol 1. Ten Cases in India* (Charlottesville: University Press of Virginia, 1975).

153i. Stevenson, I. *Cases of the Reincarnation Type. Vol. 2. Ten Cases in Sri Lanka* (Charlottesville: University Press of Virginia, 1977).

153j. Stevenson, I. *Cases of the Reincarnation Type. Vol. 3. Twelve Cases in Lebanon and Turkey* (Charlottesville: University Press of Virginia, 1980).

153k. Stevenson, I. *Cryptomnesia and Parapsychology: Some Hazards of Forgotten Knowledge* (London: Society for Psychical Research, forthcoming).

154a. Stevenson, I., and Pasricha, S. 'A Case of Secondary Personality with Xenoglossy' (*American Journal of Psychiatry*, 1979, 136, pp. 1591–1592).

154b. Stevenson, I., and Pasricha, S. 'A Preliminary Report on an Unusual Case of the Reincarnation Type with Xenoglossy' (*Journal of the American Society for Psychical Research*, 1980, 74, pp. 331–348).

155. Suringar, J. V. 'A Case of Thought-transference' (*Journal of the Society for Psychical Research*, 1923, 21, pp. 170–175).

156. Tanner, A. E. *Studies in Spiritism* (New York: Appleton, 1910).

157a. Thomas, C. D. *Some New Evidence for Human Survival* (London: Collins, 1922).

157b. Thomas, C. D. 'The Beard Case' (*Journal of the Society for Psychical Research*, 1926, 23, pp. 123–134).

157c. Thomas, C. D. 'The *Modus Operandi* of Trance-communication according to Descriptions Received through Mrs Osborne Leonard' (*Proceedings of the Society for Psychical Research*, 1928–9, 38, pp. 49–100).

157d. Thomas, C. D. 'A Consideration of a Series of Proxy Sittings' (*Proceedings of the Society of Psychical Research*, 1932–3, 41, pp. 139–185).

157e. Thomas, C. D. 'A Proxy Case Extending over Eleven Sittings with Mrs Osborne Leonard' (*Proceedings of the Society for Psychical Research*, 1935, 43, pp. 439–519).

157f. Thomas, C. D. 'A Proxy Experiment of Significant Success' (*Proceedings of the Society for Psychical Research*, 1938–9, 45, pp. 257–306).

157g. Thomas, C. D. 'A New Type of Proxy Case' (*Journal of the Society for Psychical Research*, 1939, 31, pp. 103–106, 120–123).

157h. Thomas, C. D. 'A Discourse Given through Mrs Leonard and Attributed to Sir Oliver Lodge' (*Journal of the Society for Psychical Research*, 1945, 33, pp. 134–156).

157i. Thomas, C. D. 'A New Hypothesis concerning Trance Communication' (*Proceedings of the Society for Psychical Research*, 1946–7, 48, pp. 121–163).

158. Thomas, J. F. *Beyond Normal Cognition* (Boston: Boston Society for Psychic Research, 1937).

159a. Thouless, R. H. 'A Review of Mr Whately Carington's Work on Trance Personalities' (*Proceedings of the Society for Psychical Research*, 1936–7, 44, pp. 223–275).

159b. Thouless, R. H. 'A Test of Survival' (*Proceedings of the Society for Psychical Research*, 1946–9, 48, pp. 253–263).

160. Trethewy, A. W. *The 'Controls' of Stainton Moses* (London: Hurst and Blackett, [1923]).

161. Troubridge, U. 'The "Modus Operandi" in So-called Mediumistic Trance' (*Proceedings of the Society for Psychical Research*, 1922, 32, pp. 344–378).

162a. Tyrrell, G. N. M. 'A Communicator Introduced in Automatic Script' (*Journal of the Society for Psychical Research*, 1939, 31, pp. 91–95).

162b. Tyrrell, G. N. M. 'The "Modus Operandi" of Paranormal Cognition' (*Proceedings of the Society for Psychical Research*, 1946–9, 48, pp. 65–120).

162c. Tyrrell, G. N. M. *Apparitions* (London: Duckworth, 1953).

163. Ullman, M., Krippner, S., and Vaughan, A. *Dream Telepathy* (London: Turnstone, 1973).

164a. Verrall, H. de G. (Mrs W. H. Salter). 'Report on the Junot Sittings with Mrs Piper' (*Proceedings of the Society for Psychical Research*, 1910, 24, pp. 351–664).

164b. Verrall, H. de G. (Mrs W. H. Salter). 'The Element of Chance in Cross-correspondences' (*Journal of the Society for Psychical Research*, 1911, 15, pp. 153–172)

165. Verrall, M. de G. 'A Possible Reminiscence of Plotinus in Tennyson' (*Modern Language Review*, 1906–7, 2, pp. 327–330).

166. 'Vision during a State of Coma' (*Journal of the Society for Psychical Research*, 1907, 13, pp. 87–90).

167a. Walker, N. *The Bridge* (London: Cassell, 1927).

167b. Walker, N. *Through a Stranger's Hands* (London: Hutchinson, 1935).

168. Wavell, S., Butt, A., and Epton, N. *Trances* (New York: Dutton, 1966).

169a. West, D. J. 'The Investigation of Spontaneous Cases' (*Proceedings of the Society for Psychical Research*, 1946–9, 48, p. 264–300).

169b. West, D. J. 'A Mass-observation Questionnaire on Hallucinations' (*Journal of the Society for Psychical Research*, 1948, 34, pp. 187–196).

170. Whymant, N. *Psychic Adventures in New York* (London: Morley and Mitchell, 1931).

171. Wickland, C. A. *Thirty Years among the Dead* (Los Angeles: National Psychological Institute, 1924).

172. Wilson, I. *Mind out of Time?* (London: Gollancz, 1981).

173a. Wood, F. H. *After Thirty Centuries* (London: Rider, 1935).

173b. Wood, F. H. *This Egyptian Miracle* (London: Watkins, 1955).

174. Zorab, G. 'A Case for Survival' (*Journal of the Society for Psychical Research*, 1940, 31, pp. 142–152).

Index